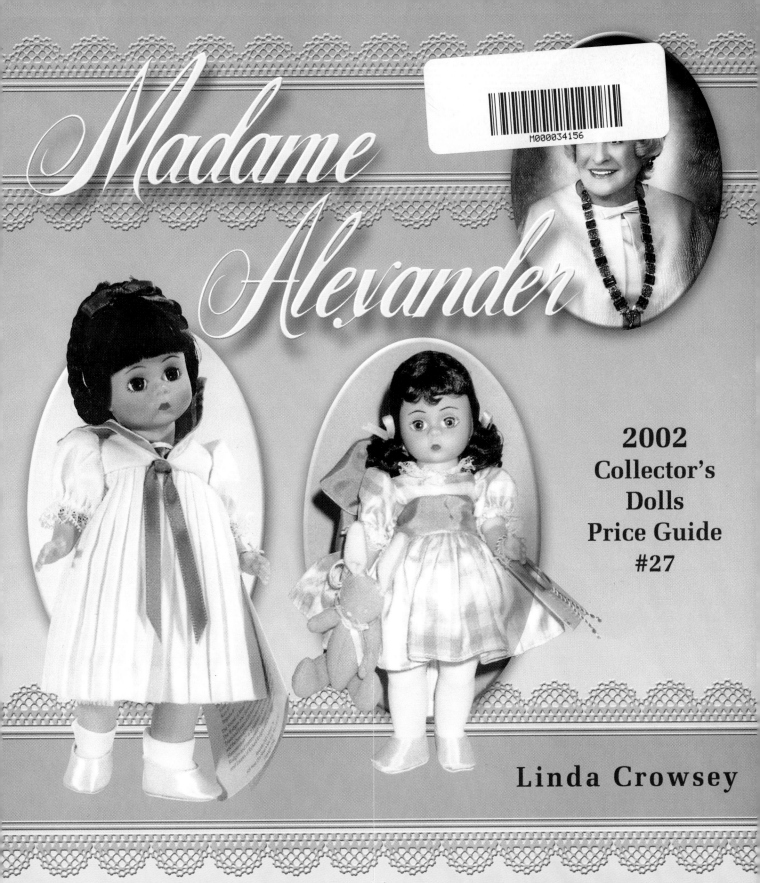

Madame Alexander

**2002
Collector's
Dolls
Price Guide
#27**

Linda Crowsey

COLLECTOR BOOKS
A Division of Schroeder Publishing Co., Inc.

Front cover:
Left: 8", 1998 Elegant Easter, $135.00.
Middle: 8", 1993 Sound of Music Marta, $200.00.
Right: 8", 1954 Bible Character, Ruth, $7,500.00.

Cover design by Beth Summers
Book design by Karen Smith

COLLECTOR BOOKS
P.O. Box 3009
Paducah, Kentucky 42002-3009

www.collectorbooks.com

Copyright © 2002 by Linda Crowsey

The current values in this book should be used only as a guide. They are not intended to set prices, which vary from one section of the country to another. Auction prices as well as dealer prices vary greatly and are affected by condition as well as demand. Neither the authors nor the publisher assumes responsibility for any losses that might be incurred as a result of consulting this guide.

Searching For A Publisher?

We are always looking for people knowledgeable within their fields. If you feel that there is a real need for a book on your collectible subject and have a large comprehensive collection, contact Collector Books.

Dedication

Madame Alexander Collector's Dolls Price Guide is dedicated to Mr. Herbert E. Brown, CEO of the Alexander Doll Company for the past five years. Madame Alexander collectors everywhere owe Mr. Brown our thanks for the hundreds of beautiful, unique dolls that were created under his leadership. Mr. Brown was receptive and always willing to take the time to listen to collectors and answer their questions. I wish Mr. Brown and his family the very best as he has decided to devote himself to endeavors and challenges that are closer to his home in Texas. The Alexander Doll Company continues to make the most beautiful dolls in the world because you were there five years ago. Thank you.

Madame Alexander Doll Club

For membership information write to:
Madame Alexander Doll Club (M.A.D.C.)
P.O. Box 330
Mundelein, IL 60060-0330

Photo credits
Johnnie Benson, Gary Green, Lahanta McIntyre,
Chris McWilliams, Florence Phelps,
Helen Thomas, and Susan York.

The Madame Alexander Doll Company

The Madame Alexander Doll Company was formed in 1923 by Madame Beatrice Alexander and her husband, Phillip Behrman. Beatrice Alexander was born on March 9, 1895, in New York City. Her father, Maurice Alexander, owned the first doll hospital in New York City. He repaired dolls and sold new dolls and fine porcelain pieces. Madame grew up seeing the joy that dolls brought to children. Madame made her first dolls of cloth.

Madame Alexander and her company manufactured the most beautiful, exquisite composition dolls in the 1930s and 1940s. Madame Alexander won Fashion Academy Gold medals in 1951, 1952, 1953, and 1954 for the fashions worn by her dolls. She was recognized with numerous honors for her achievments in the doll world and for her philanthropies. Although she died in 1990, her legacy of beautiful dolls continues to be loved and cherished by collectors.

I began collecting in 1975 when I purchased my first Madame Alexander doll, 14" Renoir, for my daughter Susan's second Christmas. I purchased other dolls for Susan, but quickly realized that I wanted to collect them also. I loved the beauty, quality, and attention to detail. Doll shows, friends, and books introduced me to the vintage dolls. Many friends that I have met through dolls have become extended family.

Mr. Herbert E. Brown, chairman and CEO of the Alexander Doll Company, has completed his five-year contract and has decided to pursue interests that would allow him to spend more time with his family in Texas. He has been commuting to New York City. He leaves the Alexander Doll Company in very capable hands. Gale Jarvis became president of the Alexander Doll Company three years ago and has worked closely with Mr. Brown. My best wishes to Ms. Jarvis and everyone at the Alexander Doll Company as they continue to create the most beautiful dolls in the world.

Linda Crowsey at the Alexander Doll Company Factory. The House was formerly located at the showroom on Fifth Avenue. The doors on the houses would open each year to reveal the new collection.

Johnnie Benson and Linda Crowsey at the Madame Alexander Doll Company showroom, February 2001.

What is a Price Guide?

Price guides must be based upon values for a perfect doll since all collectors need accurate prices for insurance purposes. Insurance companies and postal services must have a way to determine the value of a damaged or stolen doll. Collectors must also have a way to appraise and insure their collection. A price guide, while not the final word, is a starting point to determine the value of a doll. The prices listed are for perfect dolls. Imperfect dolls will bring considerably less than exceptional dolls, which collectors call "tissue mint." Original boxes are important because the information on the box helps determine the age and manufacturer of the doll. The prices quoted are for dolls without their boxes prior to 1972. Prices for dolls from 1973 to present are for dolls with their original boxes. Prices of these dolls would be adjusted lower if they are missing their boxes. Boxes can be a fire hazard. It is possible to fold most boxes and store them inside a larger box and place the boxes in an airy, dry room. Collectors will pay a higher price for a doll in its original box. Beware of storing dolls for a long time in their boxes — clothing, wigs, and vinyl can fade or change colors. Also, vinyl dolls tend to become greasy or sticky when stored in their boxes.

Swiss (right) is a BK Walker in mint condition with wrist tag. The doll on the left is missing her apron and flowers, and she has no cheek color. Her clothing is dirty and faded. The Swiss on the right is worth more than three times the doll on the left.

Perfect Dolls
❖ Complete outfit on correct doll
❖ Beautiful face color
❖ Clothes and doll in excellent condition
❖ Has all accessories, such as hats, etc.
❖ Clothes not laundered or ironed
❖ Hair in original set

Less Than Perfect Dolls
❖ Re-dressed or has part of original clothes
❖ Washed, cleaned, ironed clothes
❖ Stains, soil, faded, shelf dust, holes in fabric
❖ Faded face color
❖ Tag cut or missing
❖ Hair mussed or dirty

Exceptional Dolls
❖ Extremely rare doll
❖ Has wrist tag or original box
❖ Autographed by Madame Alexander
❖ Unique outfit or doll
❖ "Tissue Mint" condition
❖ Has wardrobe or trunk
❖ Matched set of same year
(such as "Little Women")

There is no guarantee that any doll, antique or modern, will appreciate year after year. Prices remain high on exceptional dolls and always will.

Mold Marks

Mold marks can be the same for an extended period of time. For example, 14" "Mary Ann" dolls will be marked "1965" which is the first year the doll was made. From then to now, all "Mary Ann" dolls will be marked "1965." Another example is the 21" "Jacqueline" first introduced in 1961. This doll has been used for the Portraits since 1965 and up to now still bears the 1961 date mark on head. Determining the exact year can be difficult for that reason.

Doll Names

The dolls named after real people are listed with last name first. (Example: "Bliss, Betty Taylor.") Make-believe doll names will be listed with first name first. (Example: "Tommy Snooks.")

Abbreviations

h.p. – hard plastic
compo. – composition
FAD – factory altered dress
SLNW – straight leg, non-walker
SLW – straight leg walker
BKW – bend knee walker
BK – bend knee
U.F.D.C. – United Federation of Doll Clubs
M.A.D.C. – Madame Alexander Doll Club
C.U. – Collectors United

Box Numbers

Order/box numbers for the 8" dolls with "0" prefix (example: 0742) were used in 1973 only. It must be noted the box numbers found with doll's name are from the Madame Alexander catalogs, but many dolls were placed in wrong boxes by the stores from which they were sold.

Auction Prices

Auction prices bear little or no effect on general pricing for Madame Alexander dolls. Dolls often sell at auction for exorbitant prices. It is as simple as two or more people wanting the same item — the bidders just get carried away! Another reason is the rarity or the pristine condition of a doll. This type of doll is extremely difficult to find and warrants the high auction price.

The final word is Madame Alexander dolls have always been collectible and should continue to be. They should endure in time and value. Wise collectors purchase dolls that they really like rather than purchasing dolls that are rumored to go up in value. Then, even if the doll's value doesn't go up, the collector has a beautiful doll that he or she loves. We hope you will continue to build the collections you desire, be they of older dolls or the wonderful current dolls that become available each year.

8" Alexander-Kins, Wendy Ann, Wendy, or Wendy-Kin

1953 – 1976:
Has "Alex" on back of doll.

1953:
First year of production, straight leg, non-walker. Only year Quiz-Kins were produced with two buttons on their back for the head to nod yes or no.

1954:
Straight leg walker.

1955:
Straight leg walker with no painted lashes under the eye.

1956 – 1965:
Bend knee walker.

1965 – 1972:
Bend knee, does not walk.

1973 – 1976:
Straight leg, non-walker with "Alex" on back of doll.

1977 – Present:
Has "Alexander" on back.

The Many Faces of Madame Alexander Dolls

Wendy Ann (composition)

Tiny & Little Betty

Princess Elizabeth

Maggie

Margaret (O'Brien)

Cissy

Elise (1950s – 1960s)

Lissy (1950s)

Cissette

Mary-Bel

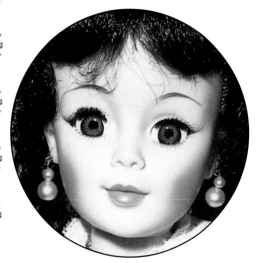

Jacqueline

Mary Ann

Elise (1960s – 1980s)

Polly & Leslie

Nancy Drew

Wendy Ann – New 1988 face

Maggie Mixup (1960 – 1961)

Wendy Ann (1953 – 1965)

Active Miss — 18" h.p., 1954 only (Violet/Cissy) $850.00

Adams, Abigail — 1976 – 1978, Presidents' Ladies/First Ladies
    Series, First Set (Mary Ann)..$150.00

Adams, Louisa — 1976 – 1978, Presidents' Ladies/First Ladies
    Series, First Set (Louisa)..$125.00

Addams Family — #31130, 1997 – 1998, set 4 dolls (8", 10") and Thing $350.00
    #31110, 1997 – 1998, 10" Gomez and Morticia..$180.00
    #31120, 1997 – 1998, 8" Wednesday and Pugsley..$160.00

Adorable Silk Victorian — 8", #26875, 2001, white dress $95.00

Africa — 8" h.p., #766, 1966 – 1971, BK (Wendy Ann) $295.00
    8" h.p., straight leg, re-issued, #523 – 583, 1988 – 1992 (Wendy Ann) $60.00

African Bride — 10", #28600, 2001, includes broom $125.00

Agatha — 18" h.p. (Cissy)
    1954 only, Me and My Shadow Series, rose taffeta dress, excellent face color ....$1,900.00 up
    8" h.p. (Wendy Ann), #00308, 1953 – 1954, black top and floral gown ....$1,300.00 up
    21" Portrait, #2171, 1967, red gown (Jacqueline) $675.00
    #2297, 1974, rose gown with full length cape (Jacqueline) $475.00
    #2291, 1975, blue with white sequin trim (Jacqueline)....................................$375.00
    #2294, 1976, blue with white rick-rack trim (Jacqueline)..................................$325.00
    #2230, 1979, 1980, lavender; #2230, 1981, turquoise blue (Jacqueline) $275.00
    #2230, 1981, turquoise blue (Jacqueline) $275.00
    10" Portrette, #1171, 1968 only, red velvet (Cissette)..$450.00

Age of Innocence — 10", #28400, 2001, dark blue vintage gown........................$120.00

Agnes — cloth/felt, 1930s $750.00

Aladdin — 8" h.p., #482, 1993; #140482, 1994 only, Storybook Series $60.00

Alaska — 8", #302, 1990 – 1992, Americana Series (Maggie smile face) $60.00

Albania — 8" straight leg, #526, 1987 only (Wendy Ann) $60.00

Alcott, Louisa May — 14", #1529, 1989 – 1990, Classic Series
    (Mary Ann) $85.00
    8" h.p., #409, 1992 only, Storyland Series (Wendy Ann) $90.00

Alegria — 10", h.p., #20118, 1996 Cirque du Soleil, silver outfit..........................$95.00

Alex — 16", plastic/vinyl, 2000, Fashion Doll Editor-in-Chief, 2000,
    #25570, brown skirt, white sweater, camel coat..$95.00
    Millennium Ball, 2000, #25580, ball gown with beading $130.00
    Museum Gala, 2000, #27280, gray sweater, beaded taffeta skirt $115.00
    Runway Review, 2000, #27275, black evening dress $90.00
    Magazine Launch, 2000, #27285, jet beaded black suit $85.00
    Alexandra Fairchild Ford, 2000, #26930, pink chiffon and taffeta dress $85.00

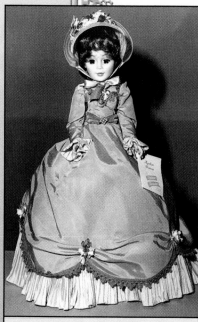

Agatha, 21", Portrait Doll, #2230, 1980, (Jacqueline).

Alexander-Kins, 8", BKW, 1959, (Wendy Ann). Polished cotton dress and pinafore. A rare doll.

Alexander-Kins, 8", 1953, SLNW, (Wendy Ann). Cotton school dress and pinafore. Came mint in original box.

Alex, continued

Lunch at 2, 2000, #27290, gray crepe dress $75.00
Woman of the Year, 2001, #30640, stunning gold gown $125.00
Tides, #30630, 2001, BK, redhead $80.00
Tides, #30620, 2001, BK, blonde $80.00
Tides, #30625, 2001, BK, brunette $80.00
Book Tour, #31625, 2001 ....$175.00
Mardi Gras, #31155, 2001 ....$250.00
Cyber Launch, #31215, 2001 ....$80.00
Sunset Grille, #31165, 2001 ....$110.00
Milano, #31221, 2001 ....$100.00
New Year's Eve, #28455, 2001 ....$150.00
Music Video Awards, #31220, 2001 ....$90.00
Santa Baby, #30635, 2001, red dress, coat with Christmas room $250.00
Paris, 16", is the new 2001 African-American Fashion Doll
   Grand Entrance, #31170, 2001, stunning orange gown with lavender accents...........$200.00
   La Concorde, #31175, 2001 ....$90.00

Alexander RagTime Dolls — cloth, 1938 – 1939 only ....$850.00 up

Alexander-Kins — 7½ – 8" h.p., must have excellent face color (Also referred to
as Wendy, Wendy Ann, or Wendy-Kin.) If doll is not listed here, see regular listing
for name. (Add more for mint or mint in box dolls. Special hairdos are higher priced.)
Straight leg non-walker, 1953 (Add more for Quiz-Kins)
Coat/hat (dress) $575.00
Cotton dress/organdy or cotton pinafore/hat...$550.00
Dresser/doll/wardrobe, mint ....$3,200.00 up
Easter doll ....$950.00 up
Felt jackets/pleated skirt dresses $550.00
Garden Party long gown ....$1,400.00 up
Jumper/one-piece bodysuit $375.00
Nightgown..$275.00
Nude/perfect doll (excellent face color) $300.00
Organdy dress/cotton or organdy pinafore/hat..$575.00
Satin dress/organdy or cotton pinafore/hat..$650.00
Sleeveless satin dress/organdy or cotton pinafore...$495.00
Taffeta dress/cotton pinafore/hat..$650.00
Robe/nightgown or P.J.'s...$300.00
Straight leg walker, 1954 – 1955, must have good face color.
(Add more for mint or mint in box dolls.)

Alexander-Kins, 8", #450, 1955, SLW. "Visitors Day at School."

Wendy's First Sailor Dress, 8", SLW, #576, 1955, (Wendy Ann). Tag: Alexander-Kin.

Alexander-Kins, *continued*

Basic doll in box/panties/shoes/socks	$425.00
Coat/hat (dress)	$475.00
Cotton dress/pinafore/hat	$450.00 up
Cotton school dress	$375.00
Day in Country	$950.00
Garden Party, long gown	$1,400.00 up
Maypole Dance	$575.00
Nightgown, robe, or P.J.'s	$275.00
Jumper dress with blouse effect, any material	$400.00
Organdy party dress/hat	$475.00 up
Riding Habit	$375.00 up
Sailor dress	$950.00 up
Sleeveless organdy dress	$375.00
Swimsuits (mint)	$350.00
Taffeta/satin party dress/hat	$550.00 up

Bend knee walker, 1956 – 1965, must have good face color. (Add more for mint or mint in box dolls.) "Alexander-Kin" dropped in 1963 and "Wendy Ann" used through 1965.

Nude (excellent face color)	$150.00
Basic doll in box/panties/shoes/socks (mint in box)	$450.00
Carcoat set	$950.00
Cherry Twin	$1,500.00 ea.
Coat/hat/dress	$425.00
Cotton dress/cotton pinafore/hat	$425.00
Cotton or satin dress/organdy pinafore/hat	$400.00 up
Easter Egg/doll, 1965, 1966 only	$1,500.00 up
Felt jacket/pleated skirt/dress/cap or hat	$425.00 up
First Dancing Dress (gown)	$750.00
Flowergirl	$875.00
French braid/cotton dress, 1965	$575.00
June Wedding	$750.00
Long party dress	$800.00 up
Nightgown/robe	$275.00

Neiman-Marcus (clothes must be on correct doll with correct hairdo)

Doll in case with all clothes	$1,400.00 up
Name of store printed on dress material	$750.00
2-pc. playsuit, navy with red trim	$575.00
Robe, navy	$325.00

Alexander-Kins, 8", BKW, 1957, #568, (Wendy Ann). A hard-to-find doll. The trim on the hat is missing from the sleeves, but there is no indication the trim was ever sewn there.

Alexander-Kins, 8", BKW, #530, 1957, (Wendy Ann). Tag: Alexander-Kin.

Alexander-Kins, 8", #569, 1958, (Wendy Ann). Polished cotton dress with velvet ribbon and lace trim. All original.

Alexander-Kins, continued

    Nude, perfect doll with excellent face color, bend knee/non-walker......................................$85.00
    Organdy dress/hat, 1965 ....$475.00
    Organdy dress/organdy pinafore/hat..$475.00
    Riding habit, boy or girl...$450.00
        Devon Horse Show...$750.00
    Riding habit, check pants, girl, 1965, boy, 1965 ....$375.00
    Sewing Kit/doll, 1965, 1966 only ....$950.00 up
    Skater..$600.00
    Sundress...$375.00
    Swimsuits, beach outfits..$325.00
    Taffeta party dress/hat $475.00
    Tennis..$450.00

Algeria — 8", straight leg, #528, 1987 – 1988 only (Maggie)..$60.00
Alice — 18" h.p., 1951 only, saran wig to waist (Maggie)..$750.00
Alice and Her Party Kit — 1965 only, included case, wardrobe and wigs,
   mint (Mary Ann) $750.00
Alice (in Wonderland) — 16" cloth, 1930 flat face, eyes painted to side $875.00
   1933 formed mask face $675.00
   7" compo., 1930s (Tiny Betty)..$400.00
   9" compo., 1930s (Little Betty)..$375.00
   11 – 14" compo., 1936 – 1940 (Wendy Ann)...$425.00 – 475.00
   13" compo., 1930s, has swivel waist (Wendy Ann) $425.00
   14½ – 18" compo., 1948 – 1949 (Margaret)..$475.00 – 750.00
   21" compo., 1948 – 1949 (Margaret, Wendy Ann) $950.00
   14" h.p., 1950 (Maggie)..$675.00
   17 – 23" h.p., 1949 – 1950 (Maggie & Margaret) ....$625.00 – 900.00
   15", 18", 23" h.p., 1951 – 1952 (Maggie & Margaret) ....$450.00 – 900.00
   14" h.p. with trousseau, 1951 – 1952 (Maggie) ....$1,600.00 up
   15" h.p., 1951 – 1952 (Maggie & Margaret) $575.00
   17" h.p., 1949 – 1950 (Maggie & Margaret) $700.00
   23" h.p., 1942 – 1952 (Maggie & Margaret) ....$875.00 up
   29" cloth/vinyl, 1952 (Barbara Jane) ....$700.00 up
   8" h.p., #465 – #590, 1955 – 1956 (Wendy Ann)...$800.00 up
   8", #494, Storyland Series, blue/white eyelet pinafore 1990 – 1992 ....$70.00
      #492, 1993, #140492, 1994 blue/white with red trim...$70.00
      8" h.p., 1972 – 1976, Disney crest colors (Disneyland, Disney World)...........................$450.00
   8" h.p., blue with lace trim, organdy pinafore, 1995 ....$70.00
   8" h.p., #13000, 1997 – 1998, Alice with calendar, blue party dress,
      gold crown, #13001, 1999 – 2000 ....$75.00

Wendy Adores A Party, 8", BKW, #566, 1958, (Wendy Ann). Tag: Alexander-Kin.

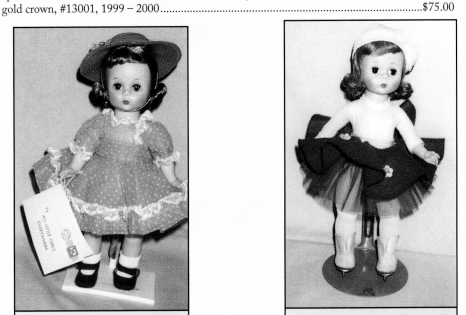

Wendy Learning to Skate, 8", BKW, #540, 1958, (Wendy Ann). Tag: Alexander-Kin.

12", Prom Party set, 1963 (Lissy) ....$950.00 up

14" plastic/vinyl, #1452 to 1974, #1552, 1966 – 1992, Literature &
Classic Series (Mary Ann) $100.00

14" plastic/vinyl, #87001, 1996 Storyland Friends...$110.00

14", h.p., #25905, (Margaret), 2000 – 2001, blue with white dot dress, organdy pinafore $140.00

10", 1991, with white rabbit (see Disney under Special Events/Exclusives)

18", #16001, 1996 Rag Doll Series (cloth doll) ....not available for sale

8", #30665, 2001, includes plush rabbit $50.00

All Star — 8" h.p., #346 – 346-1, Americana Series, 1993 white or black,
1994 white only $70.00

Allison — 18" cloth/vinyl, 1990 – 1991 ....$110.00

Alpine Boy and Girl — 1992 (see Christmas Shoppe under Special Events/Exclusives)

Altar Boy — 8" h.p., #311, 1991 only, Americana Series $70.00

Amanda — 8" h.p., #489, 1961 only, Americana Series, burnt
orange/lace trim (Wendy Ann)..$2,000.00 up

American Babies — 16 – 18" cloth, 1930s ....$175.00 – 350.00

American Beauty — 10" Portrette, #1142, 1991 – 1992, all pink $90.00

American Farm Couple — 8", 1997, #22160, 1930s rural America $130.00

American Girl — 7 – 8" compo., 1938 (Tiny Betty)...$385.00

9 – 11" compo., 1937 (Little Betty, Wendy Ann) ....$350.00 – 475.00

8" h.p., #388, #788, 1962 – 1963, became "McGuffey Ana" in
1964 – 1965 (Wendy Ann)..$395.00

American Indian — 9" compo., 1938 – 1939 (Little Betty) $350.00

American Legend, An — 10", #12510, 1999, with hardcover book $250.00

American Tots — 16 – 21" cloth, dressed in child's fashions..............$275.00 – 500.00

American Women's Volunteer Service (A.W.V.S.) — 14" compo.,
1942 (Wendy Ann) ....$850.00 up

Amish Boy — 8" h.p., BK, #727, 1966 – 1969, Americana Series (Wendy Ann) $375.00

Amish Girl — 8" h.p., BK, #726, 1966 – 1969, Americana Series (Wendy Ann)..........$375.00

Amy — (see Little Women)

Amy Goes to Paris Trunk Set — 8", #14635, 1996 ....$200.00

Amy the Bride — 10", #14622, 1996, ivory lace dress $100.00

Anastasia — 10" Portrette, #1125, 1988 – 1989 (Cissette)................................$90.00

14" (see M.A.D.C. under Special Events/Exclusives)

Anatolia — 8", straight leg, #524, 1987 only $65.00

Angel and 8" Music Box Creche — 8", #19530, 1997 – 2000, Nativity set $250.00

Angel — 8", in pink, blue, off-white gowns (Wendy & Maggie)...................$950.00 up

Baby Angel — 8" h.p., #480, 1955, multi-layered chiffon wings (Wendy Ann) ......$950.00 up

Guardian Angel — 8", #480, 1954 only (Wendy Ann)...........................$850.00 up

Guardian Angel — 8", #618, 1961 (Maggie smile face)........................$800.00 up

Guardian Angel — 10", #10602, 1995, first in series, all pink with white wings $110.00

Pristine Angel — 10", #10604, 1995, second in series, white with gold trim $110.00

Angel of Bliss — 10", #32155, 2000, pink long dress, white wings................$135.00

Angel Face — (see Shirley's Doll House under Special Events/Exclusives)

Angel Tree Topper — (see Tree Topper)

Anglund, Joan Walsh — Joy, 10", #28805 ....$45.00

Ann Estelle — 8", #17600, 1999 – 2001, Mary Engelbreit sailor outfit................$90.00

Anna and the King of Siam — 8", 1996, #14656, sold as set $160.00

Anna Ballerina — 18" compo., 1940, Pavlova (Wendy Ann) ....$950.00 up

Annabelle — 14 – 15" h.p., 1951 – 1952 only, Kate Smith's
stories of Annabelle (Maggie)...$600.00

14 – 15" trousseau/trunk, 1952 only, FAO Schwarz (Maggie)...........$1,500.00 up

18" h.p., 1951 – 1952 (Maggie) $750.00

20 – 23" h.p., 1951 – 1952 (Maggie) ....$700.00 – 875.00

Annabelle at Christmas — (see Belks & Leggett under Special Events/Exclusives)

Anna Karenina — 21" Portrait, #2265, 1991 (Jacqueline) $350.00

10", #21900, (Cissette) bustle dress, 1998 – 1999................................$125.00

10", #21910, (Cissette) Trunk set, doll, 3 outfits, 1998 – 1999 ....$275.00

Anne of Green Gables — 14", #1530, 1989 – 1990 only (Mary Ann) $100.00

14", #1579, 1992 – 1994, Goes to School, with trunk/wardrobe (Louisa/Jennifer)..........$200.00

14", #1570 in 1993 only, #261501 in 1995, Arrives at Station $125.00

14", 1993, Becomes the Teacher..$125.00

8" h.p., 1994 – 1995, #260417, At the Station (Wendy Ann)................$90.00

8" h.p., #260418, 1994, puff sleeve dress $100.00
8" h.p., #26423, 1995, concert dress $85.00
8" h.p., #26421, 1995, trunk playset $250.00
8" h.p., #13830, 1998 – 1999, floral dress, drawstring bag, straw hat..............$80.00
Annette — 1993 (see Disney under Special Events/Exclusives)
Annie the Artist — 20", #35001, 1996, artist outfit, crayons ....not available for sale
Annie Laurie — 14" compo., 1937 (Wendy Ann) $650.00
   17" compo., 1937 (Wendy Ann)..$925.00
Antoinette — 21" compo., 1946, extra make-up, must be mint (Wendy Ann) ....$2,100.00 up
Antoinette, Marie — 21", 1987 – 1988 only, multi-floral with pink front insert $375.00
Antony, Mark — 12", #1310, 1980 – 1985, Portraits of History (Nancy Drew) $70.00
Apple Annie of Broadway — 8" h.p., 1953 – 1954 (Wendy Ann) ....$1,100.00 up
Apple Pie — 14", #1542, 1991 only, Doll Classics (Mary Ann) $90.00
Apple Tree — 8", #13290, 2000 – 2001, dressed as a tree trunk with
   leaves and apples $80.00
April — 14", #1533, 1990 – 1991, Doll Classics (Mary Ann & Jennifer) $95.00
April Showers Bring May Flowers — 8", #13480, 1998 – 1999,
   pink taffeta and lace, parasol $100.00
Aquarius — 8", #21310, 1998, orange and gold mermaid costume $90.00
Argentine Boy — 8" h.p., BKW & BK, #772, 1965 only (Wendy Ann) $525.00
Argentine Girl — 8" h.p., BK, #0771-571, 1965 – 1972 (Wendy Ann) $150.00
   BKW, #771 (Wendy Ann) $175.00
   8" h.p., straight legs, #571, 1973 – 1976, marked "Alex" $70.00
   8" h.p., straight legs, #571, 1976 – 1986 (1985 – 1986 white face) $50.00
Aries — 8", #21330, 1998, gray furry ram outfit $90.00
Armenia — 8", #507, 1989 – 1990 (Wendy Ann) $70.00
Arriving in America — 8" h.p., #326, 1992 – 1993 only, Americana Series (Wendy Ann)........$75.00
Artie — 12" plastic/vinyl, 1962, sold through FAO Schwarz (Smarty) $285.00
Artiste Wendy — 8", #31250, 1998 – 1999, pink smock and black beret.............$75.00
Ashley — 8", #628, 1990 only, Scarlett Series, tan jacket/hat $100.00
   8" h.p., #633, 1991 – 1992 only, Scarlett Series, as Confederate officer $125.00
Astor — 9" early vinyl toddler, 1953 only, gold organdy dress & bonnet $150.00
Astrological Month Dolls — 14 – 17" compo., 1938 (Wendy).................$525.00
Aunt Agatha — 8" h.p., #434, 1957 (Wendy Ann), checked taffeta gown...........$1,300.00 up
Aunt Betsy — cloth/felt, 1930s $900.00
Aunt March — 8", #14621, 1996 ....$70.00
Aunt Pitty Pat — 14 – 17" compo., 1939 (Wendy Ann) from
   "Gone with the Wind"...$1,500.00 up
   8" h.p., #435, 1957 (Wendy Ann) from "Gone with the Wind" ....$1,800.00 up
   8" h.p., straight leg, #636, 1991 – 1992, Scarlett Series $100.00
Auntie Em — 8" h.p., #14515, 1995 only, Wizard of Oz series.........$90.00
Australia — 8", #504, 1990 – 1991 only (Wendy Ann)........................$60.00
Austria Boy* — 8" h.p., 1974 – 1989 (Wendy Ann)
   Straight legs, #599 – #533, 1973 – 1975, marked "Alex"...............$70.00
   #599, 1976 – 1989, marked "Alexander" $55.00
Austria Girl* — 8" h.p., 1974 – 1993 (Wendy Ann)
   Straight legs, #598, 1973 – 1975 marked "Alex"........................$75.00
   #598 – #532, 1976 – 1990, marked "Alexander".........................$55.00
   Reintroduced #110539 (Maggie), 1994 only $65.00
Autumn — 14", 1993, Changing Seasons Doll with four outfits.................$150.00
   5", porcelain, #25860, 2000, brown dress & jacket, black hat.............$65.00
Autumn in N.Y. — (see First Modern Doll Club under Special Events/Exclusives)
Autumn Leaves — 14", 1994, Classic Dolls $125.00
Avril, Jane — 10" (see Marshall Fields under Special Events/Exclusives)
Babbie — Cloth with long thin legs, inspired by Katharine Hepburn ....$1,000.00 up
   16", cloth child doll, 1934 – 1936 ....$775.00 up
   14" h.p. (Maggie)...$800.00 up
Babette — 10" Portrette, #1117, 1988 – 1989, black short dress (Cissette)........$75.00
Babs — 20" h.p., 1949 (Maggie)..$850.00
Babs Skater — 18" compo. (Margaret)...$1,250.00 up
   15" h.p., 1948 – 1950 (Margaret) ....$1,200.00 up
   17 – 18" h.p. ....$1,300.00 up
   21" h.p. ....$1,500.00 up

* Formerly Tyrolean Boy and Girl.

Aunt Agatha, 8", #434, 1957, (Wendy Ann), checked taffeta gown, black jacket, hat, and purse.

Babsie Baby — Compo./cloth, moving tongue $550.00
Babsie Skater (roller) — 15", 1941 (Princess Elizabeth)...$850.00
Baby Betty — 10 – 12" compo., 1935 – 1936..$300.00
Baby Brother and Sister — 20", cloth/vinyl, 1977 – 1979, (Mary Mine) ....$125.00 ea.
    14", 1979 – 1982...$75.00 ea.
    14", re-introduced 1989 only ....$65.00 ea.
Baby Clown — See Clowns
Baby Ellen — 14", 1965 – 1972 (black Sweet Tears) $125.00
Baby Genius — 11" all cloth, 1930s..$425.00
    11 – 12" compo./cloth, 1930s – 1940s..$250.00 up
    16" compo./cloth, 1930s – 1940s..$275.00
    22" compo./cloth, 1940s $550.00
    15", 18", h.p. head, vinyl limbs, 1949 – 1950
      (some get sticky or turn dark) ....$125.00 – 150.00
    21" h.p. head, vinyl limbs, 1952 – 1955 ....$350.00
    8" h.p./vinyl, 1956 – 1962 (see Little Genius)
Baby Jane — 16" compo., 1935 ....$950.00 up
Baby Lynn — 20" cloth/vinyl, 1973 – 1976...$135.00
    14" cloth/vinyl, 1973 – 1976..$125.00
Baby Madison — 14", #29750, 1999, vinyl, with layette $105.00
Baby McGuffey — 22 – 24" compo., 1937 ....$325.00
    20" cloth/vinyl, 1971 – 1976..$175.00
    14" cloth/vinyl, 1972 – 1978..$150.00
Baby Precious — 14" cloth/vinyl, 1975 only...$150.00
    21" cloth/vinyl, 1974 – 1976..$175.00
Baby in Louis Vuitton trunk/wardrobe
    or wicker basket with legs — Any year ....$900.00 up
Baby Shaver — 12", cloth h.p., 1941 – 1943,
    yellow floss wig, round painted eyes (Little Shaver) ....$650.00 up
Baby Sister — 18", #30300, cloth, 2001, pink check dress...$45.00
Bad Little Girl — 16" cloth, 1966 only, blue dress,
    eyes and mouth turned down, looking sad..$250.00
Bali — 8" h.p., #533, 1993 only $70.00
Ballerina — (Also see individual dolls – Leslie, Margaret, etc.)
    9" compo., 1935 – 1941 (Little Betty) $375.00
    11 – 13", 1930s (Betty) $400.00
    11 – 14" compo., 1936 – 1938 (Wendy Ann)..$425.00

Baby McGuffey, 14", 1940s, composition. Tag: Madame Alexander/New York.

Ballerina, 8", 1956, BKW, (Wendy Ann). All original. Tag: Alexander-Kins.

Ballerina, continued

17" compo., 1938 – 1941 (Wendy Ann) ....$700.00 up

21" compo., 1947, "Debra" ("Deborah") Portrait ballerina in
    mint condition (Wendy Ann) ....$5,500.00 up

8" h.p., must have excellent face color, (Wendy Ann)

(Also see Enchanted Doll House under Special Events/Exclusives)

(Also see M.A.D.C. under Special Events/Exclusives)

SLNW, #354, 1953 – 1954, lavender, yellow, pink, or blue ....$750.00 up

    8" straight leg, #0730, #530, #430, 1973 – 1992 (1985 – 1987 white face) $85.00

SLW, #454, 1955, lavender, yellow, pink, or white ....$675.00 up

BKW, #564, 1954 – 1960, golden yellow $575.00

    #454, 1955, white $475.00

    #564, 1956, rose $625.00

    #564 – 631, 1956, yellow $650.00

    #364, 1957, blue $400.00

    #544, 1958, pink $375.00

    #420, 1959, gold ....$750.00 up

    #420, 1961, lavender $750.00

    #640, 1964, pink $450.00

    BK, #620-730, 1965 – 1972, yellow $375.00

    #440-730, 1962 – 1972, blue $275.00

    #440-730, 1962 – 1972, pink $250.00

SLNW, #330, 1990 – 1991 (black or white dolls, 1991), Americana Series,
    white/gold outfit (Wendy Ann) $70.00

    #331 – 331-1, 1992, black or white doll in pink/silver outfit (Wendy Ann) $70.00

    #331, 1993, white doll only pink/silver outfit $65.00

    #100331, 1994 – 1995, white doll, pink tutu $65.00

    #13900 – 1998, lace tutu over pink tulle $85.00

    #17640, 1999 – 2000, blue Ballet Recital, wears silver crown $75.00

    #17660, 2000 – 2001, pink Ballet Class $70.00

    #17650, 1999 – 2000, lilac Ballet Recital, lilac and silver $75.00

    #17690, 1999 – 2000, pink Ballet Recital, pink knit outfit $75.00

    #25030, 2000, Irish Dream, green bodice, white tutu with shamrocks $80.00

    #26810, 2000, pink petal, light pink costume $80.00

10 – 11" h.p., #813, 1957 – 1960, must have excellent face color (Cissette) $385.00

12", 1964 only (Janie) $300.00

12", 1989 – 1990, "Muffin," (Janie) $85.00

12", 1990 – 1992 only, Romance Collection (Nancy Drew) $85.00

12", 1993 only, in lavender (Lissy) $175.00

14", 1963 only (Melinda) $325.00

15 – 18" h.p., 1950 – 1952, must have good face color (Margaret) ....$625.00 – 850.00

16½" h.p., 1957 – 1964, jointed ankles, knees & elbows,
    must have good face color (Elise) $400.00

    1957, yellow, rare $900.00

    1958, white $395.00

    1959, gold $425.00

    1960, pink $385.00

    1961, upswept hairdo, pink $425.00

    1962, blue $375.00

    1963 – 1964 only, small flowers in 1963; large flowers in 1964 (Mary-Bel) (18" also Elise) $400.00

17" plastic/vinyl, 1967 – 1989, discontinued costume (Elise) $140.00

17" plastic/vinyl, 1990 – 1991, "Firebird" and "Swan Lake" (Elise) $150.00

17", 1966 – 1971 only (Leslie - black doll) $450.00

16", classic ballerina, #22700, 2000 only $170.00

Barbara Jane — 29" cloth/vinyl, 1952 only, mint $500.00

Barbara Lee — 8", 1955, name given by FAO Schwarz $650.00

Barbary Coast — 10" h.p., 1962 – 1963, Portrette (Cissette) ....$1,500.00 up

Barton, Clara — 10", #1130, 1989 only, Portrette, wears nurse's outfit (Cissette) $125.00

Baseball Boy — 8", #16313, 1997, red, white baseball outfit $60.00

Baseball Girl — 8", #16300, baseball outfit with ball glove $60.00

Bathing Beauty — (see U.F.D.C. under Special Events/Exclusives)

Beary Best Friends — 8" with 2½" bear, #32160, 2000, white dress $70.00

Beast — 12", 1992 only, Romance Series (Nancy Drew) $100.00

    8", #140487 Storyland Series - 1994, Fairy Tales Series - 1995 ....$70.00

Beau Brummel — cloth, 1930s...$750.00
Beauty — 12", 1992 only, Romance Series (Nancy Drew).......................................$100.00
    8", #140486 Storyland Series - 1994, Fairy Tales Series - 1995 ....$80.00
Beauty Queen — 10" h.p., 1961 only (Cissette)..$375.00
Beaux Arts Dolls — 18" h.p., 1953 only (Margaret, Maggie)................................$2,200.00 up
Beddy-Bye Brooke — (see FAO Schwarz under Special Events/Exclusives)
Beddy-Bye Brenda — (Brooke's sister) (see FAO Schwarz under Special Events/Exclusives)
Being a Prom Queen — (see Wendy Loves)
Being Just Like Mommy — (see Wendy Loves)
Belgium — 8" h.p., BK, #762, 1972 only (Wendy Ann)..$125.00
    8" straight legs, #0762, #562, 1973 – 1975, marked "Alex".................................$70.00
    8" straight legs, #562, 1976 – 1988, marked "Alexander"..................................$60.00
    7" compo., 1935 – 1938 (Tiny Betty)...$275.00
    9" compo., 1936 only (Little Betty)...$300.00
Belle — 14", #18402, 1996 Dickens, red jacket, long skirt.................................$125.00
Belle Brummel — cloth, 1930s $775.00
Belle of the Ball — 10", #1120, 1989 only, Portrette, deep rose gown (Cissette) $130.00
Belle Watling — 10", 1992 only, Scarlett Series (Cissette)................................$125.00
    21", #16277, 1995 only, red outfit with fur trim (Jacqueline) $350.00
    10", #30820, 2001, gold satin dress, brown trim $150.00
Bellows' Anne — 14" plastic/vinyl, #1568, 1987 only, Fine Arts Series $75.00
Belk & Leggett Department Stores — (see Special Events/Exclusives)
Bernhardt, Sarah — 21", #2249, 1987 only, dressed in all burgundy.........................$325.00
Berries and Cream — 8", #28475, 2001, pink stripe dress, hat $90.00
Bessy Bell — 14" plastic/vinyl, #1565, 1988 only, Classic Series (Mary Ann) $75.00
Bessy Brooks — 8", #487, 1988 – 1991, Storybook Series (Wendy Ann) $70.00
    8", 1990 (see Collectors United/Bride under Special Events/Exclusives)
Best Man — 8" h.p., #461, 1955 only (Wendy Ann) $875.00
Best Friend — 8", #26090, 2000, blue silk dress with smocking.............................$110.00
    8", #26085, 2000 – 2001, pink silk dress with smocking $110.00
Beth — (see Little Women)
    10" (see Spiegel's under Special Events/Exclusives)
Betty — 14" compo., 1935 – 1942..$425.00
    12" compo., 1936 – 1937 only $350.00
    16 – 18" compo., 1935 – 1942 ....$425.00
    19 – 21" compo., 1938 – 1941 ....$550.00

Best Man, 8", h.p., #461, 1955 only. SLW with Wendy Ann face. All original.

Queen Esther, 8", SLW, (Wendy Ann). One of eight Bible characters made in 1954 only in extremely limited quantities. One of the rarest 8" dolls made.

Binnie, 18", #1820, 1964 only. Replaced shoes.

Betty, continued
    14½ – 17½" h.p., 1951 only, made for Sears (Maggie) $575.00
    30" plastic/vinyl, 1960 only $400.00
Betty, Tiny — 7" compo., 1934 – 1943 ....$325.00 up
Betty, Little — 9" compo., 1935 – 1943 ....$350.00 up
Betty Blue — 8" straight leg, #420, 1987 – 1988 only, Storybook Series (Maggie) $70.00
Betty Boop — 10", #17500, (Cissette) red dress, 1999 – 2001...$130.00
    21", #25125, 2000, doll with two outfits...$225.00
    10", #26450, 2000 – 2001, Razzle Dazzle, white long dress, hat....................$130.00
Bible Character Dolls — 8" h.p., 1954 only, (Wendy Ann)
    (Mary of Bethany, David, Martha, Ruth, Timothy, Rhoda,
        Queen Esther, and Joseph) ....$7,500.00 up
    1995 (see Delilah, Joseph, Queen Esther, and Samson)
Bill/Billy — 8" h.p., #320, #567, #420, 1955 – 1963, has boy's clothes and hair style
    (Wendy Ann) ....$475.00 up
    #577, #464, #466, #421, #442, #488, #388, 1953 – 1957, as groom ....$475.00 up
Billie Holiday — 10", #22070, 1997, silver long gown...$110.00
Billy-In-The-Box — 8" jester, 1996, Alexander signature box $125.00
Binnie — 18" plastic/vinyl toddler, 1964 only...$375.00
Binnie Walker — 15 – 18" h.p., 1954 – 1955 only (Cissy) ....$200.00 – 375.00
    15", 1955 only, in trunk with wardrobe..$750.00
    15", 1955 only, h.p. skater ....$700.00 up
    18", toddler, plastic/vinyl, 1964 only ....$325.00 up
    25", 1955 only in formals ....$550.00 up
    25", h.p., 1954 – 1955 only, dresses $450.00
Birds, The — 10", #14800, green dress, fur coat pictured 1998 catalog ....not available for sale
Birthday Dolls — 7" compo., 1937 – 1939 (Tiny Betty)...$375.00 up
Birthday, Happy — 1985 (see M.A.D.C. under Special Events/Exclusives)
Bitsey — 11 – 12" compo., 1942 – 1946 ....$250.00
    11 – 16" with h.p. head, 1949 – 1951 ....$250.00
    19 – 26", 1949 – 1951 ....$150.00 – 300.00
    12" cloth/vinyl, 1965 – 1966 only $150.00
Bitsey, Little — 9" all vinyl, 1967 – 1968 only $125.00
    11 – 16"...$75.00 – 175.00
Black Forest — 8", #512, 1989 – 1990 (Wendy Ann) $70.00
Blast Off 2000 — 8", #17830, 2000 only, (Maggie), silver and gold costume $85.00
Bliss, Betty Taylor — 1979 – 1981, 2nd set Presidents' Ladies/First Ladies
    Series (Mary Ann) $125.00
Blooming Rose — 8", #28470, 2001, pink stripe dress, hat $90.00
Blue Boy — 16" cloth, 1930s $650.00
    7" compo., 1936 – 1938 (Tiny Betty) $350.00
    9" compo., 1938 – 1941 (Little Betty) $375.00
    12" plastic/vinyl, #1340, 1972 – 1983, Portrait Children (Nancy Drew) $75.00
    1985 – 1987, dressed in blue velvet...$75.00
    8", #22130, 1997 – 1998, blue satin outfit $70.00
Blue Danube — 18" h.p., 1953 only, pink floral gown (#2001B - blue
    floral gown) (Maggie) ....$1,800.00 up
    18" h.p., 1954 only, Me and My Shadow Series, blue taffeta dress (Margaret) .....$1,600.00 up
Blue Edwardian Lady — 5", porcelain, #27025, blue long gown, 2000 ....$75.00
Blue Fairie — 10", #1166, 1993; #201166, 1994, Portrette,
    character from Pinocchio (Cissette) $125.00
Blue Fairy — 8", #32135, 2000, blue gown, wings...$80.00
Blue Gingham Chloe — 14", #25350, vinyl, 2001 ....$70.00
Blue Hat Doll — 8", #25310, 2000, Maud Humphrey design $85.00
Blue Mist Angel — 10", #25290, 2000 – 2001, Caucasian doll, blue costume $130.00
    10", #25291, 2000 – 2001, African-American doll, blue costume $130.00
Blue Moon — 14", #1560, 1991 – 1992 only, Classic Series (Louisa) $125.00
Blue Zircon — 10", #1153, 1992 only, Birthday Collection, gold/blue flapper $100.00
Blynkin — (see Dutch Lullaby)
Bobby — 8" h.p., #347, 1957 only (Wendy Ann) $575.00
    8" h.p., #361, #320, 1960 only (Maggie Mixup)..$600.00
Bobby Q. — cloth, 1940 – 1942 ....$750.00
Bobby (Bobbie) Soxer — 8" h.p., 1990 – 1991 (see Disney
    under Special Events/Exclusives)

Bobo Clown — 8", #320, 1991 – 1992, Americana Series (Wendy Ann) $85.00
Bohemia — 8", #508, 1989 – 1991 (Wendy Ann)..$60.00
Bolivia — 8" h.p., BK & BKW, #786, 1963 – 1966 (Wendy Ann)...$375.00
Bonnet Top Wendy — 8", #14487, 1995, Toy Shelf Series,
    yarn braids and large bonnet $70.00
Bonnie (Baby) — 16 – 19" vinyl, 1954 – 1955 $125.00 – 250.00
    24 – 30", 1954 – 1955...$125.00
Bonnie Blue — 14", #1305, 1989 only, Jubilee II (Mary Ann)..$150.00
    8" h.p., #629, #630, 1990 – 1992 (Wendy Ann)..$125.00
    8", #16649, 1995, side-saddle riding outfit $100.00
Bonnie Goes to London — 8", #640, 1993, Scarlett Series #160640-1994 ....$125.00
Bonnie Toddler — 18" cloth/h.p. head/vinyl limbs, 1950 – 1951..$175.00
    19" all vinyl, 1954 – 1955...$200.00
    23 – 24"...$250.00
Bon Voyage — 8" and 10" (see I. Magnum under Special Events/Exclusives)
Boone, Daniel — 8" h.p., #315, 1991 only, Americana Series,
    has no knife (Wendy Ann) $70.00
Bo Peep, Little — 7" compo., 1937 – 1941, Storybook Series (Tiny Betty) $375.00
    9 – 11" compo., 1936 – 1940 (Little Betty, Wendy Ann) $350.00
    7½" h.p., SLW, #489, 1955 only (Wendy Ann) $675.00
    8" h.p., BKW, #383, 1962 – 1964 (Wendy Ann)..$350.00
    8" h.p., BK, #783, 1965 – 1972 (Wendy Ann)...$150.00
    8" h.p., straight leg, #0783-483, 1973 – 1975, marked "Alex" (Wendy Ann) $75.00
    8" h.p., 1976 – 1986, #483 – #486, marked "Alexander" (Wendy Ann) $70.00
    14", #1563, 1988 – 1989, Classic Series (Mary Ann) $100.00
    14", #1567, 1992 – 1993 only, candy stripe pink dress (Mary Ann) $115.00
    12" porcelain, #009, 1990 – 1992 ....$200.00
    10" Portrette Series, 1994 ....$100.00
    8" (see Dolly Dears under Special Events/Exclusives)
    8", #25960, 2000 – 2001, long blue dress and hat with staff....................................$70.00
Boys Choir of Harlem — 8", #20170, 1997 – 1998, maroon blazer, Kufi hat $75.00
Brazil — 7" compo., 1937 – 1943 (Tiny Betty)...$325.00
    9" compo., 1938 – 1940 (Little Betty) $350.00
    8" h.p., BKW, #773, 1965 – 1972 (Wendy Ann)..$125.00
    BK, #773...$100.00
    8" h.p., straight leg, #0773, #573, 1973 – 1975, marked "Alex" (Wendy Ann) $70.00
    8" h.p., straight leg, #573, #547, #530, 1976 – 1988, marked "Alexander" $60.00
        #573, #547, #530, 1985 – 1987...$60.00

Brenda Starr, 12", 1964. All original in her rainy day outfit.

Brenda Starr, 12", 1964.

Wendy Pink Bride, 8", 1959, BKW, #483, (Wendy Ann). Rare pink all original bride. Pleated tulle gown and veil.

Brazil, continued

8" straight leg, #11564, 1996 International, carnival costume $65.00

Brenda Starr — 12" h.p., 1964 only (became "Yolanda" in 1965) $350.00

    Bride $375.00

    Street dresses..$400.00

    Ball gown $450.00

    Beach outfit $225.00

    Raincoat/hat/dress $350.00

Briar Rose — (see M.A.D.C. under Special Events/Exclusives)

    10", #14101, 1995, Brothers Grimm Series, blue floral with apron (Cissette) $95.00

Brick Piggy — 12", #10010, 1997, denim overalls, maize felt cap $90.00

Bride — Tiny Betty: Composition 7" compo., 1935 – 1939 ....$295.00

    9 – 11" compo., 1936 – 1941 (Little Betty) $325.00

  Wendy Ann: Composition 13", 14", 15" compo., 1935 – 1941 (Wendy Ann) ....$300.00 – 450.00

    17 – 18" compo., 1935 – 1943 (Wendy Ann) $450.00

    21 – 22" compo., 1942 – 1943 (Wendy Ann) ....$600.00 up

    In trunk/trousseau (Wendy Ann) ....$1,650.00 up

    21" compo., 1945 – 1947, Royal Wedding/Portrait (Wendy Ann) ....$2,400.00 up

  Margaret, Maggie: Hard plastic

    15" h.p., 1951 – 1955 (Margaret) ....$675.00 up

    17" h.p., 1950, in pink (Margaret) $850.00

    18" h.p., tagged "Prin. Elizabeth" (Margaret)..$700.00

    18" h.p., 1949 – 1955 (Maggie, Margaret) $675.00

    21" h.p., 1949 – 1953 (Margaret, Maggie) ....$1,200.00 up

    18" – 21", pink bride, 1953 (Margaret) ....$1,200.00 up

    23" h.p. 1949, 1952 – 1955 (Margaret)..$850.00

    25" h.p., 1955 only (Margaret) $875.00

Elise: 16½" h.p., 1957 – 1964, jointed ankles, elbows & knees,

must have good face color (also see 17" below)

    1957, nylon tulle, chapel length veil..$425.00

    1958, wreath pattern hem of skirt $500.00

    1959, tulle puffed sleeves, long veil (pink) $625.00

    1960, satin gown, lace bodice with sequins & breads..$425.00

    1961, short bouffant hair, tulle with puff sleeves $400.00

    1962, lace pattern bodice & trim on tulle skirt $425.00

    1963, tulle, rows of lace on bodice $425.00

    1964, lace bodice & sleeves, lace on skirt, chapel length veil $400.00

    2000, 16", Classic Bride, white lace and tulle gown...$210.00

Elise, 16½", 1959, (Elise). Jointed elbows, knees, and ankles. Mint, rare Pink Bride.

Cissy Bride, 21", 1962, #2170, (Cissy). Very elaborate gown of lace over pleated tulle. A very rare doll.

Bride, continued

Cissy: 20" h.p., 1955 – 1958
- 1955 only, Dreams Come True Series, brocade gown with floor length veil ....$1,200.00 up
- 1956 only, tulle gown, tulle cap & chapel length veil, Fashion Parade Series ....$1,000.00 up
- 1957 only, Models Formal Gowns Series, nylon tulle with double train of satin...............$900.00 up
- 1958 only, Dolls To Remember Series, lace circles near hem (wreath pattern) ....$950.00 up
- 1959 only, tulle over white satin $750.00

Cissette: 10" h.p., 1957 – 1963 must have good face color
- 1957, tulle gown, short veil or lace & tulle cap veil..$375.00
- 1958, lace wreath pattern, matches Elise & Cissy..$425.00
- 1959 – 1960, tulle gown, puff sleeves...$375.00
- 1961, tulle, rhinestones on collar & veil..$375.00
- 1962, lace bodice & trim on skirt, long veil...$350.00
- 1963, tulle, rows of lace on bodice & at hem (matches Elise the same year) $425.00
- In trunk/trousseau, various years..$900.00 up
- #1136, 1990 – 1991, Portrette $115.00
- #14103, 1995, 1920s style $100.00
- #22470, 10" Empire Bride, 1998, lace gown, straw bonnet $140.00
- #22460, 10" Rococo Bride, 1998, peach gown, lace train $150.00
- #22480, 10" Victorian Bride, 1998, blue satin gown...$140.00
- #26880, 10", Contemporary Bride, (blonde)..$130.00
- #26881 (brunette), 2000 ....$130.00

Lissy: 12" h.p., 1956 – 1959
- 1956, jointed knees & elbows, tulle, tulle cap veil...$625.00
- 1957, same as 1956, except long veil...$525.00
- 1958 – 1959, dotted net, tulle veil...$575.00
- Porcelain, 1991 – 1992 only (version of 14" head)..$200.00

Jacqueline: 21" Portrait
- #2151, 1965, full lace, wide lace edge on veil (Jacqueline) $950.00
- #2192, 1969, full lace overskirt and plain veil $750.00

Alexander-Kin (Wendy Ann): 8" h.p. or plastic/vinyl
- 8" h.p., #315, 1953 only, Quiz-Kin ....$725.00 up
- 8" h.p., 1954...$650.00 up
- SLW, BKW, #735 in 1955, #615 in 1956, #410 in 1957; #582 in 1958 ....$375.00 – 525.00
- BKW, #482, 1959, pink...$1,100.00 up
- BKW, #735, 1960...$400.00
- BKW, #480, 1961..$375.00
- BKW, #760 (#630 in 1965), 1963 – 1965 ....$375.00
- BK, #470 in 1966; #735 in 1967 – 1972 ....$200.00
- Straight leg, #0735-435, 1973 – 1975, marked "Alex"...$100.00
- Straight leg, #435, 1976 – 1994, marked "Alexander" $75.00
- #337, white doll; #336-1, black doll, 1991 – 1992..$70.00
- #337, 1993, white only...$60.00
- #435, 1985 – 1987 ....$60.00

Collectors United (see under Special Events/Exclusives)
- #10395, 1995, Special Occasion Series – African-American $70.00
- #10392, 1995, Special Occasion Series, three hair colors..$70.00
- #17016, 1996 white lace and satin gown...$70.00
- #21030, 1997 – 1998, white gown, comes with cake top, #21033 – African-American ...$100.00
- #21171, 1999, blonde or brunette, satin ribbon at hem $80.00
- #25015 (blonde), #25016 (brunette), 2000 ....$80.00
- #25017, 2000, African-American $80.00
- #30650 (blonde), #30652 (brunette), 2001, white dress, sequin trim................................$70.00
- #30651, African-American, 2001 ....$70.00

Mary Ann, Jennifer, Louisa: 14" plastic/vinyl
- #1465 (#1565 in 1974, #1565 in 1977, #1570 in 1976), 1973 – 1977 (Mary Ann)...........$100.00
- #1589 in 1987 – 1988; #1534 in 1990, Classic Series (Mary Ann, Jennifer) $100.00
- #1566, reintroduced 1992 only, ecru gown (Louisa, Jennifer) $150.00

Elise, Leslie, Polly: 17" plastic/vinyl or 21" porcelain
- 1966 – 1988 (Elise)...$175.00
- 1966 – 1971 (Leslie)..$325.00
- 1965 – 1970 (Polly)...$300.00
- Porcelain, 1989 – 1990, satin and lace look like bustle $425.00
- Porcelain, Portrait Series, 1993 – 1994..$425.00

Bridesmaid — 9" compo., 1937 – 1939 (Little Betty)...$350.00
    11 – 14" compo., 1938 – 1942 (Wendy Ann) ....$350.00 – 450.00
    15 – 18" compo., 1939 – 1944 (Wendy Ann) ....$375.00 – 600.00
    20 – 22" compo., 1941 – 1947, Portrait (Wendy Ann)......................$1,800.00 up
    21½" compo., 1938 – 1941 (Princess Elizabeth) ....$950.00 up
    15 – 17" h.p., 1950 – 1952 (Margaret, Maggie) ....$450.00 – 700.00
    15" h.p., 1952 (Maggie) $650.00
    18" h.p., 1952 (Maggie) ....$700.00 up
    21" h.p., 1950 – 1953, side part mohair wig, deep pink or lavender gown (Margaret) ....$800.00 up
    19" rigid vinyl, in pink, 1952 – 1953 (Margaret) ....$550.00 up
    15" h.p., 1955 only (Cissy, Binnie) $375.00
    18" h.p., 1955 only (Cissy, Binnie) $400.00
    25" h.p., 1955 only (Cissy, Binnie) $475.00
    20" h.p., 1956 only, Fashion Parade Series, blue nylon tulle & net (Cissy) ....$1,400.00 up
    10" h.p., 1957 – 1963 (Cissette) $450.00
    12" h.p., 1956 – 1959 (Lissy) ....$750.00 up
    16½" h.p., 1957 – 1959 (Elise) ....$475.00 up
    8", h.p. SLNW, 1953, pink, blue, or yellow ....$900.00 up
    8" h.p., SLW, #478, 1955 (Wendy Ann) ....$800.00 up
        BKW, #621, 1956 ....$750.00 up
        BKW, #408, #583, #445, 1957 – 1959 ....$700.00 up
    8", 2000, Little Gardenia, #26855 (Wendy), white tulle & satin $80.00
    8", 2000, Little Pearl, #26800, (Wendy), lace bodice $80.00
    17" plastic/vinyl (Elise) 1966 – 1987 ....$175.00
    17" plastic/vinyl, 1966 – 1971 (Leslie)..$325.00
Brigitta — 11" & 14" (see Sound of Music)
Brooke — (see FAO Schwarz under Special Events/Exclusives)
Bubbles Clown — 8" h.p., #342, 1993 – 1994, Americana Series $85.00
Buck Rabbit — Cloth/felt, 1930s ....$650.00 up
Bud — 16 – 19" cloth/vinyl, 1952 only (Rosebud head) $175.00
    19" & 25", 1952 – 1953 only....................................$150.00 – 300.00
Bulgaria — 8", #557, 1986 – 1987, white face (Wendy Ann) $60.00
Bumble Bee — 8" h.p., #323, 1992 – 1993, only Americana Series...................$75.00
Bunny — 18" plastic/vinyl, 1962 only, mint..$250.00
Bunny Tails — 8", #28200, 2000, yellow dress......................................$80.00
Burma — 7" compo., 1939 – 1943 (Tiny Betty).....................................$350.00
Butch — 11 – 12" compo./cloth, 1942 – 1946 ....$150.00
    14 – 16" compo./cloth, 1949 – 1951 ....$175.00
    14" cloth, vinyl head & limbs, 1950 only $175.00
    12" cloth/vinyl, 1965 – 1966 only $125.00
Butch, Little — 9" all vinyl, 1967 – 1968 only...................................$125.00
Butch McGuffey — 22" compo./cloth, 1940 – 1941 ....$275.00
Butterfly Queen — 8", #25670, 2000 – 2001, (Wendy), lavender costume...........$75.00
C.U. — (see Collectors United under Special Events/Exclusives)
Cafe Rose and Ivory Cocktail Dress — 10", #22200 – white, #22203 – black,
    1997 – 1998 ....$125.00
Calamity Jane — 8" h.p. Americana Series, 1994 only (Wendy Ann)..................$75.00
Calla Lilly — 10", #22390, 1998 (Cissette), white gown, hand beaded jewels $230.00
Cameo Lady — (see Collectors United under Special Events/Exclusives)
Camelot — (see Collectors United under Special Events/Exclusives)
Camille — 21" compo., 1938 – 1939 (Wendy Ann)...........................$3,500.00 up
Canada — 8" h.p., BK, #760, 1968 – 1972 (Wendy Ann)...........................$100.00
    Straight leg, #0706, 1973 – 1975, marked "Alex" $70.00
    Straight legs, #560 (#534 in 1986), 1976 – 1988 (white face 1985 – 1987),
        marked "Alexander" $60.00
    Straight legs, #24130, 1999, hockey skater $90.00
Cancer — 8", #21360, 1998, red crab costume $90.00
Candy Kid — 11 – 15" compo., 1938 – 1941 (Wendy Ann)
    red/white striped dress ....$275.00 – 450.00
    8", #27060, 2000, h.p., Peter Pan series, red coat, black pants $85.00
Candy Land Game — Princess Lolly – 8", #25250, 2000, yellow costume $80.00
Capricorn — 8", #21300, 1998 (Maggie), fuchsia snakeskin body...................$90.00
Captain Hook — 8" h.p., #478, 1992 – 1993 only, Storyland Series
    (Peter Pan) (Wendy Ann) $90.00

Captain Hook, continued

    8", #27060, 2000 – 2001, h.p., Peter Pan series, red coat, black pants $95.00

Careen — (see Carreen)

Carhop Takes Your Order — 8", #17710, 2000, black check dress $75.00

Carmen — Dressed like Carmen Miranda, but not marked or meant as such.

    7" compo., 1938 – 1943 (Tiny Betty) $350.00

    9 – 11" compo., 1938 – 1943, boy & girl (see also "Rumbera/Rumbero") (Little Betty)..........$275.00 ea.

    11" compo., 1937 – 1939, has sleep eyes (Little Betty)..............................$350.00

    14" compo., 1937 – 1940 (Wendy Ann) $450.00

    17" compo., 1939 – 1942 (Wendy Ann) $650.00

    21" compo., 1939 – 1942, extra make-up, mint (Wendy Ann) ....$1,400.00 up

    21" compo., 1939 – 1942, Portrait with extra make-up ....$1,900.00 up

    14" plastic/vinyl, #1410, 1983 – 1986, Opera Series (Mary Ann) $80.00

    10" h.p., #1154, 1993 only, Portrette Series (Miranda), yellow/red $90.00

    16", #28395, 2001, red Spanish dress, black lace $250.00

Carmen Miranda Lucy — 10", #25760, 2000, white dress with ruffles $140.00

Carnavale Doll — (see FAO Schwarz under Special Events/Exclusives)

Carnival in Rio — 21" porcelain, 1989 – 1990 ....$475.00

Carnival in Venice — 21" porcelain, 1990 – 1991 ....$475.00

Caroline — 15" vinyl, 1961 – 1962 only, in dresses, pants/jacket $400.00

    In riding habit $400.00

    Dressed as Kurt of Sound of Music $475.00

    In case/wardrobe ....$900.00 up

    8", 1993 (see Belk & Leggett under Special Events/Exclusives)

    8", 1994 (see Neiman-Marcus under Special Events/Exclusives)

Carreen/Careen — 14 – 17" compo., #1593, 1937 – 1938 (Wendy Ann) ....$750.00 up

    14" plastic/vinyl, 1992 – 1993 only (Louisa/Jennifer) $125.00

    8" plaid, two large ruffles at hem, #160646, 1994 only $100.00

    8", #15190, 1999 (Wendy), blue dress, straw hat $85.00

Carrot Kate — 14", #25506, 1995, Ribbons & Bows Series,

    vegetable print dress (Mary Ann) $140.00

Carrot Top — 21" cloth, 1967 only $125.00

Casey Jones — 8" h.p., 1991 – 1992 only, Americana Series $70.00

Casper's Friend Wendy — 8", (Maggie) #15210, 1999, red costume, broom $80.00

Caterpillar — 8" h.p., #14594, 1995 – 1996, has eight legs,

    Alice In Wonderland Series $100.00

Cats — 16", plush, dressed, glass eyes, long lashes, felt nose $350.00

Cat on a Hot Tin Roof — 10", #20011, "Maggie," white chiffon dress $125.00

Celia's Dolls — (see Special Events/Exclusives)

Celtic Bride — 10", #28595, 2001, white gown, gold trim, red rose

    headpiece and bouquet $125.00

Century of Fashion — 14" & 18" h.p., 1954 (Margaret,

    Maggie & Cissy) ....$2,000.00 up

Changing Seasons — (Spring, Summer, Autumn, Winter)

    14", 1993 – 1994 ....$140.00 ea.

Chanukah Celebration — 8", #27330, 2001, blue dress $95.00

Charity — 8" h.p., #485, 1961 only, Americana Series, blue cotton

    dress (Wendy Ann) ....$1,900.00 up

Charlie Brown — 10", #26425, 2001, Peanuts Gang, includes

    Snoopy and ballglove $40.00

Champs-Elysées — 21" h.p., black lace over pink,

    rhinestone on cheek ....$5,000.00 up

Charlene — 18" cloth/vinyl, 1991 – 1992 only $100.00

Chatterbox — 24" plastic/vinyl talker, 1961 only $275.00

Cheerleader — 8", #324, 1990 – 1991 only, Americana

    Series (Wendy Ann) $70.00

    8", 1990 (see I. Magnin under Special Events/Exclusives)

    8" h.p., #324, #324-1, 1992 – 1993 only, Americana Series,

      black or white doll, royal blue/gold outfit $75.00

Chef Alex — 8", #31260, 1998 (Maggie) chef attire $85.00

Cheri — 18" h.p., 1954 only, Me and My Shadow Series,

    white satin gown, pink opera coat (Margaret) ....$1,800.00 up

Cherry Blossom — 14", #25504, 1995, Ribbons & Bows Series,

    cherry print dress (Mary Ann) $135.00

Carreen O'Hara, 8", #15190, 1999, (Wendy).
Blue dress with straw hat with feathers.

Cherry Girl — 8", #17590, 1999 – 2001, Mary Engelbreit,
  comes with basket and card $90.00
Cherry Twins — 8" h.p., #388E, 1957 only (Wendy Ann) ....$1,500.00 up ea.
  8", BK, #17700, 1999, pair, remake of 1957 set $130.00
Cherub — 12" vinyl, 1960 – 1961...$250.00
  18" h.p. head/cloth & vinyl, 1950s $350.00
  26", 1950s...$375.00
Cherub Babies — cloth, 1930s $450.00
Cheshire Cat — 8", #13070, 1997 – 1999 Storyland Series,
  pink velvet cat suit $75.00
Chile — 8" h.p., #528, 1992 only (Maggie) $70.00
Child at Heart Shop — (see Special Events/Exclusives)
Child's Angel — 8", #14701, 1996, gold wings, harp, halo $70.00
Children's Prayer — 8", #28385, pink gown, bonnet $80.00
China — 7" compo., 1936 – 1940 (Tiny Betty) $325.00
  9" compo., 1935 – 1938 (Little Betty) $300.00
  8" h.p., BK, #772, 1972 (Wendy Ann)..$100.00
  8" (Maggie smile face) $125.00
  Straight leg, #0772 – #572, 1973 – 1975, marked "Alex" $70.00
  Straight leg, #572, 1976 – 1986, marked "Alexander" (Wendy Ann) $60.00
  #572, 1987 – 1989 (Maggie)...$70.00
  8", #11550, 1995 only, 3 painted lashes at edges of eyes (Wendy Ann) ...$60.00
  8", #11561, 1996 International, Little Empress costume $75.00
  8", #26280, 2000 – 2001, (Wendy), red silk costume with panda bear....$70.00
Chinese New Year — 8", 2 dolls, #21040, 1997 – 1998 ....$130.00
  8", 3 dolls, dragon, #21050, 1997 – 1998..$230.00
Chloe — Blue gingham - 14", #25350, 2000, dress and hat....................$60.00
  Pink gingham, 14", #25345, 2000, white dress with pink check $60.00
Christening Baby — 11 – 13" cloth/vinyl, 1951 – 1954 ....$150.00
  16 – 19"...$150.00
Christmas Angels — (see Tree Toppers)
Christmas at Grandma's — 8", #27445, 2000, red coat and hat.............$85.00
Christmas Candy — 14", #1544, 1993 only, Classic Series $115.00
Christmas Carol — 8" (see Saks Fifth Avenue under Special Events/Exclusives)
Christmas Caroler — 8", #19650, 1997, red velvet cape, print skirt $85.00
Christmas Caroling — 10", #1149, 1992 – 1993 only, Portrette, burnt orange/gold dress.......$115.00
Christmas Cookie — 14", #1565, 1992 (Also see 'Lil Christmas Cookie, 8")
  (Louisa/Jennifer) $125.00
Christmas Eve — 14" plastic/vinyl, #241594, 1994 only (Mary Ann) $115.00
  8", #10364, 1995, Christmas Series $75.00
Christmas Holly — 8", #19680, 1998 – 1999, print dress, red coat..........$85.00
Christmas Shoppe — (see Special Events/Exclusives)
Christmas Stocking — Dancing Wendy, 20" stocking, #28530, 2001 ......$56.00
  Skating Maggie, 20" stocking, #31255, 2001.....................................$56.00
Christmas Tree Topper — 8" (see Spiegel's under Special Events/Exclusives;
  also Tree Topper)
Chrysanthemum Garden Ball — 10", #31245, 2001, green and pink ball gown $125.00
Churchill, Lady — 18" h.p., #2020C, 1953 only, Beaux Arts Series, pink gown with
  full opera coat (Margaret) ....$2,300.00 up
Churchill, Sir Winston — 18" h.p., 1953 only, has hat (Margaret) ....$1,250.00 up
Cinderella — (see also Topsy Turvy for two-headed version)
  7 – 8" compo., 1935 – 1944 (Tiny Betty)..$325.00
  9" compo., 1936 – 1941 (Little Betty) $350.00
  13" compo., 1935 – 1937 (Wendy Ann) $395.00
  14" compo., 1939 only, Sears exclusive (Princess Elizabeth)................$500.00
  15" compo., 1935 – 1937 (Betty) $475.00
  16 – 18" compo., 1935 – 1939 (Princess Elizabeth).............................$550.00 up
  8" h.p., #402, 1955 only (Wendy Ann)..$900.00
  8" h.p., #498, 1990 – 1991, Storyland Series (Wendy Ann) $65.00
  8", #476, 1992 – 1993, blue ball gown, #140476, 1994 Storyland Series $75.00
  8", #475, 1992 only, "Poor" outfit in blue w/black strips $70.00
  8" h.p., #14540, 1995 – 1996, pink net gown with roses, Brothers Grimm Series,
    #13400, 1997 – 2000...$75.00
    8", h.p., #13410, 1997 – 1999, calico skirt with broom and pumpkin..............$75.00

Poor Cinderella, 14", plastic/vinyl (Mary Ann). In production from 1967 to 1992.

Cinderella, continued

8", h.p., #13490, 1999 – 2001, Cinderella's wedding, white gown $100.00
8", At the Ball, #30670, 2001, white dress, blue long cape......................................$80.00
12" h.p., 1966 only, Literature Series (Classic Lissy)......................................$950.00 up
12" h.p., 1966, "Poor" outfit $675.00
   1966, in window box with both outfits ....$1,600.00 up
14" h.p., 1950 – 1951, ball gown (Margaret)..$900.00 up
14" h.p., 1950 – 1951, "Poor" outfit (Margaret) ....$675.00 up
14", h.p., #25940, 2000, pink, lace trimmed long gown $140.00
18" h.p., 1950 – 1951 (Margaret) ....$800.00 up
21", #45501, 1995, pink and blue, Madame's Portfolio Series.............................$300.00
14" plastic/vinyl (#1440 to 1974; #1504 to 1991; #1541 in 1992) 1967 – 1992,
   "Poor" outfit (can be green, blue, gray, or brown) (Mary Ann) $80.00
14", #140 on box, 1969 only, FAO Schwarz, all blue satin/gold
   trim, mint (Mary Ann) $425.00
14" plastic/vinyl, #1445, #1446, #1546, #1548, 1970 – 1983, Classic Series,
   dressed in pink (Mary Ann)...$100.00
#1548, #1549, 1984 – 1986, blue ball gown, two styles (Mary Ann)..........................$100.00
14", #1546, #1547, 1987 – 1991, Classic Series, white or blue ball gown
   (Mary Ann, Jennifer) $125.00
14", #1549, 1992 only, white/gold ball gown (Jennifer)..............................$125.00
14", 1985, with trunk (see Enchanted Doll House under Special Events/Exclusives)
14", 1994, has two outfits (see Disney World under Special Events/Exclusives)
14", 1996, #87002, white gown, gold crown (Mary Ann) $125.00
14", #25940, 2001, (Margaret), long pink ball gown $150.00
10", 1989 (see Disney Annual Showcase of Dolls under Special Events/Exclusives)
10", #1137, 1990 – 1991, Portrette, dressed in all pink (Cissette) $100.00
Cinderella's Carriage — #13460, 1999 – 2000, white metal carriage....................$175.00
Cinderella's Footmouse — 8", #13470, 1999 – 2000, painted face $105.00
Cissette — 10 – 11" h.p., 1957 – 1963, high heel feet, jointed elbows & knees,
   must have good face color, in various street dresses. Allow more for M.I.B.,
   rare outfits & fancy hairdos..$350.00
   In formals, ball gowns..$550.00 up
   Coats & hats $350.00
   1961 only, beauty queen with trophy..$350.00
   Special gift set/three wigs ....$950.00 up

Dating Cissette Dolls

Eyelids: 1975, beige; 1958, pale pink; 1959 – 1963,

Clothes: 1957 – 1958, darts in bodice; 1959 – 1963, no darts except ball gowns

Fingernails: 1962 – 1963, polished

Eyebrows: 1957 – 1963, single stroked

Body and legs: 1957 – 1963, head strung with hook and rubber band; legs jointed with plastic socket

Feet: 1957 – 1963, high heels

Wigs: 1957 – 1958, three rows of stitching; 1959 – 1963, zigzag stitches except 1961 – 1962 with fancy hairdos, then three rows; 1963, few have rooted hair in cap, glued to head or removable wigs

Tags: 1957 – 1962, turquoise; 1963, dark blue

Portrette: 1968 – 1973. Two or three stroke eyebrows, blue eyelids, no earrings, strung head with hook, high heels.

Jacqueline: 1961 – 1962. Two or three stroke eyebrows, side seam brunette wig, small curl on forehead, blue eyelids, eyeliner, painted lashes to sides of eyes, polished nails, head strung, socket jointed hips with side seams, high heels.

Sleeping Beauty: 1959 only. Three stroke eyebrows, pink eyelids, no earrings, mouth painted wider, no knee joints, flat feet, jointed with metal hooks.

Sound of Music: 1971 – 1973. (Brigitta, Liesl, Louisa). Two stroke eyebrows, the rest same as Portrettes.

Tinker Bell: 1969 only. Two stroke eyebrows, blue eyelids, painted lashes to side of eyes, no earrings, hair rooted into wig cap, head and legs strung with metal hooks.

Margot: 1961. Same as Jacqueline, except has three stroke eyebrows and elaborate hairdos.

Cissette, continued

Doll only, clean with good face color $125.00

1957, Queen/trunk/trousseau ....$1,200.00 up

Slacks or pants outfits $350.00

Cissette Barcelona — 10", Spanish costume, black lace, 1999 ....$165.00

Cissy — 20" h.p. (also 21"), 1955 – 1959, jointed elbows & knees, high heel feet,
must have good face color, in various street dresses $550.00 – 750.00

Dress & full-length coat $500.00

In ball gowns..$900.00 up

Trunk/wardrobe..$1,200.00 up

Pants suits ....$450.00 up

1950s magazine ads using doll (add 10.00 if framed) $25.00

21", reintroduced in the following 1996 MA Couture Collection

    #67303, aquamarine evening column and coat $275.00

    #67302, cafe rose and ivory cocktail dress $325.00

    #67306, cafe rose and ivory cocktail dress, African-American $400.00

    #67301, coral and leopard travel ensemble..$325.00

    #67601, ebony and ivory houndstooth suit $600.00

Cissette, 10", wearing a dress available as a boxed outfit in 1962.

Cissette, 1959, 10", (Cissette). Elaborate gold ball gown.

Cissy, 1957, #2160, 21", (Cissy). Gown of dotted net accented with flowers over pink taffeta.

Cissy, 21", 1958, #2252, (Cissy). Wearing a pink satin cocktail dress. She is missing her pink roses in her hair.

Vienna Cissy, 21", #25585, 2000 only.

Cissy, continued

#67603, ebony and ivory houndstooth suit, African-American $700.00
#67304, onyx velvet lace gala gown and coat $375.00
#67602, pearl embroidered lace bridal gown...$650.00
#86003, limited edition red sequined gown $375.00

21", 1997 MA Couture Collection
#22210, daisy resort ensemble, limited to 2,500 ....$375.00
#22230, tea rose cocktail ensemble $350.00
#22220, calla lily evening ensemble..$700.00
#22240, peony and butterfly wedding gown $450.00
#22290, gardenia gala ball gown $400.00
#22250, Cissy's secret armoire trunk set (1997 – 1998) $750.00

21", 1998 MA Couture (each limited to 1,500)
#22300 Cissy Paris, gold houndstooth outfit, sable, feathered hat $625.00
#22330 Cissy Barcelona, coral charmeuse with black lace $625.00
#22333 Cissy Barcelona, African-American $625.00
#22320 Cissy Milan, long fur coat and fur-trimmed hat $625.00
#22310 Cissy Venice, brocade gown, blue taffeta cape $625.00
#22340 Cissy Budapest, blue dress and coat trimmed with fur............................$625.0

21", 1999, Cissy Designer Originals (see Madame Alexander Doll Company
   under Specials/Exclusives)

21", 2000, #25555, Rome Cissy...$400.00
#26980, New York Cissy $350.00
#25585, Vienna Cissy $400.00
#25560, Cairo Cissy...$350.00
#25565, Shanghai Cissy...$325.00
#26865, Hollywood Cissy $450.00
#26866, Hollywood Cissy, African-American $450.00
#27005, Romantic Dreams Cissy...$350.00
#28450, Peacock Rose, limited to 600 ....$1,000.00
#27370, Yardley Cissy, blue dress, blonde $600.00

21", 2001, all limited to 500 pieces
#28415, Society Stroll Cissy, (Caucasian)..$500.00
#28415, Society Stroll Cissy, (African-American)...$500.00
#28441, Royal Reception Cissy..$550.00
#28430, Black and White Ball Cissy..$450.00
#28420, A Day in the Life of Cissy, trunk set $550.00
#28435, Haute Couture, black suit, hat with feathers $500.00
#28440, On the Avenue Yardley Cissy, green suit, plush dog $500.00
#31235, Promise of Spring Cissy $800.00

21", Cissy Amethyst, #32070, limited to 350 ....$500.00
21", Manhattan Gothic, #31965, 2001, limited to 100...$1,200.00
21", Madame Du Pompador Cissy, #31520, 2001, limited to 100 ....$1,700.00
21", Prima Donna Cissy, #31970, 2001, limited to 100 ....$1,200.00

Cissy Bride — 21", #52011, porcelain portrait, 1994 only $500.00
Cissy By Scassi — (see FAO Schwarz under Special Events/Exclusives)
Cissy Godey Bride — 21", #011, porcelain, 1993 only $525.00
Civil War — 18" h.p., #2010B, 1953 only, Glamour Girls Series, white taffeta
   with red roses (Margaret)...$1,800.00 up
Clara — 8", #25330, 2000 – 2001, blue long gown with nutcracker $90.00
Clara & The Nutcracker — 14", #1564, 1992 only (Louisa/Jennifer) $110.00
Clara's Party Dress — 8", #14570, 1995, Nutcracker Series....................................$70.00
Clarabell Clown — 19", 1951 – 1953 ....$350.00
   29"...$575.00
   49"...$1,000.00
Classic Ballerina — 16", #22700, white tulle and satin (1999)..................................$170.00
Classic Bride — 16", #22690, white tulle and lace gown (1999) $190.00
Claudette — 10", #1123 (in peach), 1988 – 1989, Portrette (Cissette) $85.00
Cleopatra — 12", #1315, 1980 – 1985, Portraits of History Series $75.00
   10", #86002, 1996 Platinum Collection..$100.00
Cleveland, Frances — 1985 – 1987, 4th set Presidents' Ladies/First Ladies Series
   (Mary Ann)..$125.00
Clover Kid — 7" compo., 1935 – 1936 (Tiny Betty)..$375.00
Clown — 8", #305, 1990 – 1992 only, Americana Series, has painted face (Wendy) ...$85.00

Clown, *continued*

Baby — 8", #464-1955, has painted face (Wendy Ann)...$1,200.00 up
Bobo — 8" h.p., #310, 1991 – 1992 (Wendy Ann)..$100.00
Pierrot — 8", #561, 1956 only (Wendy Ann)...$1,000.00 up
  14", 1991 only, #1558, white costume with red trim $85.00
Stilts — 8", #320, 1992 – 1993, doll on stilts $125.00
Clue Game Doll — 8", #25255, 2000, maid costume $70.00
Coca-Cola 1920s — 10", #28280, 2001, long white dress with lace $150.00
Coca Cola Carhop — 10", #17400, 1997 – 2000, roller skates, #17401, brunette..........$115.00
Coca Cola Celebrates American Aviation — 10", #17380, 1998 – 1999 ....$175.00
Coca Cola Fantasy — 10", #31210 – white, #31213 – black, 1997 – 1998........$150.00
Coca Cola Nostalgia — 16", #17490, 1999, white lace dress $220.00
Coca-Cola Off to the North Pole — 8", #25245, 2001, with bear $100.00
Coca-Cola School Days — 8" #28275, 2001, includes lunch box $110.00
Coca-Cola Sock Hop — 10", #26255, 2001, red-checked skirt $120.00
Coca Cola Victorian Calendar Doll — 10", #17360, 1998 – 1999 ....$165.00
Coca Cola Winter Fun Wendy — 8", #17370, 1999, red ski outfit $100.00
Coco — 21" plastic/vinyl, 1966, in various clothes (other than Portrait)...........$2,000.00 up
  In sheath style ball gown...$2,200.00 up
  14", #1558, 1991 – 1992, Classic Series (Mary Ann)...................................$85.00
  10", #1140, 1989 – 1992, Portrette, dressed in all black (Cissette)..............$85.00
  16", #31240, 1997 – 1998, travel wardrobe and dog, Cleo.............................$450.00
  16", #22400, 1998, Belle Epoque, includes houndstooth and glitter gown outfits $325.00
Collecting Butterflies — 8", #28240, 2001, lavender dress with butterflies $50.00
Collecting Buttons — 8", #28245, 2001, white dress trimmed in pink.............$50.00
Collecting Dolls — 8", #30940, 2001, pink lacy dress with doll and dollhouse case $75.00
Collecting Seashells — 8", #28250, 2001, yellow dress with seashells............$50.00
Collecting Trains — 8", #28585, 2001, striped overalls with Bachmann train $110.00
Collector Pin Series — 1999, 2½" polyresin miniature doll $10.00
Collectors United — (see Special Events/Exclusives)
Colleen — 10", #1121, 1988 only, Portrette, in green (Cissette) $85.00
Colonial — 7" compo., 1937 – 1938 (Tiny Betty)...$325.00
  9" compo., 1936 – 1939 (Little Betty) $350.00
  8" h.p., BKW, #389, #789, 1962 – 1964 (Wendy Ann)................................$350.00
Columbian Sailor — (see U.F.D.C. under Special Events/Exclusives)
Columbine — 8", #14575-1995, Nutcracker Series $65.00
Columbus, Christopher — 8" h.p., #328, 1992 only, Americana Series $125.00
Comedienne — 10", #20120, clown, 1996 Cirque du Soleil Series $85.00
Computer Age Wendy — 8", #17820, 1999, comes with laptop and cell phone $70.00
Confederate Officer — 12", 1990 – 1991, Scarlett Series (Nancy Drew) $80.00
  8" h.p., 1991 – 1992, Scarlett Series (see Ashley)
Congratulations — 8" h.p., #21180, 1998 (Maggie), pink dress, balloons $80.00
Contemporary Bride — 10", 2001 ....$140.00
Cookie — 19" compo./cloth, 1938 – 1940, must be in excellent condition $650.00
Coolidge, Grace — 14", 1989 – 1990, 6th set Presidents' Ladies/First Ladies
  Series (Louisa) $125.00
Coppertone Beach Set — 8", #12110, 1998 – 1999, bikini, umbrella, suntan lotion $140.00
Coppelia — 16", #28390, 2001, pink ballerina $200.00
Coral and Leopard Travel Ensemble — 10", #22180, 1997 ....$125.00
Cornelia — Cloth & felt, 1930s ....$700.00 up
  21", #2191, 1972, Portrait, dressed in pink with full cape, (Jacqueline)..............$450.00
  #2191, 1973, pink with ¾ length jacket $375.00
  #2296, 1974, blue with black trim $350.00
  #2290, 1975, rose red with black trim and hat...$375.00
  #2293, 1976, pink with black trim and hat...$350.00
  #2212, 1978, blue with full cape $325.00
Cossack — 8" h.p. #511, 1989 – 1991 (Wendy Ann).....................................$70.00
Country Christmas — 14", #1543, 1991 – 1992 only, Classic Series (Mary Ann) $135.00
  8", #20190, 1999 – 2000, calico dress, snowman $75.00
Country Cousins — 10" cloth, 1940s $575.00
  26" cloth, 1940s $650.00
  30" cloth, 1940s $750.00
  16½", 1958, mint (Mary-Bel) $375.00
Country Fair — (see Wendy Loves)

Coppertone Beach Set, 8", #12110, 1998 – 1999, (Wendy). Comes with umbrella and accessories shown.

Courtney and Friends — (see Madame Alexander Doll Company under Special Events/Exclusives)

Cousin Grace — 8" h.p., BKW, #432, 1957 only (Wendy Ann) ....$1,900.00 up

Cousin Karen — 8" h.p., BKW, #620, 1956 only (Wendy Ann) ....$1,800.00 up

Cousin Marie & Mary — 8" h.p. (Marie, #465; Mary, #462) 1963 only (Wendy Ann), each.....$1,000.00 up

Cowardly Lion — 8", #431, 1993, Storybook Series, #140431, 1994 – 1996 ....$70.00
    #13220, 1997 – 2001 ....$70.00
    5", #28695, 2001, porcelain $70.00

Cowboy — 8" h.p., BK, #732, 1967 – 1969, Americana Series (Wendy Ann) $425.00
    8", 1987 (see M.A.D.C. under Special Events/Exclusives)

Cowgirl — 8" h.p., BK, #724, 1967 – 1970, Americana/Storybook Series (Wendy Ann) $395.00
    10", #1132, 1990 – 1991, Portrette, white/red outfit (Cissette)...............$75.00

Crayola, Americana — 8", #17840-17873, felt outfits, with Crayolas ....$70.00 ea.

Crayola Meagan — 14", #25470, 2000, brown dress, with Crayolas $75.00

Crete — 8" straight leg, #529, 1987 only..$85.00

Croatia — 8", h.p., #110543, 1994 (Wendy Ann) $65.00

Crockett, Davy, Boy or Girl — 8" h.p., 1955 only (Boy - #446; Girl - #443)
    (Wendy Ann)...$700.00 up

Cry Dolly — 14 – 16" vinyl, 1953, 12-piece layette..............................$225.00
    14", 16", 19" in swimsuit ....$100.00 – 175.00
    16 – 19" all vinyl, dress or rompers..................................$150.00 – 225.00

Cuba — 8", #11548, 1995 only, has round brown face..............................$70.00

Cuddly — 10½" cloth, 1942 – 1944 ....$375.00
    17" cloth, 1942 – 1944 ....$400.00

Cupid — 8", #13860, 1998 – 1999, (Maggie), white costume, bow, arrow $80.00

Curly Locks — 8" h.p., #472, 1955 only (Wendy Ann) ....$850.00 up
    8" straight leg, #421, 1987 – 1988, Storybook Series, 1997 (Wendy Ann) $75.00
    8", #28315, 2001, print dress $95.00

Cute Little Baby — 14", 1994 – 1995, doll only, $100.00. With layette and basket....$225.00

Cutie Patootie — 18", #28320, 2001, cloth, Mary Engelbreit, pink dress $45.00

Cynthia — 15" h.p., 1952 only (black "Margaret") ....$850.00 up
    18", 1952 only..$850.00 up
    23", 1952 only..$1,200.00 up

Cyrano — 8" h.p., #140505, 1994 only, Storyland Series (Pinocchio)..............$75.00

Czarina Alexandra — 8", #12620, 1999, blue satin and gold $80.00

Czechoslovakia — 7" compo., 1935 – 1937 (Tiny Betty) $325.00
    8" h.p., BK, #764, 1972 (Wendy Ann) $100.00
    Straight leg, #0764, #564, 1973 – 1975, marked "Alex" $70.00
    Straight leg, #536, 1976 – 1987, marked "Alexander" $60.00

Cousin Grace, 8", BKW, #432, 1957, (Wendy Ann). All original. Tag: Alexander-Kin.

Cousin Marie, 8", BKW, #465, 1963, (Wendy Ann). All original. Tag: Wendy-Kin.

Curly Locks, 8", #472, 1955, SLW. A hard-to-find doll.

Czechoslovakia, continued

8", #536, 1985 – 1987 ....$60.00
8", #521, reintroduced 1992 – 1993 only (Wendy Ann) $60.00

Daffy Down Dilly — 8" straight legs, #429, 1986 only, Storybook Series
(Wendy Ann or Maggie) $85.00

Dahl, Arlene (Pink Champagne) — 18" h.p., 1950 – 1951, red wig, lavender gown
(Maggie), mint ....$5,500.00 up

Daisy — 10", #1110, 1987 – 1989, Portrette Series, white lace over yellow (Cissette) $75.00

Daisy Munchkin — 8", #28770, 2001, white outfit with daisies $65.00

Daisy Resort Cissette Ensemble — 10", #22380, 1998, silk, linen outfit, chair $160.00

Dance of the Flowers — 8", #25225, 2000 – 2001, blue embroidered tutu $75.00

Dancing Princess Blue — 10", #32050, 2000, blue tulle gown $135.00

Dancing Princess Gold — 10", #32055, 2000, gold tulle gown $135.00

Dancing Princess Magenta — 10", #32045, 2000, tulle and lace gown $135.00

Danish — 7" compo., 1937 – 1941 (Tiny Betty) $325.00
9" compo., 1938 – 1940 (Little Betty) $350.00

Dare, Virginia — 9" compo., 1940 – 1941 (Little Betty) $450.00

Darlene — 18" cloth/vinyl, 1991 – 1992 ....$100.00

David and Diana — 8" (see FAO Schwarz under Special Events/Exclusives)

David Copperfield — 7" compo., 1936 – 1938 (Tiny Betty) $350.00
14" compo., 1938 only (Wendy Ann) $725.00
16" cloth, early 1930s, Dickens character ....$800.00 up

David, The Little Rabbi — 8" (see Celia's Dolls under Special Events/Exclusives)

David Quack-a-Field or Twistail — cloth/felt, 1930s ....$700.00 up

Day of Week Dolls — 7", 1935 – 1940 (Tiny Betty) ....$350.00 ea.
9 – 11" compo., 1936 – 1938 (Little Betty) ....$375.00 ea.
13" compo., 1939 (Wendy Ann) $425.00

Day to Remember — 10", 2001, bride $145.00

Dear America Series — 18" recreations from *Dear America* Book Series
Abigail Jane Stewart, 1999 – 2000, 18", blue print dress $80.00
Catherine Carey Logan, 1999 – 2000, 18", Pilgrim costume $80.00
Margaret Ann Brady, 1999 – 2000, 18", pink dress $80.00
Remember Patience Whipple, 1999 – 2000, 18", red vest, skirt $80.00
Clotee, a Slave Girl, 2000, #25665, African-American, brown outfit $80.00
Emma Simpson, a Southern Belle, 2000, #25660, beige long dress $80.00
Sara Nita, a Navajo Girl, 2000, #25655, black Indian outfit $80.00
Zipporah Feldman, a Jewish Immigrant — 2000, #25650 ....$80.00

Dearest — 12" vinyl baby, 1962 – 1964 ....$125.00

Debra (Deborah) — 21", 1949 – 1951, Portrette, ballerina with
extra make-up (Margaret) ....$5,000.00 up
21", 1949 – 1951, bride with five-piece layered bustle in back ....$5,500.00 up

Deborah Bride — 16", #25595, 2000, remake of 1949 – 1951 costume $200.00

Debutante — 18" h.p., 1953 only (Maggie) ....$1,250.00 up

December — 14", #1528, 1989 only, Classic Series (Mary Ann) $100.00

DeFoe, Dr. Allen — 14 – 15" compo., 1937 – 1939 ....$1,600.00 up

Degas — 21" compo., 1945 – 1946, Portrait (Wendy Ann) ....$2,250.00 up

Degas Ballerina (The Star) — 10", #13910, 1998 – 1999,
(Cissette), white tutu $95.00
10", #25305, 2000 – 2001, pink long tutu with flowers $100.00

Degas "Dance Lesson" — 14", #241598, 1994 ....$95.00

Degas Girl — 14", #1475 (#1575 from 1974), 1967 – 1987 (20-year production),
Portrait Children and Fine Arts Series (Mary Ann) $75.00

Degas' Rehersal Shadow Box — 10", 2001, #28410, white costume,
gold shadow box $150.00

Delightful Afternoon — 10", #30410, 2001, pink long gown $125.00

Delilah — 8" h.p., #14583, 1995 only, Bible Series $100.00

Denmark — 10" h.p., 1962 – 1963 (Cissette) $700.00
8" h.p., BK, #769, 1970 – 1972 (Wendy Ann) $125.00
8" h.p., straight leg, #0769-569, 1973 – 1975, marked "Alex" (Wendy) $75.00
8" h.p., straight leg, #546, 1976 – 1989, marked "Alexander"
(1985 –1987 white face) (Wendy) $70.00
8" reintroduced, #519, 1991 only (Wendy Ann) $60.00

Desert Storm — (see Welcome Home)

Dewdrop Fairy — 8", #28495, 2001, blue tulle costume $85.00

Denmark, 8", 1975, (Wendy). Pinafore came in a variety of prints.

Diana — 14", 1993 – 1994, Anne of Green Gables Series, trunk and wardrobe.........................$275.00
    Tea dress, came with tea set, 1993 only $150.00
    Sunday Social, 8", #260417, 1994 – 1995 (Wendy Ann) $100.00
    Sunday Social, 14", #261503, 1994.......................................$125.00
Diamond Dance — 8", #26030, 2000, pink long gown, rhinestones $100.00
Diamond Lil — 10" (see M.A.D.C. under Special Events/Exclusives)
Dickinson, Emily — 14", #1587, 1989 only, Classic Series (Mary Ann) $100.00
Dicksie & Ducksie — Cloth/felt, 1930s ....$700.00 up
Dilly Dally Sally — 7" compo., 1937 – 1942 (Tiny Betty) $325.00
    9" compo., 1938 – 1939 (Little Betty) $350.00
Ding Dong Bell — 7" compo., 1937 – 1942 (Tiny Betty) $325.00
Dinner at Eight — 10", #1127, 1989 – 1991, Portrette, black/white dress (Cissette).................$75.00
Dinosaur — 8" h.p., #343, 1993 – 1994, Americana Series $75.00
Dion, Celine — 10", 1999, (Cissette), long gown, heart necklace $125.00
Dionne Quints — Original mint or very slight craze. Each has own color:
    Yvonne – pink, Annette – yellow, Cecile – green, Emilie –lavender, Marie – blue
    20" compo. toddlers, 1938 – 1939 ....$700.00 ea., $4,200.00 set
    19" compo. toddlers,1936 – 1938 ....$700.00 ea., $4,200.00 set
    16 – 17" compo. toddlers, 1937 – 1939 ....$650.00 ea., $3,600.00 set
    14" compo. toddlers, 1937 – 1938 ....$500.00 ea., $2,500.00 set
    11" compo. toddlers, 1937 – 1938, wigs & sleep eyes....................$400.00 ea., $2,200.00 set
    11" compo. toddlers, 1937 – 1938, molded hair & sleep eyes...................$400.00 ea., $2,200.00 set
    11" compo. babies, 1936, wigs & sleep eyes......................$400.00 ea., $2,200.00 set
    11" compo. babies, 1936, molded hair & sleep eyes...............$400.00 ea., $2,200.00 set
    8" compo. toddlers, 1935 – 1939, molded hair or wigs & painted eyes ....$300.00 ea., $1,500.00 set
    8" compo. babies, 1935 – 1939, molded hair or wigs & painted eyes ....$300.00 ea., $1,500.00 set
    14" cloth/compo., 1938.............................$475.00 ea., $3,100.00 set
    17" cloth/compo., 1938.............................$575.00 ea., $3,600.00 set
    22" cloth/compo., 1936 – 1937 ....$750.00 ea.
    24" all cloth, 1935 – 1936, must be mint ....$1,200.00 ea.
    16" all cloth, 1935 – 1936, must be mint ....$900.00 up
    8" h.p., 1998, 75th Anniversary Set with carousel, #12230 ....$450.00
    8" Yvonne, Marie, Annette, Cecile, Emilie, 1998 ....$85.00 ea.
Dionne furniture — (no dolls)
    Scooter, holds 5 ....$300.00 up
    Basket case, holds 5 ....$250.00
    Divided high chair, holds 5..$300.00 up
    Table and chairs, 5 piece set $400.00
    Ferris wheel, holds 5 ....$450.00 up
    Bath/shower ....$250.00 up
        Wagon, holds 5 ....$400.00 up
        Playpen, holds 5 ....$300.00 up
        Crib, holds 5 ....$300.00 up
        Tricycle ....$125.00 up
        Merry-go-round, holds 5 ....$350.00 up
        High chair for 1 ....$100.00
Disney — (see Special Events/Exclusives)
Dogs — (see Poodles)
Doll Finders — (see Special Events/Exclusives)
Dolls of the Month — 7 – 8" compo., 1937 – 1939,
    Birthday Dolls (Tiny Betty) $350.00
Dolls 'n Bearland — (see Special Events/Exclusives)
Dolly — 8", #436, 1988 – 1989, Storybook Series
    (Wendy Ann), 1997.....................................$90.00
Dolly Dears — (see Special Events/Exclusives)
Dolly Dryper — 11" vinyl, 1952 only, 7-piece layette $300.00
Dolly Levi (Matchmaker) — 10" Portrette, 1994 only $75.00
Dominican Republic — 8" straight leg, #544,
    1986 – 1988 (1985 – 1986 white face) $70.00
Dormouse — 8", #13090, 1998 – 2000, mouse in sugar
    bowl w/spoon.......................................$100.00
Dorothy — 14", #1532, 1990 – 1993, all blue/white
    check dress and solid blue pinafore (Mary Ann).................$95.00

Dionne Quints, 8", composition, 1930s. Playpen not original.

8" h.p., #464, 1991 – 1993, #140464, 1994 – 1995, blue/white check,
white bodice (Wendy Ann) $70.00
8" h.p., emerald green dress special, mid-year special (see Madame Alexander
Doll Co. under Special Events/Exclusives)
8" h.p., #13200, 1997 – 1999, blue-checked dress, basket with Toto, #13201, 2000 – 2001 .....$60.00
14" plastic/vinyl, #87007, 1996 ....$125.00
15", #25545, cloth, 2000 – 2001, blue-checked dress, with Toto $50.00
5", #27065, porcelain, 2000 – 2001, blue-checked dress $80.00

Dottie Dumbunnie — cloth/felt, 1930s ....$800.00 up
Dream Dance — 10", #26180, 2000, (Cissette) blue, short party dress $100.00
10", #26175, 2000, (Cissette) black bodice, long tulle gown $110.00
Dressed for Opera — 18" h.p., 1953 only (Margaret) ....$1,800.00 up
Dressed Like Daddy — 8", #17002, 1996, white or black.......................$75.00
Dressed Like Mommy — 8", #17001, 1996 – 1998, white or black $75.00
Drucilla — (see M.A.D.C. under Special Events/Exclusives)
Drum Majorette — (see Majorette)
Duchess, The — 8", #14613, 1996, Alice in Wonderland Series $75.00
Duchess Eliza, The — 10", #20114, 1996 Classics $115.00
Dude Ranch — 8" h.p., #449, 1955 only (Wendy Ann).........................$700.00 up
Dudley Do-Right and Nell — 8", #15140, 1999,
Dudley in Monty outfit (Maggie), Nell (Wendy) includes rope, train track, and backdrop $180.00
Dumplin' Baby — 20 – 23½", 1957 – 1958 ....$185.00
Dutch — 7" compo., 1935 – 1939 (Tiny Betty) $300.00
9" compo. boy or girl, 1936 – 1941 ....$325.00
8" h.p., BKW, #777, 1964, boy* (Wendy) $150.00
BK, #777, #0777, 1965 – 1972 ....$125.00
8" h.p., straight leg, #777, *0777, 1972 – 1973, marked "Alex" $75.00
8" h.p., BKW, #391-791, 1961 – 1964, girl* $150.00
8" h.p., BK, #791, 1965 – 1972 ....$125.00
8" BKW, #791, 1964 only (Maggie smile face) $185.00
Dutch Lullaby — 8", #499, 1993, #140499, 1994, Wynkin, Blynkin & Nod,
in wooden shoe $200.00
Easter — 8", h.p. #21020, 1998, hat with bunny ears, floral dress $70.00
Easter Bonnet — 14", #1562, 1992 (Louisa/Jennifer) $150.00
8" h.p., #10383 – 10385, 1995 – 1996, three hair colors, Special Occasions Series $70.00
8" h.p., #10401, 1996, African-American...$70.00

Easter Bunny — 8", (see Child at Heart
under Special Events/Exclusives)
8", #26675, 2001, blue dress, hat, basket
with bunny $100.00
Easter Doll — 8" h.p., 1968 only, special for
West Coast, in yellow dress (Wendy Ann),
limited to 300..$1,300.00 up
7½", SLNW, #361, 1953, organdy dress,
doll carries basket with chicken ....$925.00 up
14" plastic/vinyl, 1968 only (Mary Ann),
limited to 300..$600.00 up
Easter Egg Hunt — 8", #25020, 2000 – 2001,
white dress, straw hat, basket................................$90.00
Easter of Yesterday — 1995 (see C.U.
under Special Events/Exclusives)
Easter Sunday — 8" h.p., #340 or #340-1, 1993
only, Americana Series, black or white doll $70.00
8", #21510 (white), #21513 (black), 1998 – 2000,
yellow print dress, straw hat, basket $90.00
Ebony and Ivory Houndstooth Suit — 10",
#22190, 1997 – 1998 ....$150.00
Ecuador — 8" h.p., BK & BKW, #878,
1963 – 1966 (Wendy Ann)..............................$350.00
Edith, The Lonely Doll — 16" plastic/vinyl,
1958 – 1959 (Mary-Bel) $375.00
22", 1958 – 1959...$400.00
8" h.p., #850, 1958 only (Wendy Ann)...............$750.00 up
Both became Netherlands in 1974.

Easter Doll, 8", BK, (Wendy Ann).
Made in 1968 only in a limited
production of 300 pieces.

Edith with Golden Hair — 18" cloth, 1940s..$675.00
Edwardian — 18" h.p., #2001A, 1953 only, pink embossed cotton,
  Glamour Girl Series (Margaret) ....$2,000.00 up
  8" h.p., #0200, 1953 only (Wendy Ann)...$1,000.00 up
Eisenhower, Mamie — 14", 1989 – 1990, 6th set Presidents' Ladies/First
  Ladies Series (Mary Ann)...$125.00
Egypt — 8" straight leg, #543, 1986 – 1989 (round brown face) $70.00
Egypt with Sarcophagus — 8", #24110, 1998 – 2000, Pharaoh costume..............$110.00
Egyptian — 7 – 8" compo., 1936 – 1940 (Tiny Betty) $350.00
  9" compo., 1936 – 1940 (Little Betty) $375.00
Elaine — 18" h.p., 1954 only, Me and My Shadow Series, blue organdy dress (Cissy) ....$1,700.00 up
  8" h.p., #0035E, 1954 only, matches 18" (Wendy Ann) ....$950.00 up
Elegant Emerald — 8", #32085, 2000, green long ball gown $85.00
Elise — 16½" h.p./vinyl arms (18", 1963 only), 1957 – 1964, jointed ankles & knees, face color
  In street clothes or blouse, slacks & sash ....$450.00 up
  In ball gown, formal, or Portrait ....$750.00 up
  In riding habit, 1963 (Mary-Bel head) $425.00
  Ballerina, rare yellow tutu, red hair $875.00
  With Mary-Bel head, 1962 only $425.00
  18", 1963 only, with bouffant hairstyle $450.00
  17" h.p./vinyl, 1961 – 1962, one-piece arms & legs, jointed ankles & knees....$300.00
  18" h.p./vinyl, 1963 – 1964, jointed ankles & knees $350.00
  In riding habit $375.00
  17" plastic/vinyl, 1966 only, street dress $275.00
  17", 1966 – 1972, in trunk/trousseau ....$650.00 up
  17", 1972 – 1973, Portrait...$225.00
  17", 1966, 1976 – 1977, in formal $225.00
  17", 1966 – 1987, Bride $175.00
  17", 1966 – 1991, Ballerina $140.00
  17", 1966 – 1989, in any discontinued costume ....$100.00 up
  16", 1997, #22060, Firebird, red and gold tutu.......................................$150.00
  16", 1997, #22050, Giselle, aqua tutu, rose tiara $150.00
  16", 1997, #22040, Swan Lake, white tulle tutu $150.00
Elise/Leslie — 14", #1560, 1988 only (Mary Ann) $85.00
Eliza — 14", #1544, 1991 only, Classic Series (Louisa) $125.00
Eliza the Flower Girl — 10", #20113, 1996 Classics....................................$100.00
Elizabethan Bride — 10", #25005, 2000, Cissette $150.00
Elizabethan Pin Cushion — 2000 – 2001, pink #26480, gold #25645, 8", Wendy,
  brocade as a pin cushion $100.00
Eloise — 8", #80680, 2000, vinyl, Eloise lace, white blouse, navy pleated skirt $35.00

Elise Ballerina, 17", #1600, 1988.

Elise Bride, 17", #1685, 1981 – 1985.

Fairy Godmother, 14", #1550, 1983 – 1990, (Mary Ann).

Eloise, continued

18", #80690, 2000 – 2001, cloth, Eloise face, same costume as 8" doll $45.00

36", Just Like Me, #30936, 2001, cloth with rag doll $200.00

8", Eloise Tea Party, #30810, 2001, vinyl, white dress $45.00

8", Eloise Loves to Dance, #30815, 2001, ballet.................$45.00

12", Eloise Loves to Dance, #30935, 2001, cloth $40.00

Emerald City Guard — 8", #31395, 2001, black costume with sequin hat $85.00

Emerald Lass — 8", #27870, 2001, green dress $80.00

Emily — cloth/felt, 1930s $600.00

Emily Elizabeth — 8", #26370, 2000 – 2001, (Maggie) with cloth, 16" Clifford dog.................$90.00

Emma — 10", #25335, 2000, (Cissette) long blue gown, straw hat $125.00

Empire Bride — 10", (Cissette), white lace gown (1999) $135.00

Empress Elizabeth of Austria — 10" (see My Doll House under Special Events/Exclusives)

Enchanted Doll House — (see Special Events/Exclusives)

Enchanted Evening — 21" Portrait, 1991 – 1992 only, different necklace than
shown in catalog (Cissy) $325.00

England — 8", #24040, 1997 – 1999, Beefeater guard outfit $85.00

8", #28560, 2001, Queen costume $85.00

English Guard — 8" h.p., BK, #764, 1966 – 1968, Portrait Children Series (Wendy Ann) $350.00

8", #515, reintroduced 1989 – 1991, marked "Alexander" (Wendy Ann) $70.00

Entertaining the Troops — 8", #17550, 1999, red outfit, microphone $75.00

Eskimo — 8" h.p., BK, #723, 1967 – 1969, Americana Series (Wendy Ann) $375.00

9" compo., 1936 – 1939 (Little Betty) $300.00

With Maggie Mixup face $400.00

Estonia — 8" straight leg, #545, 1986 – 1987 only (Wendy Ann) $70.00

Estrella — 18", h.p. (Maggie), lilac gown, 1953 ....$1,200.00 up

Eva Lovelace — 7" compo., 1935 only (Tiny Betty).................$350.00

cloth, 1935 only $600.00

Eva Peron — 10", #22030, 1997, white long lace dress (Cissette).................$125.00

Evangeline — 18" cloth, 1930s ....$650.00 up

Evening Star — 15", porcelain, blace lace over pink satin (1999 – 2000) $180.00

Evening of Romance — 10", #27010, 2000, (Cissette) black lace gown $140.00

Evil Sorceress — 8", #13610, 1997, long black velvet dress.................$75.00

FAO Schwarz — (see Special Events/Exclusives)

Fairy Godmother — 14", #1550, #1551, #1568, 1983 – 1992,
Classic Series (Mary Ann, Louisa).................$100.00

Fairy Godmother outfit, 1983, M.A.D.C. (see Special Events/Exclusives)

10" Portrette, #1156, 1993 only, blue/gold gown (Cissette) $100.00

10", #14549, 1995 only, purple gown, white wig (Cissette).................$85.00

8", #13430, 1997 – 1999, dark blue hooded cloak $75.00

8", #25920, 2000 – 2001, (Maggie) dark blue over light blue gown $90.00

Fairy of Beauty — 8", #13620, 1997 – 2001, pink tulle gown $90.00

Fairy of Song — 8", #13630, 1997 – 2001, green tulle gown $90.00

Fairy of Virtue — 8", #13640, 1997 – 2001, blue tulle gown $90.00

Fairy Princess — 7 – 8" compo., 1940 – 1943 (Tiny Betty) $350.00

9" compo., 1939 – 1941 (Little Betty) $375.00

11" compo., 1939 only (Wendy Ann) $375.00

15 – 18" compo., 1939 – 1942 (Wendy Ann) $650.00

21 – 22" compo., 1939, 1944 – 1946 (Wendy Ann) $900.00

Fairy Queen — 14½" compo., 1940 – 1946 (Wendy Ann).................$700.00

18" compo., 1940 – 1946 (Wendy Ann).................$800.00

14½" h.p., 1948 – 1950 (Margaret) $800.00

18" h.p., 1949 – 1950 (Margaret) $950.00

Fairy Tales – Dumas — 9" compo., 1937 – 1941 (Little Betty) $375.00

Faith — 8" h.p., #486, 1961 only, Americana Series, plaid jumper/organdy
blouse (Wendy Ann).................$1,800.00 up

8" h.p. (see Collectors United under Special Events/Exclusives)

Fall Angel — 8", #28360, 2001, rust gown with leaves $80.00

Fantasy — 8", 1990 (see Doll Finders under Special Events/Exclusives)

Fannie Elizabeth — 8" (see Belks & Leggett under Special Events/Exclusives)

Farmer's Daughter — 8", 1991 (see Enchanted Doll House under Special Events/Exclusives)

Fashions of the Century — 14 – 18" h.p., 1954 – 1955 (Margaret, Maggie).................$2,000.00 up

Father Christmas — 8" h.p., #100351 Americana Series $75.00

Father of the Bride — 10", #24623, 1996, white satin wedding gown $110.00

Father of Vatican City, The — 8", #24190, 1999, gold silk robe...$80.00
Figurines — 1999, 6", polyresin replica of Alexander dolls ....$25.00 – 28.00
Fillmore, Abigail — 1982 – 1984, 3rd set Presidents' Ladies/First
    Ladies Series (Louisa) $125.00
Findlay, Jane — 1979 – 1981, 1st set Presidents' Ladies/First
    Ladies Series (Mary Ann)...$135.00
Finland — 8" h.p., BK, #767, 1968 – 1972 (Wendy Ann)......................................$100.00
    8" h.p., straight leg, #0767-567, 1973 – 1975, marked "Alex"............................$75.00
    8" h.p., straight leg, #567, 1976 – 1987, marked "Alexander" $60.00
Finnish — 7" compo., 1935 – 1937 (Tiny Betty) $300.00
Fire Fighter Wendy — 8", #31270, 1998 – 1999, yellow coat, red hat, and dog.......................$85.00
Fireplace Stocking Holder — #91005, 6¼", red fireplace..$60.00
First Communion — 8" h.p., #395, 1957 only (Wendy Ann)..................................$675.00
    8" h.p., reintroduced 1994, #100347 Americana Series $75.00
    8", #10347 – 10349, 1995, three hair colors, Special Occasions Series...................$70.00
    8", #17012 – 17015, 1996, black, three hair colors (Wendy Ann) #21100, 1997 – 1998 ....$70.00
    8", #21530 (white), #21534 (black), white dress, veil, Bible, 1999 – 2000 ....$75.00
    8", #30656, 2001, Latin American, lacy white dress, veil $80.00
    8", #30655, 2001, Caucasian...$80.00
    14", #1545, 1991 – 1992 only, Classics Series (Louisa) $110.00
First Dance Pair — 8", 1996...$200.00
First Ladies — (see Presidents' Ladies)
First Modern Doll Club — (see Special Events/Exclusives)
First Recital — 8", #17024 (white), #17037 (black), lacy dress $60.00
Fischer Quints — 7" h.p./vinyl, 1964 only, one boy and four girls (Little Genius) ....$550.00 set
Five Little Peppers — 13" & 16" compo., 1936 only ....$750.00 ea.
Flapper — 10", Portrette, 1988 – 1991 (Cissette), red dress..$75.00
    10", #1118, 1988, black dress (all white dress in 1991)
    (see M.A.D.C. under Special Events/Exclusives)
    8", #14105, 1995, three-tiered rose colored dress with matching headband,
        Nostalgia Series..$60.00
Flora McFlimsey — (with and without "e")
    9" compo., 1938 – 1941 (Little Betty) $425.00
    22" compo., 1938 – 1944 (Princess Elizabeth) ....$800.00 up
    15 – 16" compo., 1938 – 1944 (Princess Elizabeth) ....$550.00 up
    16 – 17" compo., 1936 – 1937 (Wendy Ann)...$550.00
    14" compo., 1938 – 1944 (Princess Elizabeth) ....$500.00 up
    12" compo., 1944 only, holds 5" "Nancy Ann" doll, tagged "Margie Ann" (Wendy Ann).......$950.00 up
    15" Miss Flora McFlimsey, vinyl head (must have good color), 1953 only (Cissy) ....$700.00 up

First Communion, 8", #395, 1957, BKW, (Wendy Ann). Original organdy dress and veil.

Flowergirl, 8", BKW, #602, 1956, (Wendy Ann). Satin gown with pink sash. Tag: Alexander-Kin.

Flora McFlimsey, continued

14", #25502, 1995, tiers of pink, white, and black, Button & Bows Series (Mary Ann) $125.00
Flower Child — 8", #17790, 1999, (Maggie) $65.00
Flowergirl — 16" – 18" compo., 1939, 1944 – 1947 (Princess Elizabeth) $550.00
  20 – 24" compo., 1939, 1944 – 1947 (Princess Elizabeth)..$650.00 up
  15 – 18" h.p., 1954 only (Cissy)..$450.00 – 850.00
  15" h.p., 1954 only (Margaret) ....$600.00 up
  8" h.p., #602, 1956 (Wendy Ann) ....$900.00 up
  8", h.p., #445, 1959, (Wendy) blue nylon pleated dress...$675.00 up
  8", h.p., #334, 1992 – 1993, Americana Series, white doll (Wendy Ann) $75.00
  8", #334-1, 1992 only, black doll $70.00
  10", #1122, 1988 – 1990, Portrette, pink dotted Swiss dress (Cissette)........................$85.00
  8", #22620, 1999, mauve satin, rose crown, limited to 2,700.....................................$80.00
Forrest — 8", h.p., #10750, 1998, Tyrolean outfit $75.00
Forget-Me-Not — 8", #28465, 2001, yellow, pink dress with flowers, hat.......................$90.00
France — 7" compo., 1936 – 1943 (Tiny Betty) $300.00
  9" compo., 1937 – 1941 (Little Betty) $325.00
  8" h.p., BKW, #390, #790, 1961 – 1965 (Wendy Ann) $150.00
  8" h.p., BK, #790, 1965 – 1972 ....$125.00
  8" h.p., straight leg, #0790, #590, 1973 – 1975, marked "Alex" $75.00
  8" straight leg, #590, #552, #517, #582, 1976 – 1993, marked "Alexander" (1985 – 1987)
    1985 – 1987, #590, #552...$65.00
  8" h.p., reissued 1994 – 1995, #110538 (Wendy) $65.00
  8" h.p., #11557, 1996 International, cancan costume (#24020 – 1998) $65.00
French Aristocrat — 10" Portrette, #1143, 1991 – 1992 only, bright pink/white (Cissette) $150.00
French Flowergirl — 8" h.p., #610, 1956 only (Wendy Ann)......................................$750.00 up
Friar Tuck — 8" h.p., #493, 1989 – 1991, Storybook Series (Maggie Mixup) $85.00
Friday's Child — 8", #27790, 2001, lavender dress $110.00
Friedrich — (see Sound of Music)
Frog Princess — 8", #27755, 2001, includes frog $100.00
Frost Fairy Boy — 8", #25140, 2000, silver costume and crown $70.00
Frost Fairy Girl — 8", #25145, 2000, silver ballerina costume...................................$70.00
Frou-Frou — 40" all cloth, 1951 only, ballerina with yarn hair,
  dressed in green or lilac...$800.00 up
Fun Fun Chloe — 14", #30115, 2001, vinyl..$75.00
Funny — 18" cloth, 1963 – 1977...$75.00
Funny Maggie — 8" (Maggie) #140506, 1994 – 1995, Storyland Series, yarn hair.....................$70.00
Gainsborough — 20" h.p., 1957, Models Formal Gowns Series, taffeta gown,
  large picture hat (Cissy) ....$1,500.00 up
  #2184, 21" h.p./vinyl arms, 1968, blue with white lace jacket (Jacqueline) ..$650.00
  #2192, 21", 1972, yellow with full white lace overskirt (Jacqueline)............$650.00
  #2192, 21", 1973, pale blue, scallop lace overskirt (Jacqueline) $600.00
  #2211, 21", 1978, pink with full lace overdress (Jacqueline)........................$450.00
  10" pink gown & hat, 1957 Portrette (Cissette) $700.00
  10", #45201, 1995, pink with lace overlay, Madame's Portfolio Series........$110.00
Gardenia — 10", #22360, 1998 (Cissette), yellow satin long gown $150.00
Garden Fairy — 8", #28500, 2001, pink costume with roses $85.00
Garden Party — 18" h.p., 1953 only (Margaret).......................................$1,600.00 up
  20" h.p., 1956 – 1957 (Cissy) ....$1,200.00 up
  8" h.p., #488, 1955 only (Wendy Ann) ....$1,800.00 up
Garden Rose — 10", (Cissette), #22530, 1999, pink tulle with roses............$130.00
Garfield, Lucretia — 1985 – 1987, 4th set Presidents'
  Ladies/First Ladies Series (Louisa) $115.00
Gemini — 8", #21350, 1998, African-American, 2 dolls, yellow outfit..........$175.00
  8", #21351, 1998, white, 2 dolls $175.00
Genius Baby — 21" – 30" plastic/vinyl, 1960 – 1961, has flirty eyes ...$125.00 – 250.00
  Little, 8" h.p. head/vinyl, 1956 – 1962 (see Little Genius)
Geppetto — 8", #478, 1993, #140478, 1994, Storybook Series $75.00
Geppetto and Pinocchio — 8", 5", #32130, 2000, navy jacket, hat ....
Geranium — 9" early vinyl toddler, 1953 only, red organdy dress & bonnet .$125.00
German (Germany) — 8" h.p., BK, #763, 1966 – 1972 (Wendy Ann).......$125.00
  8" h.p., straight leg, #0763-563, 1973 – 1975, marked "Alex" $75.00
  10" h.p., 1962 – 1963 (Cissette) $925.00
  8" straight legs, #563, #535, #506, 1976 – 1989, marked "Alexander"...........$65.00

Gainsborough, 21", #2192, 1972, (Jacqueline). Mint and all original.

German (Germany), continued

8", 1990 – 1991, marked "Alexander" $60.00

8", #535, 1986 ....$60.00

8" h.p., #110542, 1994 – 1995, outfit in 1994 Neiman-Marcus trunk set (Maggie) $65.00

8", #25800, 2000 – 2001, (Maggie) blue print dress, beer stein $150.00

Get Well — 8", h.p. #21090, 1998 – 1999, red stripe outfit, vase of flowers $80.00

Get Well Wishes — #10363 – 10365, 1995, 3 hair colors, nurse with bear,
Special Occasions Series $65.00

Ghost of Christmas Past — 8", #18002, 1996, Dickens, long white gown $60.00

Ghost of Christmas Present — 14", #18406, 1996, Dickens, sold as set only with
8" Ignorance (boy) and 8" Want (girl) $325.00

Gibson Girl — 10" h.p., 1962, eyeshadow (Cissette) ....$800.00 up

10", 1963, plain blouse with no stripes ....$800.00 up

16" cloth, 1930s $850.00

10", #1124, 1988 – 1990, Portrette, red and black (Cissette) $75.00

10", #17750, 1999, navy blue gown $125.00

Gidget — 14" plastic/vinyl, #1415, #1420, #1421, 1966 only (Mary Ann) $275.00

Gigi — 14", #1597, 1986 – 1987, Classic Series (Mary Ann) $100.00

14", #87011, 1996, plaid dress, straw hat (Mary Ann) $100.00

8", h.p., #13990, 1998 – 1999, pleated plaid dress, straw hat (Maggie) $80.00

Gilbert — 8", #260420, 1994 – 1995, Anne of Green Gables Series $85.00

Gingerbread House — candy-trimmed house $130.00

Girl on Flying Trapeze — 40" cloth, 1951 only, dressed in pink satin tutu
(sold at FAO Schwarz) $950.00

Girl on a Swing — 8", #28640, 2001, white dress with swing $90.00

Giselle — 16", #22050, 1998, aqua tutu $195.00

Glamour Girls — 18" h.p., 1953 only (Margaret, Maggie) ....$1,800.00 up

Glamour Girl 1953 — 10", h.p., 2000, (Cissette) pink and black gown $110.00

Glinda, The Good Witch — 8", #473, 1992 – 1993, Storyland Series (Wendy Ann),
#140473, 1994 – 1995 ....$100.00

14" plastic/vinyl, #141573, 1994 only $100.00

10", #13250, 1997 – 2001, pink tulle and taffeta dress (Cissette) $115.00

15", #25546, 2001, cloth, pink gown $65.00

Glorious Angel — 10½" h.p., #54860 (see Tree Toppers)

Godey — 21" compo., 1945 – 1947 (Wendy Ann) white
lace over pink satin ....$2,700.00 up

14" h.p., 1950 – 1951 (Margaret) ....$1,500.00 up

21" h.p., 1951 only, lace ¾ top with long sleeves, pink
satin two-tiered skirt (Margaret) ....$1,800.00 up

18" h.p., #2010A, 1953 only, Glamour Girl Series, red gown
with gray fur stole (Maggie) ....$1,700.00 up

21" h.p., vinyl straight arms, 1961 only, lavender
coat & hat (Cissy) $1,500.00

21", 1962, bright orange gown, white lace ruffles on bodice $1,500.00

21", #2153, 1965, dressed in all red, blonde hair (Jacqueline) $800.00

21" plastic/vinyl, 1966 only, red with black short jacket
& hat (Coco) ....$2,300.00 up

21" h.p., vinyl arms, #2172, 1967, dressed in pink
& ecru (Jacqueline) $650.00

#2195, 1969, red with black trim $650.00

#2195, 1970, pink with burgundy short jacket $375.00

#2161, 1971, pink, black trim, short jacket $425.00

#2298, 1977, ecru with red jacket and bonnet $350.00

8" SLW, #491, 1955 only (Wendy Ann) ....$1,400.00 up

10" h.p., #1172, 1968, dressed in all pink with ecru lace,
with bows down front (Cissette) $450.00

#1172, 1969, all yellow with bows down front $475.00

#1183, 1970, all lace pink dress with natural straw hat $450.00

Godey Bride — 14" h.p., 1950, lace ¾ top over satin gown
with long train (Margaret) ....$1,000.00 up

18" h.p., 1950 – 1951 (Margaret) ....$1,400.00 up

21" porcelain, 1993 (Cissy) $525.00

Godey Groom/Man — 14" h.p., 1950, has curls over ears,
wearing black jacket and tan pants (Margaret) ....$975.00 up

Godey, 21", (Margaret). 1951 only. Lace and pink satin dress.

Godey Groom/Man, continued

18" h.p., 1950 – 1951 (Margaret) ....$1,200.00 up
Godey Lady — 14" h.p., 1950, green velvet dress with pink/bright orange pleated ruffles,
peach/white bodice (Margaret) ....$1,000.00 up
18" h.p., 1950 – 1951 (Margaret) ....$1,500.00 up
Goldfish — 8" h.p., #344, Americana Series 1993 – 1994 ....$80.00
Gold Rush — 10" h.p., 1963 only (Cissette) $1,600.00
Goldilocks — 18" cloth, 1930s..$875.00
7 – 8" compo., 1938 – 1942 (Tiny Betty) $325.00
18" h.p., 1951 only (Maggie) $1,300.00
14" plastic/vinyl, #1520, 1978 – 1979, Classic Series, satin dress (Mary Ann) $115.00
14", #1520, 1980 – 1983, blue satin or cotton dress (Mary Ann) $100.00
14", #1553, 1991 only, Classic Series, long side curls tied with ribbon (Mary Ann) $100.00
8", #497, 1990 – 1991 only, Storyland Series (1991 dress in different plaid) (Wendy Ann) $75.00
8", #140500, 1994 – 1995, Storyland Series, floral print dress, has bear..$85.00
8", #25965, 2000, (Wendy), blue dress, eyelet apron with bear $60.00
Golden Girl 1920 — 10", #17740, 1999, black and gold dress $110.00
Golf Boy — 8", 1998, #16402 (Maggie) green coat, checked hat, pants, golf club $75.00
Golf Girl — 8", 1998, #16412 (Wendy) ivory sweater, navy skirt, golf club $75.00
Gone Fishing — 8", #28190, 2001, green dress, hat, fishing pole..$85.00
Gone With the Wind (Scarlett) — 14", #1490, #1590, 1969 – 1986, all white dress/green
sash, made 17 years without a change (Mary Ann) (dress must be mint) $150.00
Good Fairy — 14" h.p., 1948 – 1949 (Margaret) ....$725.00 up
Good Little Girl — 16" cloth, 1966 only, mate to "Bad Little Girl," wears pink dress $150.00
Goya — 8" h.p., #314, 1953 only (Wendy Ann) ....$1,000.00 up
21" h.p./vinyl arms, #2183, 1968, multi-tiered pink dress (Jacqueline) $550.00
21", #2235, 1982 – 1983, maroon dress with black Spanish lace (Jacqueline) $300.00
Graceful Garnet — 8" #32170, 2000, red and gold ball gown..$90.00
Graduation — 8" h.p., #399, 1957 only (Wendy Ann)..$900.00 up
12", 1957 only (Lissy) ....$1,000.00 up
8", #307, 1990 – 1991, Americana Series (white doll only) (Wendy Ann)..$75.00
8", #307, #307-1, 1991 – 1992, Americana Series, white or black doll..$70.00
8", #10307 – 10309 (black), #10310 (white), 1995, blue robe, Special Occasions Series..$70.00
8", #26105 (blonde), #26106 (brunette), #26107 (African-American),
2000 – 2001, white robe, hat $85.00
Grand Ole Opry Boy — 8", #77005, 1996 Classic $80.00
Grand Ole Opry Girl — 8", #77004, 1996 Classic..$80.00
Grandma Jane — 14" plastic/vinyl, #1420, 1970 – 1972 (Mary Ann)..$250.00

Gold Rush, 10", h.p. (Cissette). Made in 1963 only. Orange long dress with bustle and straw hat with net, feathers, and orange ribbon.

Goya, 21", #2183, 1968, (Jacqueline). A hard-to-find doll.

Grant, Julia — 1982 – 1984, 3rd set Presidents' Ladies/First Ladies Series (Louisa) $125.00
Grave, Alice — 18" cloth, 1930s ....$750.00 up
Grayson, Kathryn — 20 – 21" h.p., 1949 only (Margaret) ....$5,500.00 up
Great Britain — 8" h.p., #558, 1977 – 1988 (Wendy Ann) $60.00
Great Gatsby Pair — 10", #15310, 1997, Classic characters...$180.00
Greece Boy — 8" h.p., #527, 1992 – 1993 only (Wendy Ann) $55.00
Greek Boy — 8" h.p., BK, 1965, & BKW, 1966 – 1968, #769 (Wendy Ann) $350.00
Greek Girl — 8" h.p., BK, #765, 1968 – 1972 (Wendy Ann) $125.00
    8" h.p., straight leg, #0765, #565, 1973 – 1975, marked "Alex" $75.00
    8" h.p., straight leg, #565, #527, 1976 – 1987 (1985 – 1987), marked "Alexander" $65.00
Gretel — 7" compo., 1935 – 1942 (Tiny Betty) $325.00
    9" compo., 1938 – 1940 (Little Betty) $350.00
    18" h.p., 1948 only (Margaret) ....$1,000.00 up
    7½ – 8" h.p., SLW, #470, 1955 (Wendy Ann) ....$500.00 up
    8" h.p., BK, #754, 1966 – 1972, Storybook Series (Wendy) $125.00
    8" h.p., straight leg, #0754, #454, 1973 – 1975, marked "Alex" $75.00
    8" h.p., straight leg, #454, 1976 – 1986, marked "Alexander" $65.00
    8" h.p., #462, 1991 – 1992 only, Storyland Series, reintroduced doll (Wendy Ann) $65.00
    8", h.p., #26600, 2001, red stripe skirt $80.00
Gretel Brinker — 12", 1993 only (Lissy) $175.00
    8", #14650, 1996 ....$70.00
Gretl — (see Sound of Music)
Groom — 18" – 21" compo., 1946 – 1947, mint (Margaret) ....$975.00 up
    18 – 21" h.p., 1949 – 1951 (Margaret)....................................$975.00 – 1,200.00
    14 – 16" h.p., 1949 – 1951 (Margaret) ....$750.00 up
    7½" h.p., SL & SLW, #577, #464, #466, 1953 – 1955 (Wendy Ann) ....$450.00 up
    8", BKW, #577, 1956 ....$425.00
    8", BKW, #377, 1957 ....$425.00
    8", BKW, #572, 1958 ....$425.00
    8" h.p., BKW, #421, #442, 1961 – 1963 (Wendy Ann) $375.00
    8", #488, #388, reintroduced 1989 – 1991 only (Wendy Ann) $70.00
    8", #339, 1993, only black pants, peach tie, white jacket $70.00
    8", #17020, 1996, black velvet tails, black pants, pink tie $70.00
    8", #17023, 1996, black velvet tails, etc., black doll $70.00
    8", #21071, 1997 – 2001, velvet tailcoat, top hat, #21073 — African-American (1997 – 1998) $90.00
Groovy Girl 1970 — 8", #17800, 1999, BK, denim pants, hat $75.00
Guardian Angel — 10", #10602 – 1995, first in series, 100th Anniversary Special,
    all pink with white wings $125.00
    10" #10720, 1998, rose print brocade gown, feather wings...$125.00
    10", of Harmony, #10691, 1996 ....$100.00
    10", of Hope, #10609, 1996 ....$100.00
    10", of Love, frosted ivy, #10605, 1996 ....$100.00
    10", of Love, heather blue #10607, 1996 ....$100.00
    10", of Love, misty rose, #10603, 1996..$100.00
    10", Pink Pristine, #10700, 1997 – 2000, pink tulle dress $130.00
    10", #10720, 1999, pink print brocade gown, feather wings $110.00
Guatemala — 8", #24180, 1999, red and black outfit $80.00
Guinevere — 10", #1146, 1992 only, Portrette, forest green/gold $125.00
    8", #13570, 1999, blue dress with white brocade overdress $75.00
Gypsy of the World — 8", #28570, 2001, purple costume, tarot cards $85.00
Halloween Witch — 8" (see Collectors United under Special Events/Exclusives)
Hamlet — 12", Romance Series (Nancy Drew) $90.00
    12", 1993 only (Lissy) $125.00
Hans Brinker — 12", 1993 only (Lissy)...$150.00
    8", #14649, 1996 ....$60.00
Hansel — 7" compo., 1935 – 1942 (Tiny Betty)...$300.00
    9" compo., 1938 – 1940 (Little Betty) $350.00
    18" h.p., 1948 only (Margaret) ....$800.00 up
    8" h.p., SLW, #470, 1955 only (Wendy Ann)...$650.00 up
    8" h.p., BK, #753, 1966 – 1972, Storybook Series (Wendy Ann) $100.00
    8" h.p., straight leg, #0753, #543, 1973 – 1975, marked "Alex" $75.00
    8" h.p., straight leg, #543, 1976 – 1986 (1986 white face), marked "Alexander" $65.00
    8" h.p., #461, 1991 – 1992 only, Storyland Series, reintroduced doll (Wendy Ann) $60.00
    8" h.p., #26605, 2001, green costume $80.00

Happy — 20" cloth/vinyl, 1970 only $225.00
Happy Birthday — 1985 (see M.A.D.C. under Special Events/Exclusives)
    8" h.p., #325, #325-1, 1992 – 1993, Americana Series, black or white doll (Wendy Ann) $65.00
    8" h.p., #100325, 1994, white only $65.00
    8", #10325 – 10327, 1995, three hair colors, Special Occasions Series $65.00
    8", #17004 – 17010, 1996, three hair colors, black or white doll (Wendy, Maggie) $65.00
    14" plastic/vinyl, #241596, 1994 only $90.00
    8", #21520 (blonde), #21521 (brunette), #21523 (black), pink print dress, 1999 – 2000 ....$70.00
    8", #27240 (blonde), #27240 (brunette), #27242, African-American, 2001 ....$90.00
Happy Birthday Billie — 8" h.p., #345, #345-1, Americana Series, black or
    white boy, 1993 only $65.00
Happy Birthday Maggie — 8", #21080 – white, #21083 – black, 1997 – 1998 ....$65.00
Happy Chanukah — 8", #10367, 1996 Holiday, #19630, 1997 – 1999 ....$75.00
Happy the Clown — 8", #10414, 1996 Classic Circus $65.00
Harding, Florence — 1988, 5th set Presidents' Ladies/First Ladies Series (Louisa) $125.00
Harlequin — 8", #14574, 1995, Nutcracker Series
Harley-Davidson — 8", h.p., #77002, 1996 (Wendy) Classic American, #17420, 1997 ....$100.00
    8", h.p., #77005, 1996 (Billy) Classic American, #17410, 1997 ....$100.00
    10", h.p. #77102, 1996, pictured 1996 catalog ....not available for sale
    10", #17440, 1997, Cissette, black leather coat, boots $125.00
    10", #17430, 1997, David, jeans, black leather jacket $125.00
    10", #17390, 1998, Cissette, faux leather halter and skirt and backpack $160.00
Harrison, Caroline — 1985 – 1987, 4th set Presidents' Ladies/First Ladies Series (Louisa) $125.00
Hawaii — 8", #301, 1990 – 1991 only, Americana Series (Wendy Ann) $75.00
Hawaiian — 8" h.p., BK, #722, 1966 – 1969, Americana Series (Wendy Ann) $375.00
    7" compo., 1936 – 1939 (Tiny Betty) $300.00
    9" compo., 1937 – 1944 (Little Betty) $350.00
Hayes, Lucy — 1985 – 1987, 4th set Presidents' Ladies/First Ladies Series (Louisa) $125.00
Heavenly Pink Angel — 8", #26285, 2000 – 2001, pink costume, white feather wings $100.00
Heather — 18" cloth/vinyl, 1990 only $100.00
    8", h.p., #10760, 1998, Tyrolean outfit with basket $90.00
Heidi — 7" compo., 1938 – 1939 (Tiny Betty) $325.00
    8" h.p., #460, 1991 – 1992, Storyland Series (Maggie) $75.00
    14" plastic/vinyl, #1480, #1580, #1581, 1969 – 1985 (16-year production),
        Classic Series (Mary Ann) $75.00
    14", #1581, 1986 – 1988, solid green dress, floral apron $75.00
    14", #25503, 1995, Ribbons & Bows Series (not on order sheet) ....not available for sale
    8", h.p., #15100, 1998 – 2000, green dress, lace apron, straw hat, goat $80.00
Hello Baby — 22", 1962 only $175.00
Henie, Sonja — 13 – 15" compo., 1939 – 1942 ....$600.00
    7" compo., 1939 – 1942 (Tiny Betty) $450.00
    9" compo., 1940 – 1941 (Little Betty) $575.00
    11" compo. (Wendy Ann) $550.00
    14" compo. $675.00
    14" in case/wardrobe ....$1,800.00 up
    17 – 18" compo. $950.00
    20 – 23" compo. ....$1,200.00 up
    13 – 14" compo., jointed waist $750.00
    15 – 18" h.p./vinyl, 1951 only, no extra joints, must have good face color (Madeline) $750.00
Her First Day at School — (see Wendy Loves Series)
Her Lady and Child (Thumbelina) — 21" porcelain, 8" h.p., #010, 1992 – 1994,
    limited to 2,500 ....$500.00
Her Sunday Best — (see Wendy Loves Series)
Hershey's Kisses Doll — 8", #17880, 2000, pink and silver costume $75.00
Hiawatha — 8" h.p., #720, 1967 – 1969, Americana Series (Wendy Ann) $375.00
    7" compo. (Tiny Betty) $300.00
    18" cloth, early 1930s $800.00
Hickory Dickory Dock — 8", #11650, 1998 – 1999, clock costume $85.00
Highland Fling — 8" h.p., #484, 1955 only (Wendy Ann) $750.00
Holiday Ballerina — 8", #28525, 2001, white long dress with gold and red trim $75.00
Holiday on Ice — 8" h.p., #319, 1992 – 1993 only, red with white fur hat and muff,
    some tagged "Christmas on Ice" $125.00
Holiday Skater — 8", #28520, 2001, (Maggie), red skating outfit $95.00
Holland — 7" compo., 1936 – 1943 (Tiny Betty) $300.00

Holly — 10", #1135, 1990 – 1991, Portrette, white/red roses Cissette)..........$100.00
Hollywood Glamour 1930 — 10", #17760, 1999, blue taffeta dress $125.00
Hollywood Trunk Set — 8", #15340, 1997..$250.00
Homecoming — 8", 1993 (see M.A.D.C. under Special Events/Exclusives)
Home for Holidays — 14", #24606, 1995, Christmas Series $105.00
Honeybea — 12" vinyl, 1963 only...$175.00
Honeyette Baby — 16" compo./cloth, 1941 – 1942..............................$225.00
　　7" compo., 1934 – 1937, little girl dress (Tiny Betty)......................$275.00
Honeybun — 18 – 19", 1951 – 1952 only $200.00
　　23 – 26"..$300.00
Honeymoon in New Orleans — 8" (see Scarlett)
Hoover, Lou — 14", 1989 – 1990, 6th set Presidents' Ladies/First Ladies Series (Mary Ann)..$125.00
Hope — 8" (see Collectors United under Special Events/Exclusives)
Howdy Doody Time, It's — 8", #15230, 1999 – 2000, marionette $100.00
Huckleberry Finn — 8" h.p., #490, 1989 – 1991 only, Storybook Series (Wendy Ann) $85.00
Hug Me Pets — #76001 – 76007, plush animal bodies, Huggums face $60.00
Huggums, Big — 25", 1963 – 1979, boy or girl.....................................$100.00
Huggums, Little — 14", 1986 only, molded hair....................................$50.00
　　12", 1963 – 1995, molded hair, available in 7 – 10 outfits (first black version available in 1995)...$50.00
　　12", 1963 – 1982, 1988, rooted hair $40.00
　　1991, special outfits (see Imaginarium Shop under Special Events/Exclusives)
　　1996 – 2000, variety of outfits ....$40.00 up
　　12", #29700, 1998, 75th Anniversary Huggums, white dress with flowers..........$75.00
Huggums, Lively — 25", 1963 only, knob makes limbs and head move $150.00
Huggums Man in the Moon Mobile — #14700, 8" boy, star costume,
　　cloth moon, star mobiles...$70.00
Hulda — 18" h.p., 1949 only, lamb's wool wig, black doll (Margaret)............$1,900.00 up
　　14" h.p., 1948 – 1949, lamb's wool wig, black doll ....$1,300.00 up
Humpty Dumpty — 8", #13060, 1997 – 1998, plaid tailcoat, brick wall.........$70.00
Hungarian (Hungary) — 8" h.p., BKW, #397, #797, 1962 – 1965 (Wendy Ann)..........$150.00
　　BK, #397, with metal crown $150.00
　　BK, #797, 1965 – 1972..$100.00
　　8" h.p., straight leg, #0797, #597, 1973 – 1976, marked "Alex"............$70.00
　　8" h.p., straight leg, #597, 1976 – 1986, marked "Alexander" $60.00
　　8" h.p., #522, reintroduced 1992 – 1993 only (Wendy).......................$60.00
　　8", #11547, 1995 only..$60.00
Hush-You-Bye — 8", #25235, 2000 – 2001, comes with rocking horse $100.00
Hyacinth — 9" early vinyl toddler, 1953 only, blue dress & bonnet..............$150.00
Ibiza — 8", #510, 1989 only (Wendy Ann)...$80.00
Ice Capades — 1950s (Cissy) ....$1,400.00 up
　　　　1960s (Jacqueline) ....$1,600.00 up
　　Ice Skater — 8" h.p., BK & BKW, #555, 1955 – 1956 (Wendy Ann) .....$700.00 up
　　8", #303, 1990 – 1991 only, Americana Series, purple/silver (Wendy Ann) ..$75.00
　　8", #16371, 1997, boy, brocade vest, black pants $70.00
　　8", #16361, 1997 – 1998, girl, pink knit and silver outfit $65.00
　　Iceland — 10", 1962 – 1963 (Cissette) ....$750.00 up
　　Ignorance — 8", #18406 (see Ghost of Christmas Present) (sold as set)
　　I Love My Kitty — 8", #30420, 2001, blue check dress, kitty $70.00
　　I Love My Puppy — 8", #30430, 2001, red check dress, puppy...............$70.00
　　I Love My Teddy — 8", #30425, 2001, white, red dress, with teddy.........$70.00
　　I Love You — 8", #10386 – 10388, 1995, three hair colors,
　　　Special Occasions Series $60.00
　　I. Magnin — (see Special Events/Exclusives)
　　I'll Love You Forever Valentine — 8", #25025, 2000,
　　　pink dress, lace front $75.00
　　I'm a Little Teapot — 8", #28870, 2001, (Maggie), blue print teapot
　　　with tea bag...$60.00
　　Imaginarium Shop — (see Special Events/Exclusives)
　　India — 8" h.p., BKW, #775, 1965 (Wendy Ann) $150.00
　　8" h.p., BK, #775, 1965 – 1972 (Wendy) $100.00
　　8" h.p., straight leg, #0775, #575, 1973 – 1975, marked "Alex" $70.00
　　8" h.p., straight leg, #575, #549, 1976 – 1988, marked
　　　"Alexander" (1985 – 1987) $60.00

Ingres, 14", 1987, #1567, plastic/vinyl, (Mary Ann).

India, continued

8" h.p., straight leg, #11563, 1996 International, #24030, 1997 ....$60.00
Indian Boy* — 8" h.p., BK, #720, 1966 only, Americana Series (Wendy Ann) $500.00
Indian Girl* — 8" h.p., BK, #721, 1966 only, Americana Series (Wendy Ann)................$450.00
Indonesia — 8" h.p., BK, #779, 1970 – 1972 (Wendy) $100.00
    8" h.p., straight leg, #779, #0779, #579, 1972 – 1975, marked "Alex" $75.00
    8" h.p., straight leg, #579, 1976 – 1988, marked "Alexander" $60.00
    8" BK, with Maggie Mixup face $175.00
Ingalls, Laura — 14", #1531, 1989 – 1991, Classic Series, burnt orange dress/blue
    pinafore (Mary Ann)..$100.00
    14", #24621, 1995, green with rose floral, Favorite Books Series (Mary Ann) $100.00
Ingres — 14" plastic/vinyl, #1567, 1987 only, Fine Arts Series (Mary Ann) $90.00
Iris — 10" h.p., #1112, 1987 – 1988, pale blue (Cissette).....................................$85.00
Irish (Ireland) — 8" h.p., BKW, #778, 1965 only (Wendy Ann).............................$125.00
    8" BK, #778, 1966 – 1972, long gown $100.00
    8" straight leg, #0778, #578, 1973 – 1975, marked "ALEX," long gown $75.00
    8" straight leg, #578, #551, 1976 – 1985, marked "Alexander" $65.00
    8" straight leg, #551, 1985 – 1987, short dress $60.00
    8" straight leg, #551, 1987 – 1993, marked "Alexander," short dress (Maggie)........$60.00
    8" h.p., #100541, re-issued 1994 only, green skirt with white top $60.00
    8" h.p., #17028, 1996 International, Leprechaun outfit, #21000, 1997 – 1999 ....$60.00
Irish Lass — 8", #11555, 1995 only $60.00
Isolde — 14", #1413, 1985 – 1986 only, Opera Series (Mary Ann) $90.00
Israel — 8" h.p., BK, #768, 1965 – 1972 (Wendy Ann) $100.00
    8" h.p., straight leg, #0768, 1973 – 1975, marked "Alex" $75.00
    8" h.p., straight leg, #568, 1976 – 1989, marked "Alexander" $65.00
Italy — 8" h.p., BKW, #393, 1961 – 1965 (Wendy Ann) $125.00
    8" h.p., BK, #793, 1965 – 1972 ....$100.00
    8" h.p., straight leg, #0793, #593, 1973 – 1975, marked "ALEX".......................$70.00
    #593, 1985 ....$65.00
    8" straight leg, #593, #553, #524, 1976 – 1994 (#110524), marked "Alexander" ...$65.00
    8", #11549, 1995 only $65.00
    8", #24050, 1997 – 1998, gondolier outfit, with decorated oar $70.00
It's Good to Be Queen — 8", #25270, 2000 – 2001, (Maggie) Mary Engelbreit $90.00
Ivana — 16", #25635, 2000 – 2001, Ivana Trump in black velvet gown $185.00
Ivory Victorian Lady — 5", porcelain, #27030, 2000, long white gown $80.00
Jabberwocky — 8", #13580, 1999 – 2000, gold costume,
    comes with brick tower $75.00
Jack & Jill — 7" compo., 1938 – 1943 (Tiny Betty) ....$325.00 ea.
    9" compo., 1939 only (Little Betty)..$350.00 ea.
    8" straight leg (Jack - #455, #457. Jill - #456, #458), 1987 – 1992,
      Storybook Series (Maggie) $65.00
    8" straight leg, sold as set, #14626, 1996 (Wendy)......................................$100.00
Jack Be Nimble — 8" (see Dolly Dears under Special Events/Exclusives)
Jackie — 10", #45200, 1995, Madame's Portfolio Series, pink suit $85.00
    10" h.p., #20115, 1996, wedding gown, Classic American $105.00
    21", #17450, 1997, 3 outfits, 3 pieces luggage, jewelry, etc. $650.00
    10", #17460, 1997 – 1998, pink luncheon suit $105.00
    10", #17470, 1998, opera coat, evening dress $120.00
    10", #17480, 1998, beaded cocktail dress $120.00
Jackie and John — 10", #20117, 1996, limited edition ....$225.00 set
Jackson, Sarah — 1979 – 1981, 2nd set Presidents' Ladies/First
    Ladies Series (Louisa) $125.00
Jacqueline in Riding Habit — 21" h.p./vinyl arms, 1961 – 1962,
    street dress or suit, pillbox hat ....$950.00 up
    In sheath dress and hat or slacks and top $675.00
    In gown from cover of 1962 catalog $950.00
    Ball gown other than 1962 catalog cover $900.00
    10" h.p., 1962 only (Cissette) $700.00
Jacqueline — 1962, 1966 – 1967, exclusive in trunk with wardrobe ....$1,800.00 up
Jamaica — 8" straight leg, #542, 1986 – 1988 (round brown face) $80.00
Janie — 12" toddler, #1156, 1964 – 1966 only $275.00
    Ballerina, 1965 only..$325.00
    14" baby, 1972 – 1973 ....$65.00

* *Became Hiawatha and Pocahontas in 1967.*

Jacqueline, 21", #2130, 1962.

43

    20" baby, 1972 – 1973 ....$75.00

Japan — 8" h.p., BK, #770, 1968 – 1972 (Wendy) $100.00
    8" h.p., straight leg, #0770, #570, 1973 – 1975, marked "Alex" $75.00
    8" h.p., straight leg, #570, 1976 – 1986, marked "Alexander" $65.00
    8", #570, 1987 – 1991 (Maggie) $65.00
    8" BK, #770, 1960s (Maggie Mixup)..$225.00
    8" h.p., #526, reintroduced 1992 – 1993 only, white face (Wendy Ann) $65.00
    8", #28545, 2001, geisha costume..$110.00

Japanese Bride — 10", #28590, kimono $125.00

Jasmine — 10", #1113, 1987 – 1988, Portrette, burnt orange (Cissette), 1997 ....$80.00

Jeannie Walker — 13 – 14" compo., 1940s, unique jointed legs, excellent face color,
    mint condition ....$675.00 up
    18" compo., 1940s...$750.00 up

Jennifer's Trunk Set — 14" doll, #1599, 1990 only $250.00

Jessica — 18" cloth/vinyl, 1990 only $150.00

Jingles the Juggler — 8", #10404, 1996, jester's outfit.............................$75.00

Jo — (see Little Women)

Jo Goes to New York — 8", #14522, 1995 only, trunk set, Little Women Series.......$250.00 set

Joanie — 36" plastic/vinyl, 1960 – 1961, allow more for flirty eyes, 36", 1960,
    nurse dressed in all white with black band on cap............................... $475.00 up
    36", 1961, nurse in colored uniform, all white pinafore and cap.............$425.00 up

John — 8", #440, 1993 only, Peter Pan Series, wears glasses.......................$75.00

John Powers Models — 14" h.p., 1952 only, must be mint (Maggie & Margaret) ....$1,700.00 up
    18", 1952 only...$1,900.00 up

Jones, Casey — 8" h.p., Americana Series, 1991 – 1992 only (Wendy Ann)...........$60.00

Johnson, Lady Bird — 14", 1994 only $125.00

Jolly Old Saint Nick — 16", #19620, 1997 ....$190.00

Joseph, The Dream Teller — 8", #14580, 1995 only, Bible Series.............$85.00

Josephine — 12", #1335, 1980 – 1986, Portraits of History (Nancy Drew).........$75.00
    21" Portrait, 1994 only...$325.00

Joy — 12" (see New England Collectors Society under Special Events/Exclusives)

Joy Noel — 8" (see Spiegel's under Special Events/Exclusives)

Joyous Tulip Ball Gown — 10", 2001, #28515, fancy ball gown $125.00

Judy — 21" compo., 1945 – 1947, pinch pleated flowers at hem (Wendy Ann).........$3,200.00 up
    21" h.p./vinyl arms, 1962 only (Jacqueline)...$1,800.00 up

Judy Loves Pat the Bunny — 14", blue dress, plush bunny $95.00

Jugo-Slav — 7" compo., 1935 – 1937 (Tiny Betty) $275.00

Janie, 21", #1124, 1965. All original.

Jeannie Walker, 18", composition. Made in the 1940s. Marked on back of doll: Alexander Doll Co. Pat. No. 2171231. Unique walker mechanism.

John Powers Model, hard plastic, 1952 only. Maggie face.

Juliet — 21" compo., 1945 – 1946, Portrait (Wendy Ann) ....$2,500.00 up

    18" compo., 1937 – 1940 (Wendy Ann)..$1,250.00 up

    8" h.p., #473, 1955 only (Wendy Ann) ....$950.00 up

    12" plastic/vinyl, 1978 – 1987, Portrait Children Series (Nancy Drew) $65.00

    12", reintroduced 1991 – 1992, Romance Collection (Nancy Drew) $65.00

    8" (see Madame Alexander Doll Co. under Special Events/Exclusives)

June Bride — 21" compo., 1939, 1946 – 1947, Portrait Series, embroidered

    flowers near hem (Wendy Ann)..$2,500.00 up

June Wedding — 8" h.p., 1956 (Wendy Ann)..$675.00

Karen — 15 – 18" h.p., 1948 – 1949 (Margaret) ....$850.00 up

Karen Ballerina — 15" compo., 1946 – 1949 (Margaret) ....$900.00 up

    18" compo., 1948 – 1949 (Margaret) ....$1,200.00 up

    18 – 21", h.p., can be dressed in pink, yellow, blue, white, or lavender ....$950.00 up

    15", porcelain, (1999 – 2000), #90200, remake of 1940s Ballerina...........................$160.00

    10", h.p., 2000, #25551, (Cissette), remake of 1940s Ballerina $120.00

Kate Greenaway — 7" compo., 1938 – 1943 (Tiny Betty)...$375.00

    9" compo., 1936 – 1939 (Little Betty) $400.00

    16" cloth, 1936 – 1938 ....$900.00

    13", 14", 15" compo., 1938 – 1943 (Princess Elizabeth)..$800.00

    18", 1938 – 1943 (Wendy Ann/Princess Elizabeth)..$850.00

    24", 1938 – 1943 (Princess Elizabeth) ....$900.00 up

    14" vinyl, #1538, 1993 only, Classic Series $100.00

Kathleen Toddler — 23" rigid vinyl, 1959 only $150.00

Kathy — 17 – 21" compo., 1939, 1946 (Wendy Ann) ....$650.00 – 850.00

    15 – 18" h.p., 1949 – 1951, has braids (Maggie) ....$550.00 – 700.00

Kathy Baby — 13 – 15" vinyl, 1954 – 1956, has rooted or molded hair ....$75.00 – 125.00

    11 – 13" vinyl, 1955 – 1956, has rooted or molded hair ....$75.00 – 125.00

    18 – 21", 1954 – 1956, has rooted or molded hair ....$100.00 – 150.00

    11" vinyl, 1955 – 1956, doll has molded hair and comes with trousseau $175.00

    21", 1954 only $150.00

    21" & 25", 1955 – 1956 ....$100.00 – 175.00

Kathy Cry Dolly — 11 – 15" vinyl nurser, 1957 – 1958 ....$75.00 – 150.00

    18", 21", 25"..$100.00 – 175.00

Kathy Tears — 11", 15", 17" vinyl, 1959 – 1962, has closed mouth ....$75.00 – 125.00

    19", 23", 26", 1959 – 1962 ....$100.00 – 175.00

    12", 16", 19" vinyl, 1960 – 1961 (new face) ....$75.00 – 150.00

Katie (black Smarty) — 12" plastic/vinyl, 1963 only...................................$325.00

    12" (black Janie), #1156, #1155, 1965 only..$300.00

    12" h.p., 1962, 100th Anniversary doll for FAO Schwarz (Lissy) $1,000.00

    12", Shopping in Paris, 2000, #26475, white dress,

        red check jacket $60.00

Keane, Doris — cloth, 1930s $750.00

    9 – 11" compo., 1936 – 1937 (Little Betty).$250.00– 300.00

Kelly — 12" h.p., 1959 only (Lissy) ....$475.00 up

    15 – 16", 1958 – 1959 (Mary-Bel) $325.00

    16", 1959 only, in trunk/wardrobe $800.00

    18", 1958 ....$375.00

    22", 1958 – 1959 ....$425.00

    8" h.p., #433, 1959, blue/white dress

      (Wendy Ann) $575.00

    15", Shopping in Paris, #26470, 2000,

      black check outfit $85.00

Kelly and Kitty — 20", #29770, 1999,

    pink check outfit with kitten $135.00

Kelly Blue Gingham — 18", #29100,

    1997 – 1998, vinyl.............................$125.00

Kelly Blue Dupionne — 20", #29380,

    1998, blue silk dress $160.00

Kelly Good Morning — 20", #29930, 1999,

    white dress trimmed in blue $105.00

Kelly Happy Birthday — 18", #29230, 1997,

    vinyl...$125.00

Kelly's Little Sister, Katie — 12", #29940, 1999,

    pink plaid dress $55.00

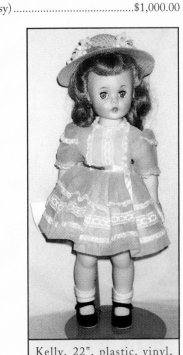

Kelly, 22", plastic, vinyl, #1912, 1958.

Kelly, 12", #1102, 1959 only. Lissy face with non-jointed arms and legs. All original.

Kelly Pink Butterfly — 20", #29920, 1999, pink dress and pinafore.....................................$105.00
Kelly Pink Dot Tulle — 18", #29230, 1997, vinyl..$125.00
Kelly Pink Snowflake — 18", #29110, 1997, vinyl $125.00
Kelly Teacher's Pet — 15", #29760, 1999, plaid dress and hat $75.00
Kelly Teatime — 15", #29300, 1998, blue dress, straw hat $85.00
Kelly Tree Trimming — 18", #29240, 1997, vinyl..$125.00
Kelly White Floral Party — 15", vinyl #29390, 1998 – 1999...$105.00
Kennedy, Jacqueline — 14", 1989 – 1990, 6th set Presidents' Ladies/First
    Ladies Series (Mary Ann)...$175.00
Kenya — 8", 1994, outfit tagged, in Neiman-Marcus trunk set $70.00
    8", issued 1995 only, same outfit but sold as Nigeria ....no price available
King — 21" compo., 1942 – 1946 , extra make-up, red chest ribbon,
    gold trimmed cape (Wendy Ann) ....$2,700.00 up
King of Hearts — 8", #14611, 1996, Alice in Wonderland Series $65.00
Kitten — 14 – 18" cloth/vinyl, 1962 – 1963...$50.00 – 85.00
    24", 1961 only, has rooted hair $95.00
    20" nurser, 1968 only, has cryer box, doesn't wet..$100.00
    20", 1985 – 1986 only, dressed in pink $90.00
    8", 1998, #29310 Powder Pink or #29423 Sunny $60.00
Kitty Baby — 21" compo., 1941 – 1942 ....$175.00
Kitten Kries — 20" cloth/vinyl, 1967 only $100.00
Kitten, Littlest — (see Littlest Kitten)
Kitten, Lively — 14", 18", 24", 1962 – 1963, knob moves head and limbs................$100.00 – 200.00
Kitten, Mama — 18", #402, 1963 only, same as "Lively" but also has cryer box $150.00
Klondike Kate — 10" h.p., 1963 only, Portrette (Cissette) ....$1,400.00 up
Knave — 8", #13040, 1997 – 1998, brocade suit, large playing card, 5 of Spades......................$75.00
Knight — 8", #25915, (Wendy), 2000 – 2001 Alice in Wonderland Series $75.00
Korea — 8" h.p., BK, #772, 1968 – 1970 (Wendy)...$195.00
    BKW & BK, #772 (Maggie Mixup)...$225.00
    #522, reintroduced 1988 – 1989 (Maggie Mixup) $75.00
Kukla — 8", #11101, 1995 only, International Folk Tales (Russia), (Wendy) $65.00
Kwanzaa Celebration — 10" h.p., #10368, 1996 Holiday $95.00
Lady and Her Child — 21" porcelain, 8" h.p., 1993...$500.00 set
Lady Bird — 8", #438, 1988 – 1989, Storybook Series (Maggie) $85.00
Lady Hamilton — 20" h.p./vinyl arms, 1957 only, Models Formal Gowns Series,
    picture hat, blue gown w/ shoulder shawl effect (Cissy) ....$1,000.00 up
    11" h.p., 1957, pink silk gown, picture hat with roses (Cissette) ....$750.00 up
    21", #2182, 1968, beige lace over pink gown (Jacqueline) $475.00

Lady in Waiting, 8", h.p., #487, (Wendy Ann), 1955 only. All original.

Leslie, 17", vinyl/plastic, #1651, 1965. Beautiful mint doll.

Lady Hamilton, continued

12" vinyl, #1338, 1984 – 1986, Portraits of History (Nancy Drew)................................$75.00
Lady in Red — 20", #2285, 1958 only, red taffeta (Cissy) ....$2,100.00 up
    10", 1990, Portrette (Cissette) $90.00
Lady in Waiting — 8" h.p., #487, 1955 only (Wendy Ann) ....$1,600.00 up
Ladybug — 8", #27725, 2001, red check dress, green jacket and hat.............................$80.00
Lady Lee — 8", #442, 1988 only, Storybook Series $70.00
Lady Lovelace — cloth/felt, 1930s $650.00
Lady Valentine — 8", #140503, 1994 only (Wendy Ann) $65.00
Lady Windermere — 21" compo., 1945 – 1946, extra make-up, Portrait Series ....$2,500.00 up
Lancelot — 8", #79529, 1995, 100th Anniversary (copy of 1995 Disney auction doll) $100.00
    8", #13550, 1999, blue and black outfit with sword..$80.00
Lane, Harriet — 1982 – 1984, 3rd set Presidents' Ladies/First Ladies Series (Mary Ann)........$125.00
Laos — 8" straight leg, #525, 1987 – 1988 ....$70.00
Lapland — 8" h.p., #537, 1993 ....$70.00
Lassie — 8", #11102, 1995 only, International Folk Tales (Norway)..............................$65.00
Latvia — 8" straight leg, #527, 1987 only $75.00
Laughing Allegra — cloth, 1932 ....$650.00
Laura Ingalls Wilder — 8", #14110, 1998 – 1999, patchwork print outfit......................$75.00
Laurie, Little Men — 8" h.p., BK, #781, #755, 1966 – 1972 (Wendy Ann) $175.00
    Straight leg, #0755, #416, 1973 – 1975, marked "Alex" $95.00
    Check pants, marked "Alexander" $85.00
    Straight leg, #416, #410, 1976 – 1992 ....$75.00
    8", #14620, 1996, waistcoat, houndstooth trousers $65.00
    12" all h.p., 1966 only (Lissy) $625.00
    12" plastic/vinyl, 1967 – 1988 (Nancy Drew) $75.00
Laurie, Piper — 14" h.p., 1950 only (Margaret) ....$2,400.00 up
    21" h.p., 1950 only (Margaret)..$2,900.00 up
Lavender Bouquet — 8", #30895, 2001, white, black long gown with lavender flowers............$80.00
Laverne and Shirley Set — 10", #25755, with Boo Boo Kitty $180.00
Lazy Mary — 7" compo., 1936 – 1938 (Tiny Betty) $275.00
Leaf Fairy — 8", #28505, 2001, rust costume with leaves $85.00
Lemonade Girl — 8", #14130, 1998 – 1999 (Maggie), doll with stand, etc $90.00
Lena (Riverboat Queen) — (see M.A.D.C. under Special Events/Exclusives)
Lennox, Mary — 14" Classic Series, 1993 – 1994 ....$100.00
Leo — 8", #21370, 1998, golden lion costume $90.00
Leopard with Shopping Bag — 10", Cissette, 1997 – 1998 ....$125.00
Le Petit Boudoir — 1993 (see Collectors United under Special Events/Exclusives)
Leslie (black Polly) — 17" vinyl, 1965 – 1971, in dress...$275.00
    1966 – 1971, as bride..$300.00
    1965 – 1971, in formal or ball gown $375.00
    In trunk with wardrobe ....$650.00 up
    1966 – 1971, as ballerina $375.00
Letty Bridesmaid — 7 – 8" compo., 1938 – 1940 (Tiny Betty) $275.00
Lewis, Shari — 14", 1958 – 1959 ....$650.00
    21", 1958 – 1959..$850.00
Liberace with Candelabra — 8", #22080, 1997, velvet cape $115.00
Libra — 8", #21390, 1998, balanced scale headpiece, purple costume $90.00
Liesl — (see Sound of Music)
'Lil Christmas Candy — 8" h.p., #100348, 1994 only, Americana Series.....................$70.00
'Lil Christmas Cookie — 8", #341, 1993 – 1994, Americana Series $70.00
'Lil Clara and The Nutcracker — 8", #140480, 1994, Story-land Series $70.00
'Lil Sir Genius — 7", #701 & #400701 vinyl, painted eyes, 1993, blue jumpsuit.............$50.00
Lila Bridesmaid — 7 – 8" compo., 1938 – 1940 (Tiny Betty)....................................$325.00
Lilac Fairy — 21", 1993, Portrait Ballerina $300.00
Lilac Rococo Lady — 5", #27020, porcelain, 2000, embroidered gown $80.00
Lilibet — 16" compo., 1938 (Princess Elizabeth) ....$750.00 up
Lily — 10", #1114, 1987 – 1988, red/black (Cissette) $85.00
Lily of the Valley — 10", satin gown with lilies of the valley $130.00
Lincoln, Mary Todd — 1982 – 1984, 3rd set Presidents' Ladies/First Ladies Series (Louisa)..$150.00
Lind, Jenny — 21" h.p./vinyl arms, #2191, 1969, dressed in all pink, no trim (Jacqueline) $1,400.00
    #2181, 1970, all pink with lace trim $1,500.00
    10", #1171, 1969, Portrette, all pink, no trim (Cissette)..$600.00
    10", #1184, 1970, Portrette, pink with lace trim (Cissette) $650.00

Lind, Jenny, continued

14" plastic/vinyl, #1491, 1970 only, Portrait Children Series (Mary Ann), pink, lace trim $375.00

10", #27375, 2000, white long gown $150.00

Lind, Jenny & Listening Cat — 14", #1470, 1969 – 1971, Portrait Children Series,
blue dot dress apron & holds plush kitten (must have kitten) (Mary Ann) $350.00

Lion Tamer — 8", #306, 1990, Americana Series (Wendy Ann)..$65.00

Linus — 10", #26435, 2001, Peanuts Gang, red stripe shirt, blue blanket $30.00

Lissy — 11½" – 12" h.p., 1956 – 1958, jointed knees & elbows

1956 – 1958, as ballerina..$450.00

1956 – 1958, as bride...$425.00 up

1956 – 1957, as bridesmaid..$650.00 up

1958, dressed in formal ....$600.00 up

1956 – 1958, in street dresses ....$375.00 up

1956, in window box with wardrobe $1,500.00

21", one-piece arm, pink tulle pleated skirt (Cissy) $1,300.00

21", #2051, 1966, pink with tiara (Coco)...$2,200.00

12" h.p., 1957, jointed elbows & knees, in window box with wardrobe (Lissy) ....$1,500.00 up

12" h.p., one-piece arms & legs in window box/wardrobe, 1959 – 1966 (Lissy) ....$1,000.00 up

Classics (see individuals, examples: McGuffey Ana, Scarlett, Cinderella)

Lithuania — 8" h.p., #110544, 1994 only (Maggie)..$65.00

Little Angel — 9" latex/vinyl, 1950 – 1957...$200.00

Little Audrey — Vinyl, 1954 only...$475.00 up

Little Betty — 9 – 11" compo., 1935 – 1943, must be mint................................$250.00 – 325.00

Little Bitsey — 9" all vinyl nurser, 1967 – 1968 (Sweet Tears)..$150.00

Little Bo Peep — (see Bo Peep, Little)

Little Boop Beep — 10", #28970, 2001, (Betty Boop), pink dress......................................$130.00

Little Boy Blue — 7" compo., 1937 – 1939 (Tiny Betty)...$300.00

Little Butch — 9" all vinyl nurser, 1967 – 1968 (Sweet Tears)..$150.00

Little Cherub — 11" compo., 1945 – 1946..$275.00

7" all vinyl, 1960 only..$225.00

Little Christmas Princess — 8", #10369, 1996 Holiday..$65.00

Little Colonel — 8½ – 9" compo. (rare size), 1935, closed mouth (Betty) $650.00

11 – 13" compo. (rare size), closed mouth (Betty)..$550.00 – 700.00

17" compo., closed mouth (Betty) ....$750.00 up

14", open mouth (Betty) ....$650.00 up

17" – 23", open mouth ....$750.00 – 950.00

26 – 27", open mouth ....$1,250.00 up

Little Countess — 8", #28890, 2001, white lacy dress $110.00

Little Devil — 8" h.p., Americana Series,
1992 – 1993 only $85.00

Little Dorrit — 16" cloth, early 1930s, Dickens character ...$700.00

Little Edwardian — 8" h.p., SL, SLW, #0200,
1953 – 1955, long dotted navy gown ....$1,000.00 up

Little Emily — 16" cloth, early 1930s, Dickens character .$650.00

Little Emperor — 8" (see U.F.D.C. under
Special Events/Exclusives)

Little Gardenia Bridesmaid — 8", 2001, white dress $100.00

Little Genius — 12 – 14" compo./cloth,
1935 – 1940, 1942 – 1946 ....$200.00

16 – 20" compo./cloth, 1935 – 1937, 1942 – 1946 ....$250.00

24 – 25", 1936 – 1940..$250.00

8" h.p./vinyl, 1956 – 1962, nude (clean condition),
good face color $100.00

Dressed in cotton play dress $175.00

In dressy, lacy outfit with bonnet $275.00

Dressed in christening outfit $350.00

Sewing or Gift Set, 1950s..................................$850.00 up

7" vinyl, 1993 – 1995, reintroduced doll
with painted eyes $50.00

#701 & #400701, 1993 – 1995, dressed in
blue jumpsuit ('Lil Sir Genius) $50.00

#702 & #400702, 1993 – 1995, dressed in pink
lacy dress ('Lil Miss Genius) $55.00

1993, extra packaged outfits..............................$30.00 ea.

Jenny Lind, 10", #1171, (Cissette). Made in 1969 with no lace
on the overskirt. Made in 1970 with lace trim.

Little Genius, continued
    Christening Baby, #400703, 1994 – 1995 ....$50.00
    Super Genius, #400704, 1994 – 1995, dressed in Superman style outfit $45.00
    Birthday Party, #400705, 1994 only $50.00
    Genius Elf, #400706, 1994 – 1995, dressed in Christmas $50.00

Dating Lissy Dolls

12" Lissy and Lissy face dolls are all hard plastic with glued-on wigs. Lissy is not marked anywhere on the body. Only the clothes were tagged.

1956 – 1958: Lissy had jointed elbows and knees which allow her to sit. Her feet are slightly arched to wear sandals with hose or white socks. The 1957-1958 Lissy Little Women wear black sandals.

1959 – 1967: The Lissy face dolls have the Lissy face but have non-jointed arms and legs. The feet are flat.

1959 – 1967: Lissy face Little Women were made.

1959: Kelly (Lissy face) was produced 1959 only in a variety of outfits.

1962: Pamela (Lissy face) had three interchangeable outfits with extra clothing in a gift set. Pamela has a Velcro strip to attach the wigs. Pamela was made for several years as store specials. Pamela was also made with the later Nancy Drew vinyl head.

1962: Lissy face Katie and Tommy made for FAO Schwarz's 100th Anniversary.

1963: McGuffey Ana, Southern Belle, and Scarlett O'Hara were made using the Lissy face doll.

1965: Brigitta of the large set of Sound of Music was made using the Lissy face doll in an Alpine outfit and the rare sailor costume.

1966: Lissy face Cinderellas was available in "poor" outfit or in blue satin ball gown. A gift set featured the doll and both outfits.

1967: Only year Laurie of Little Women was made using the Lissy face.

1993: Nine Lissy face dolls were made for the regular line: Amy, Beth, Jo, Meg, Ballerina, Greta Brinker, Hans Brinker, Hamlet, and Ophelia.

1993: Special for Horchow. Pamela Plays Dress Up was a Lissy face doll with wigs, clothes, and a trunk. Lissy face Alice in Wonderland with Jabberwocky was made for Disney, and the Columbian Sailor was made for the U.F.D.C. Luncheon.

Lissy, 12", all hard plastic, #1222, 1956. All original clothes.

Lissy, 12", 1956. All hard plastic, jointed knees and elbows. All original.

Little Genius, 8", hard plastic head with caracal hair and vinyl body. All original. Little Genius was made from 1956 to 1962.

Little Genius Toddler — 8", h.p., 1954 – 1955, (Wendy Ann), caracul hair..........................$275.00
Little Girl with a Curl — 8", #28965, 2001, pink dress..........................$85.00
Little Godey — 8" h.p., #491, 1953 – 1955 (Wendy Ann) ....$1,400.00 up
Little Granny — 14" plastic/vinyl, #1431, 1966 only, floral gown (Mary Ann) $250.00
    14", #1430, 1966 only, pinstriped gown (also variations) (Mary Ann) $225.00
Little Huggums — (see Huggums)
Little Irish Dancer — 8", #32125, 2000, navy decorated dress $85.00
Little Jack Horner — 7" compo., 1937 – 1943 (Tiny Betty) $300.00
Little Jumping Joan — 8", #487, 1989 – 1990, Storybook Series (Maggie Mixup) $75.00
Little Lady Doll — 8" h.p., #1050, 1960 only, Gift Set in mint condition (Maggie Mixup).....$800.00 up
    8" doll only, must have correct hairdo and excellent face color $350.00
    21" h.p., 1949, has braids & colonial gown, extra make-up, Portrait Series (Wendy Ann)...$2,400.00
Little Lord Fauntleroy — cloth, 1930s $750.00
    13" compo., 1936 – 1937 (Wendy Ann) ....$650.00 up
Little Madeline — 8" h.p., 1953 – 1954 (Wendy Ann) ....$750.00 up
Little Love Angel — 8", #28350, 2001, pink costume with wings $100.00
    10", #28355, 2001, lavender dress, feather wings..........................$130.00
Little Maid — 8" straight leg, #423, 1987 – 1988, Storybook Series (Wendy Ann)..........................$70.00
Little Men — 15" h.p., 1950 – 1952 (Margaret & Maggie)..........................$850.00 up ea.
Little Men — Set with Tommy, Nat & Stuffy, must be in excellent condition ....$2,600.00 set
Little Mermaid — 10", #1145, 1992 – 1993, Portrette, green/blue outfit (Cissette) $115.00
    8", #14531, 1995, Hans Christian Andersen Series, has long black hair $65.00
Little Minister — 8" h.p., #411, 1957 only (Wendy Ann)..........................$3,000.00 up
Little Miss — 8" h.p., #489, 1989 – 1991 only, Storybook Series (Maggie Mixup) $75.00
Little Miss Godey — (see M.A.D.C. under Special Events/Exclusives)
Little Miss Magnin — (see I. Magnin under Special Events/Exclusives)
Little Nannie Etticoat — #428, 1986 – 1988, straight leg, Storybook Series $75.00
Little Nell — 16" cloth, early 1930s, Dickens character ....$650.00 up
    14" compo., 1938 – 1940 (Wendy Ann)..........................$675.00
Little Orphan Annie — 8", #13740, 1999 – 2001, red dress, comes with dog Sandy $50.00
Little Pearl Bridesmaid — 8", 2001, white dress, rose crown..........................$100.00
Little Princess — 14", #26415, 1995 only, has trunk and wardrobe (Louisa) $250.00
Little Princess, A — 8", #14120, 1998 – 1999, pink taffeta, with doll $90.00
Little Shaver — 10" cloth, 1940 – 1944..........................$450.00 up
    7" cloth, 1940 – 1944..........................$550.00
    15" cloth, 1940 – 1944..........................$600.00
    22" cloth, 1940 – 1944..........................$650.00 up
    12" cloth, 1941 – 1943 (see Baby Shaver)

Little Shaver, 12", plastic/vinyl, #2930, 1963.

Little Women, Beth, 12", #1321, 1983 – 1985, (Nancy Drew).

Little Women, Meg, 12", #1190, 1957, (Lissy). She wears black elastic sandals. Black side snap shoes came on later dolls.

Little Shaver, continued

12" plastic/vinyl, 1963 – 1965, has painted eyes $250.00
10", #26820, 2000, cloth, grey/cream, remake of 1940s $55.00
10", #26825, 2000 – 2001, cloth, pink/cream, remake of 1940s $55.00
6", #26830, 2000 – 2001, cloth, grey/cream, remake of 1940s $45.00

Little Southern Boy/Girl — 10" latex/vinyl, 1950 – 1951 ....$150.00 ea.
Little Southern Girl — 8" h.p., #305, 1953 only (Wendy Ann).....................$950.00 up
Little Thumbkins — 8", #14532, Hans Christian Andersen Series, lavender/pink/yellow tiers .$65.00
Little Victoria — 7½" – 8", #376, 1953 – 1954 only (Wendy Ann).................$1,200.00 up
Little Women — Meg, Jo, Amy, Beth (Marme in sets when available)

16" cloth, 1930 – 1936 ....$700.00 up ea.
7" compo., 1935 – 1944 (Tiny Betty) ....$325.00 ea.
9" compo., 1937 – 1940 (Little Betty) ....$300.00 ea.
13 – 15" compo., 1937 – 1946 (Wendy Ann) ....$350.00 ea.
14 – 15" h.p., 1947 – 1956, plus Marme (Margaret & Maggie)........................$450.00 ea., 2,200.00 set
14 – 15" h.p., widespread fingers, ca. 1949 – 1952 ....$500.00 ea.
14 – 15" h.p., BK, plus Marme (Margaret & Maggie) ....$450.00 ea., 2,200.00 set
14 – 15" Amy with loop curls, must have good face color (Margaret) ....$550.00 ea.
8" Amy with loop curls, 1991 #411 ....$95.00 ea.
7½ – 8" h.p., SL, SLW, all #609, 1955, plus Marme (Wendy Ann) ....$375.00 ea., 1,800.00 set
8" h.p., BKW, all #609, all #409, all #481, 1956 – 1959 (Wendy Ann)............$350.00 ea., 1,600.00 set
8" BKW, all #381, 1960 – 1963 (Wendy Ann)......................................$275.00 ea., 1,300.00 set
#781, 1966 – 1972 ....$125.00 ea., 650.00 set
#7811 to #7815, 1973 ....$100.00 ea., 550.00 set
8" straight leg, #411 to #415, 1974 – 1986 ....$75.00 ea., 375.00 set
#405 to #409, 1987 – 1990 ....$65.00 ea., 350.00 set
#411 to #415, 1991 – 1992 ....$65.00 ea., 350.00 set
#14523 – 14528, 1995 ....$60.00 ea., 300.00 set
Exclusive for FAO Schwarz (see Special Events/Exclusives)
#28140 – 28180, 2000 ....$80.00 – 95.00 ea., 400.00 set
10", #14630 – 14633, 1996 ....$85.00 ea., 375.00 set
11½ – 12" h.p., jointed elbows & knees, 1957 – 1958 (Lissy) ....$375.00 ea., 1,900.00 set
11½ – 12" h.p., one-piece arms & legs, 1959 – 1968 (Lissy) ....$300.00 ea., 1,500.00 set
12" plastic/vinyl, 1969 – 1982 (Nancy Drew) ....$65.00 ea., 325.00 set
12" plastic/vinyl, 1983 – 1989, new outfits (Nancy Drew) ....$65.00 ea., 325.00 set
12", 1989 – 1990 only (see Sears unders Special Events/Exclusives)
12", 1993 only, no Marme (Lissy) ....$100.00 ea.
16", 1997 – 2000, plastic/vinyl, Little Women Journal Series (no Marme)............$105.00 ea.
16", 1999 – 2000, Marme, #28040, Little Women Journals.........................$125.00

Littlest Kitten — 8" vinyl, 1963, nude, clean, good face color ....$125.00 up
Dressed in lacy dress oufit with bonnet ....$275.00 up

Littlest Kitten, 8", vinyl. Made in 1963. All original.

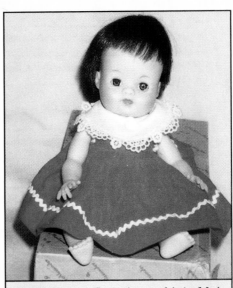

Littlest Kitten, 8", vinyl, rooted hair. Made in 1963. Original clothes.

 Dressed in christening outfit..$350.00 up
 In sewing or Gift Set ....$700.00 up
 Dressed in play attire $175.00
Lively Huggums — 25", knob makes limbs and head move, 1963 ....$150.00
Lively Kitten — 14", 18", 24", 1962 – 1963, knob makes limbs and head move........$100.00 – 175.00
Lively Pussy Cat — 14", 20", 24", 1966 – 1969, knob makes limbs and head move...$100.00 – 175.00
Lola and Lollie Bridesmaid — 7" compo., 1938 – 1940 (Tiny Betty)........................$300.00 up ea.
Lollie Baby — Rubber/compo., 1941 – 1942 ....$100.00
Lollipop Munchkin — (see Munchkin)
Looby Loo — 15½" h.p., ca. 1951 – 1954 ....$675.00 up
Lord Fauntleroy — 12", 1981 – 1983, Portrait Children (Nancy Drew) $100.00
Lord Valentine — 8", #140502, 1994 only (Wendy Ann)..$75.00
Louisa — (see Sound of Music)
Love — 8" (see Collectors United under Specials Events/Exclusives)
 8", made for public in 1994 (Only differences on C.U. doll are gold locket,
 pearls set into cap, and gold metal braids on slippers, heart box).........................$75.00
Lovey Dove (Dovey) — 19" vinyl baby, 1958 – 1959, closed mouth,
 molded or rooted hair, few are mistagged..$175.00
 19" h.p./latex, 1950 – 1951 ....$125.00
 12" all h.p. toddler, 1948 – 1951 (Precious)..$375.00 up
 1951, dressed as "Ringbearer"...$650.00 up
 "Answer Doll" with lever in back to move head..$525.00 up
Lucinda — 12" plastic/vinyl, 1969 – 1970 (Janie) $325.00
 14" plastic/vinyl, #1435, #1535, 1971 – 1982 (11-year production),
 blue gown (Mary Ann) $85.00
 14", #1535, 1983 – 1986, Classic Series, pink or peach gown (Mary Ann) $90.00
Luck of the Irish — 8", #327, 1992 – 1993 only, Americana Series (Maggie Mixup) $70.00
Lucy — 8" h.p., #488, 1961 only, Americana Series, strip cotton/poke
 bonnet (Wendy Ann)...$1,800.00 up
 10", #26420, 2001, Peanuts Gang, blue dress, includes backdrop $40.00
Lucy Bride — 14" h.p., 1949 – 1950 (Margaret)...$950.00 up
 18" h.p., 1949 – 1950 (Margaret) ....$950.00 up
 21" h.p., 1949 – 1950 (Margaret) ....$1,100.00 up
 21", #2155, 1955, (Cissy) pale pink gown, very red hair, heavily painted face ......$5,500.00 up
 14" compo., 1937 – 1940 (Wendy Ann)...$450.00
 17" compo., 1937 – 1940 (Wendy Ann)...$550.00
 21" compo., 1942 – 1944, Portrait, extra make-up (Wendy Ann)............................$2,500.00

Madelaine Du Bain. All composition. Original clothes. 1930's – 1940's.

Maggie Mixup, 8", #598, 1960, BKW. All original with green eyes and red, long straight hair.

Maggie Mixup with watering can, 8", #610, 1961, BKW, (Maggie Mixup). All original.

Lucy Gets in Pictures — 10", #31450, 2001, pink long gown, feather head piece...................$160.00
Lucy Locket — 8" straight leg, #433, 1986 – 1988, Storybook Series $75.00
    14", #25501, 1995, Ribbons & Bows Series, purple floral skirt (Louisa) $125.00
Lucy Ricardo — (see FAO Schwarz under Special Events/Exclusives)
    9", 1950s gingham dress, with bottle and spoon...$125.00
    21", #50003, 1996 Timeless Legends, black dress with black and white polka dot accents......$325.00
    10", #14071, Shadow Polka Dot Lucy, 1998 – 1999 ....$175.00
    10", #15160, 1999 – 2000, Lucy's Italian Movie, peasant outfit, grape vat.........................$160.00
Lucy and Ricky — 9" set, Vitameatavegamin episode $200.00
Lucy's Rhumba — 10", #25760, 2001, Be a Pal episode, white dress, ruffles $140.00
Lullaby Munchkin — (see Munchkin)
Mad Hatter — 8", #14510, 1995, Alice in Wonderland Series...$75.00
M.A.D.C. (Madame Alexander Doll Club) — (see Special Events/Exclusives)
Madame Butterfly — 10" (see Marshall Fields under Special Events/Exclusives)
    8", h.p., #22000, 1997 – 1998, shadow, kimono $95.00
    21", #22010, 1997, kimono over silk robe...$350.00
Madame de Pompadour — 10", #25010, 1999, (Cissette), elaborate taffeta costume $200.00
Madame Doll — 21" h.p./vinyl arms, 1966 only, pink brocade (Coco)..........................$2,200.00 up
    14" plastic/vinyl, #1460, #1561, 1967 – 1975, Classic Series (Mary Ann) $275.00
Madame (Alexander) — 21", 1984 only, one-piece skirt in pink $375.00
    21", 1985 – 1987, pink with overskirt that unsnaps...$275.00
    21", 1988 – 1990, blue with full lace overskirt $275.00
    21", #79507, 1995, 100th Anniversary, pink with lace jacket, limited edition of 500............$750.00
    8", 1993 only, introduced mid-year (see Madame Alexander Doll Co.
        under Special Events/Exclusives)
    8" in blue gown (see Doll & Teddy Bear Expo. under Special Events/Exclusives)
    8", #79527, 1995, 100th Anniversary $100.00
Madame Alexander Celebrates American Design — 10", h.p., (Cissette),
    2000, pink gown $160.00
Madame Alexander Collector's Phonograph Album —1978, Madame's voice
    reading children's stories $35.00
Madame Pompadour — 21" h.p./vinyl arms, #2197, 1970, pink lace overskirt (Jacqueline).....$120.00
Madame X, John Singer Sargent's — 10", #25300, 2000, long black gown $120.00
Madelaine — 14" compo., 1940 – 1942 (Wendy Ann)..$650.00 up
    8" h.p., 1954, FAO Schwarz special ....$800.00 up
Madelaine Du Bain — 11" compo., closed mouth, 1937 (Wendy Ann).................................$500.00
    14" compo., 1938 – 1939 (Wendy Ann)...$550.00 up
    17" compo., 1939 – 1941 (Wendy Ann)...$675.00
    21" compo., 1939 – 1941 (Wendy Ann)...$900.00 up
    14" h.p., 1949 – 1951 (Maggie) ....$950.00 up
Madeline — 17 – 18" h.p./jointed elbows & knees, 1950 – 1953....................$800.00 up
    18" h.p., 1961 only, vinyl head, extra jointed body, wears short dress,
        must be mint ....$700.00 up
    Ball gown 1961 only...$800.00 up
Madison, Dolly — 1976 – 1978, 1st set Presidents' Ladies/First
    Ladies Series (Martha) $125.00
Madonna and Child — 10", #10600, 1995, Christmas Series $105.00
Maggie — 15" h.p., 1948 – 1954 (Little Women only to 1956) $550.00
    17 – 18", 1949 – 1953 ....$650.00 up
    20 – 21", 1948 – 1954 ....$700.00 up
    22 – 23", 1949 – 1952 ....$800.00 up
    17" plastic/vinyl, 1972 – 1973 only (Elise)..$175.00
Maggie Elf — 8", #14585, 1995, Christmas Series $70.00
Maggie Mixup — 16½" h.p./vinyl, 1960 only (Elise body) $375.00
    17" plastic/vinyl, 1961 only $400.00
    8" h.p., #600, #611, #617, #627, 1960 – 1961, freckles $450.00
    8" Wendy Ann face, freckles ....$450.00 up
    8" h.p., #618, 1961, as angel $775.00
    8", #610, 1960 – 1961, dressed in overalls and has watering can $800.00
    8", #626, 1960 – 1961, dressed in skater outfit ....$750.00 up
    8", #634, 1960 – 1961, dressed in riding habit.................................$550.00
    8", #593, 1960, dressed in roller skating outfit................................$750.00
    8", #598, #597, #596, 1960, wearing dresses or skirts/blouses ......$450.00 up
    8", #31000, 1997 – 1998, Post Office commemorative, blue gingham $65.00

Maggie Mixup Angel, 8", BKW, 1961. Blue taffeta gown with silver wings.

Maggie Teenager — 15 – 18" h.p., 1951 – 1953 ....$475.00 – 600.00
  23", 1951 – 1953 ....$650.00 up
Maggie Walker — 15 – 18" h.p., 1949 – 1953 ....$400.00 – 575.00
  20 – 21", 1949 – 1953 ....$575.00
  23 – 25", 1951 – 1953 (with Cissy face) ....$650.00 up
Magnolia — 21", #2297, 1977 only, many rows of lace on pink gown........................$475.00
  21", #2251, 1988 only, yellow gown $300.00
Maid Marian — 8" h.p., #492, 1989 – 1991 only, Storybook Series (Wendy Ann) $125.00
  21", 1992 – 1993 only, Portrait Series (Jacqueline)..$325.00
Maid of Honor — 18" compo., 1940 – 1944 (Wendy Ann) ....$700.00 up
  14" plastic/vinyl, #1592, 1988 – 1989, Classic Series, blue gown (Mary Ann)........$100.00
  10", #28645, 2001, pink long dress..$125.00
Majorette — 14 – 17" compo., 1937 – 1938 (Wendy Ann) ....$850.00 up
Drum Majorette — 8" h.p., #482, 1955 only (Wendy Ann)....................................$950.00 up
  8", #314, 1991 – 1992 only, Americana Series, no baton....................................$70.00
Mali — 8", #11565, 1996 International, African-American print costume $65.00
Mambo — 8", h.p., #481, 1955 only (Wendy Ann)..$850.00 up
Mammy — 8", #402, 1989 only, Jubilee II set (black "round" face)............................$100.00
  8" h.p., #635, 1991 – 1992 only, Scarlett Series (black Wendy Ann on Cissette body)............$100.00
  10" h.p., #15010, 1997 – 1999 (black Wendy Ann) $100.00
Manet — 21", #2225, 1982 – 1983, light brown with dark brown pinstripes (Jacqueline)...........$250.00
  14", #1571, 1986 – 1987, Fine Arts Series (Mary Ann) $85.00
Marcella Dolls — 13 – 24" compo., 1936 only, dressed in 1930s fashions ....$650.00 – 900.00 ea.
March Hare — cloth/felt, mid 1930s $675.00
Margaret (O'Brien) — 14" h.p., nude with excellent color $325.00
  18" h.p., nude with excellent color..$550.00 up
  14" h.p. in tagged Alexander boxed clothes..$800.00
  18" ....$750.00 up
  21" compo., tagged Alexander clothes ....$1,300.00 up
Margaret Ann — 15", #90100, 1999, blue dress, straw hat, porcelain $140.00
Margaret Rose — (see Princess Margaret Rose)
Margot — 10 – 11" h.p., 1961 only, in formals (Cissette) ....$475.00 up
  Street dresses, bathing suit, 1961 only $375.00
Margot Ballerina — 15 – 18", 1951 – 1953, dressed in various colored
  outfits (Margaret & Maggie) ....$650.00 – 850.00
  15 – 18" h.p./vinyl arms, 1955 only (Cissy)..$375.00 – 650.00

Maggie Mixup, 8", BKW, #626, 1961, (Wendy Ann). Ice skating costume.

Maggie Mixup, Post Office Commemorative, 8", #31000, 1997 – 1998. Remake of a 1960 Maggie Mixup.

Wendy Does the Mambo, 8", #481, 1955, SLW, (Wendy Ann). All original with original fan.

Maria — (see Sound of Music)
Marie Antoinette — 21", #2248, 1987 – 1988, multi-floral print with
  pink front insert (Jacqueline) $425.00
  21" compo., 1944 – 1946, Portrait with extra make-up and in mint condition (Wendy Ann) ....$2,100.00 up
Marilla — 10", #261-168, 1994, Anne of Green Gables Series $100.00
Marine — 14" compo., 1943 – 1944 (Wendy Ann as boy) ....$800.00 up
Marionettes/Tony Sarg — 12 – 14" compo., 1934 – 1940...........................$475.00 up
  12" compo., Disney Characters...$550.00 up
Marionette Theatre — by Tony Sarg, 1938 ....$800.00 up

Manet, 21", #2225, 1982 – 1983, (Jacqueline).

Margot Ballerina, 18", #1850, 1954. Dancing costume is made of satin accented with rhinestones.

Alice in Wonderland, Marionette, 12", compostion. All original.

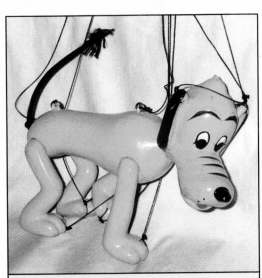

Pluto, Tony Sarg Marionette, composition. Made in the 1930s. Pluto is not marked.

Snow White Marionette, 12", compostion, 1930s. All original clothes.

Marley's Ghost — 8", #18004, 1996, Dickens, silver chains $65.00
Marme — (see Little Women)
Marme Liza — 21" compo., 1938 and 1946, extra make-up, mint condition (Wendy Ann) ..$3,200.00 up
Marshall Fields — (see Special Events/Exclusives)
Marta — (see Sound of Music)
Martin, Mary — 14 – 17" h.p., 1948 – 1952, wearing jumpsuit (Margaret)...............$700.00 – 950.00
    14 – 17", 1948 – 1952, dressed in sailor suit or ball gown (Nell from South Pacific).......$800.00 – 975.00
Mary, Joseph, Baby Jesus in Manger — 8", #19470, 1997 – 2000, Nativity set $200.00
Mary Ann — 14" plastic/vinyl, 1965, tagged "Mary Ann," in red/white dress $250.00
    Dressed in skirt and sweater $250.00
    Ballerina...$275.00
    14" ballerina, 1973 – 1982 ....$125.00
    14", reintroduced #241599, 1994 only $75.00
Mary-Bel, "The Doll That Gets Well" — 16" rigid vinyl, 1959 – 1965, doll only...............$200.00
    1959, 1961, 1965, doll in case $325.00
    1960 only, doll in case with wardrobe..$375.00
    1965 only, doll with very long straight hair, in case $350.00
    75th Anniversary, Mary-Bel Returns, 1998, #12220 ....$155.00
Mary Cassatt Baby — 14" cloth/vinyl, 1969 – 1970...$175.00
    20", 1969 – 1970...$250.00
    14" plastic/vinyl child, #1566, 1987 only, Fine Arts Series (Mary Ann) $90.00
Mary Ellen — 31" rigid vinyl, walker, 1954 only ....$600.00 up
    31" plastic/vinyl arms, 1955 only, non-walker with jointed elbows ....$500.00 up
Mary Ellen Playmate — 16" plastic/vinyl, 1965 only, Marshall Fields exclusive (Mary Ann)..$325.00
    12", 1965, in case with wigs (Lissy) ....$850.00 up
    17", 1965, exclusive $350.00
Mary Gray — 14" plastic/vinyl, #1564, 1988 only, Classic Series (Mary Ann) $75.00
Mary Had a Little Lamb — 8", #14623, 1996 Nursery Rhyme, #11610, 1997 – 1999 ....$75.00
Mary Lennox — 14", #1537, 1993 – 1994, Classic Doll Series $85.00
    8" h.p., #13850, 1998 – 1999 (Secret Garden), plaid jumper, holds key..........................$80.00
Mary Louise — 21" compo., 1938, 1946 – 1947, golden brown/burnt orange (Wendy Ann) ...$2,700.00
    18" h.p., 1954 only, Me & My Shadow Series, burnt orange & olive green (Cissy).............$1,300.00 up
    8" h.p., #0035D, 1954 only, same as 18", Me & My Shadow Series (Wendy Ann).............$1,200.00 up
Mary, Mary — 8" h.p., BKW, BK, #751, 1965 – 1972, Storybook Series (Wendy Ann)..........$125.00
    8" h.p., straight leg, #0751, #451, 1973 – 1975, marked "Alex" $75.00
    8" h.p., straight leg, #451, 1976 – 1987, marked "Alexander" (1985 – 1987 white face)............$65.00
    8", #471, reintroduced 1992 only (Wendy Ann) $65.00
    8", #14556, 1996, floral dress, straw hat, #11600, 1997 – 1999, water can...............$75.00
    8", #25930, 2000 – 2001, (Maggie), pink print dress, straw hat $80.00

Mary Louise, 8", 1954, SLW, (Wendy Ann). Godey period costume.

McGuffey Ana, 8", 1965, BKW, (Wendy Ann).

McGuffey Ana, 14", plastic/vinyl, #1526, 1987 – 1988.

14", #1569, 1988 – 1991, Classic Series (Mary Ann) $80.00

14", #241595, reintroduced 1994 only $100.00

Mary Mine — 21" cloth/vinyl, 1977 – 1989..$125.00

14" cloth/vinyl, 1977 – 1979..$100.00

14", reintroduced 1989..$75.00

Mary Muslin — 19" cloth, 1951 only, pansy eyes $500.00

26", 1951 only $575.00

40", 1951 only $850.00

Mary, Queen of Scots — 21", #2252, 1988 – 1989 (Jacqueline) $375.00

Mary Rose Bride — 17" h.p., 1951 only (Margaret)..$750.00 up

Mary Sunshine, Little — 15" plastic/vinyl, 1961 (Caroline) $375.00

Marzipan Dancer — 10", #14573, 1995, Nutcracker Series (Cissette)..$75.00

Matthew — 8", #26424, 1995, Anne of Green Gables Series $70.00

McElroy, Mary — 1985 – 1987, 4th set Presidents' Ladies/First Ladies Series (Mary Ann).....$125.00

McGuffey Ana — 16" cloth, 1934 – 1936..$675.00 up

7" compo., 1935 – 1939 (Tiny Betty) $350.00

9" compo., 1935 – 1939 (Little Betty) $375.00

15" compo., 1935 – 1937 (Betty) $650.00

13" compo., 1938 (Wendy Ann) $650.00

11", 1937 – 1939, has closed mouth $675.00

11 – 13" compo., 1937 – 1944 (Princess Elizabeth)..$675.00 – 750.00

14 – 16" compo., 1937 – 1944 (Princess Elizabeth)..$700.00 – 900.00

17 – 20" compo., 1937 – 1943 (Princess Elizabeth)..$700.00 – 1,200.00

21 – 25" compo., 1937 – 1942 (Princess Elizabeth)..$750.00 – 1,400.00

28" compo., 1937 – 1939 (Princess Elizabeth) $1,400.00

17" compo., 1948 – 1949 (Margaret)..$900.00

14½" compo., 1948, wears coat, hat & muff $950.00

18", 25", 31", 1955 – 1956, has flat feet (Cissy) ....$500.00 – 950.00

18" h.p., 1949 – 1950 (Margaret) $900.00

21" h.p., 1948 – 1950 (Margaret) $1,400.00

12" h.p. *(rare doll),* 1963 only (Lissy) ....$2,000.00 up

8" h.p., #616, 1956 only (Wendy Ann) $750.00

8" h.p., #788, #388, 1963 – 1965 (was "American Girl" in 1962 – 1963)..$375.00

8", #496, 1990 – 1991 only, Storybook Series (Wendy Ann) $75.00

29" cloth/vinyl, 1952 only (Barbara Jane) $650.00

15", porcelain, #90110, 1999 – 2000..$165.00

14" plastic/vinyl, #1450, 1968 – 1969, Classic Series, wears plaid dress/eyelet
apron (Mary Ann)..$125.00

14" plastic/vinyl, #1525, 1977 – 1986, Classic Series, wears plaid dress (Mary Ann)..$85.00

14" plastic/vinyl, #1526, 1987 – 1988, mauve stripe pinafore, Classic Series (Mary Ann) $85.00

14", #24622, 1995, red plaid dress, Nostalgia Series (Mary Ann) $85.00

McKee, Mary — 1985 – 1987, 4th set Presidents' Ladies/First Ladies Series (Mary Ann) $125.00

McKinley, Ida — 1988, 5th set Presidents' Ladies/First Ladies Series (Louisa) $125.00

Me and My Scassi — (see FAO Schwarz under Special Events/Exclusives)

Meagan — 14", #29990 or #30000, 1999 ....$80.00

Medici, Catherine de — 21" porcelain, 1990 – 1991 ....$500.00

Meg — 8", #79530, 100th Anniversary, two-tiered blue gown with white and rose
trim (also see Little Women)..$100.00

Melanie — 21" compo., 1945 – 1947 (Wendy Ann) ....$2,300.00 up

21" h.p./vinyl arms, 1961, lace bodice & overdress over satin (Cissy)..$1,100.00 up

21", #2050, 1966, blue gown with wide lace down sides (Coco) ....$2,200.00 up

#2173, 1967, blue dress with white rick-rack around hem ruffle (Jacqueline) $625.00

#2181, 1968, rust brown dress and hat $500.00

#2193, 1969, blue gown, white trim, many rows of lace, bonnet..$525.00

#2196, 1970, white gown with red ribbon trim $525.00

#2162, 1971, blue gown, white sequin trim $450.00

#2195, 1974, white gown, red jacket and bonnet..$475.00

#2220, 1979 – 1980, white dotted Swiss gown with pink trim..$350.00

1981, pink nylon with blue ribbon $350.00

#2254, 1989, all orange with lace shawl $300.00

10", #1173, 1968 – 1969, pink multi-tiered skirt (Cissette) $450.00

10", #1182, 1970, yellow multi-tiered skirt $475.00

8" h.p., #633, 1955 – 1956, green velvet (Wendy Ann)..$1,200.00 up

Melanie, continued

12", 1987 only, Portrait Children Series, aqua green gown, brown trim (Nancy Drew).............$80.00

10", #1101, 1989 only, Jubilee II, royal blue dress with black trim (Cissette)..........................$125.00

8", #627, 1990, Scarlett Series, lavender/lace (Wendy Ann) $100.00

8", #628, 1992, peach gown/bonnet with lace $90.00

8", #25775, 2000, blue gown and hat trimmed in lace..$90.00

10", #16555, 1996, Melanie's Sewing Circle, blue dress $100.00

Melinda — 10" h.p., 1968 – 1969, blue gown with white trim (Cissette) $450.00

10" h.p., 1970, yellow multi-tiered lace skirt $425.00

22", #1912, 1962 only, wears white organdy dress with red trim...$400.00

14", 16", 22" plastic/vinyl, 1962 – 1963, cotton dress...$250.00 – 400.00

14", 16", 22" plastic/vinyl, 1963, party dress ....$300.00 – 475.00

14", 1963 only, as ballerina $350.00

Melody and Friend — 25" and 8" (see Madame Alexander Doll Co.
under Special Events/Exclusives)

Merlin — 8", #13560, 1999, red velvet robe and crystal ball..$80.00

Merry Angel — 8" (see Spiegel's under Special Events/Exclusives)

Metroplex Doll Club — (see Special Events/Exclusives)

Mexico — 7" compo., 1936 (Tiny Betty) $300.00

9" compo., 1938 – 1939 (Little Betty) $325.00

8" h.p., BKW, #776, 1964 – 1965 (Wendy Ann) $125.00

8" h.p., BK, #776, 1965 – 1972 ....$100.00

8" straight leg, #0776, 1973 – 1975, marked "ALEX"..$75.00

8" straight leg, #576, #550, #520, 1976 – 1991, marked "Alexander" (1985 – 1987) $65.00

8", #11551, 1995 only (Maggie) $60.00

8", #24100, 1997 – 1998, Mariachi outfit, guitar...$75.00

Michael — 11" plastic/vinyl, 1969 only (Janie) (Peter Pan set) with teddy bear........................$375.00

8", #468, 1992 – 1993, Storybook Series (Peter Pan set) (Wendy)...$75.00

Midnight — 21", #2256, 1990, dark blue/black (Jacqueline)..$300.00

Millennium Princess — 8", #25810, 2000 only, lavender gown $100.00

Miller's Daughter — 14" with 8" Rumpelstiltskin, #1569, 1992 only, limited to 3,000 sets .....$300.00 set

Milly — 17" plastic/vinyl, 1968 only (Polly)...$375.00

Mimi — 30", h.p. in 1961 only, multi-jointed body, dressed in formal......................................$950.00

Dressed in romper suit/skirt $550.00

Dressed in Tyrolean outfit $950.00

Dressed in slacks, stripe top, straw hat...$600.00

Dressed in red sweater, plaid skirt $600.00

Melanie, 21", #2235, 1961, (Cissy). Blue satin dress with elaborate Godey hairdo. All original. She is fully jointed hard plastic with vinyl arms.

Melanie, 21", #2193, 1969, (Jacqueline).

Melinda, 16", 1963 only. Left is #1620 and right is #1612. Both have swivel waists.

21" h.p./vinyl arms, #2170, 1971, vivid pink cape & trim on white gown (Jacqueline) $600.00

14", #1411, 1983 – 1986, Opera Series (Mary Ann) $90.00

Minister, Little — 8" h.p., #411, 1957 only ....$3,200.00 up

Miracle Santa — 10", 1996, with street sign $155.00

Miracle Wendy — 8", 1996 ....$170.00

Miss America — 14" compo., 1941 – 1943, holds flag ....$850.00 up

Miss Eliza Doolittle — 10", #20112, 1996 Classic $100.00

Miss Gulch with Bicycle, Toto — 10", #13240, 1997 – 2001, Wizard of Oz Series.............$125.00

Miss Leigh — 8", 1989, made for C.U. Gathering (see Special Events/Exclusives)

Miss Liberty — 10" (see M.A.D.C. under SpecialEvents/Exclusives)

Miss Magnin — 10" (see I. Magnin under SpecialEvents/Exclusives)

Miss Muffett, Little — 8" h.p., BK, #752, 1965 – 1972, Story book Series (Wendy Ann) $125.00

8" straight leg, #0752, #452, 1973 – 1975, marked "Alex" $75.00

8" straight leg, #452, 1976 – 1986 (1985 – 1986 white face), marked "Alexander" (Wendy).....$65.00

8" straight leg, #452, 1987 – 1988 (Maggie)..$65.00

8", #493, 1993, Storybook Series #140493, 1994 ....$65.00

8", #13500, 1998 – 2000, comes with bowl, spoon, and pillow $90.00

Miss Scarlett — 14" (see Belk & Leggett under Special Events/Exclusives)

Miss Smarty — 8", #17610, 1999 – 2001, Mary Engelbreit, (Maggie) pink check outfit............$80.00

Miss Unity — 10" (see U.F.D.C. under Special Events/Exclusives)

Miss U.S.A. — 8" h.p., BK, #728, 1966 – 1968, Americana Series (Wendy Ann).....................$350.00

Miss Victory — 20" compo., 1944 – 1946, magnets in hands (Princess Elizabeth).....................$750.00 up

Misterioso — 10" h.p., #20119, 1996 Cirque du Soleil Series $85.00

Mistress Mary — 7" compo., 1937 – 1941 (Tiny Betty) $350.00

Molly — 14", #1561, 1988 only, Classic Series (Mary Ann) $85.00

Molly Cottontail — cloth/felt, 1930s $625.00

Mommy & Me — 14" and 7" compo., 1948 – 1949 (Margaret and Tiny Betty) ....$1,700.00 up set

Mommy & Me On-the-Go — 8", 10", h.p., #11010, 1997 – 1998 ....$175.00

Mommy & Me at Home — 8", 10", h.p., #11009, 1997 – 1998, pink floral outfits............$160.00

Mommy's Pet — 14 – 20", 1977 – 1986 ....$50.00 – 150.00

Mona Lisa, DaVinci's — 8", h.p., 1997, #22140, green velvet dress................................$80.00

Monday's Child — 8", #27770, 2001, pink dress, mirror..$110.00

10", #28860, 2001, print skirt, 10" goose..$135.00

Monet — 21", #2245, 1984 – 1985, black & white check gown with red jacket (Jacqueline) $275.00

Monique — 8" (see Disney under Specials Events/Exclusives)

Monroe, Elizabeth — 1976 – 1978, 1st set Presidents' Ladies/First Ladies Series (Mary Ann)....$150.00

Moonlight Dance — 10", #28900, 2001, blue tulle and brocade dress $140.00

Mop-Top Annie — 8", #14486, 1995, red dress with white dots $70.00

Mop-Top Baby Girl — 12", #29030, 1998, yarn hair, patch work dress.................$60.00

Mop-Top Wendy — 8" #140484, 1993 – 2000, Toy Shelf Series........................$80.00

Mop-Top Billy — 8" #140485, 1993 – 2000, Toy Shelf Series........................$75.00

Morisot — 21", #2236, 1985 – 1986 only, lime green gown with white
lace (Jacqueline) $275.00

Morning Glory — 14", #25505, Ribbons & Bows Series, floral dress
with lace (Mary Ann)..$150.00

8", #28476, 2001, lavender dress, bonnet with flowers $90.00

Morocco — 8" h.p., BK, #762, 1968 – 1970 (Wendy Ann) $300.00

8", h.p. #11559, 1996 International, belly dancer $65.00

Moss Rose — 14", #1559, 1991 only, Classic Series (Louisa) $150.00

Mother & Me — 14 – 15" and 9" compo., 1940 – 1943, mint condition
(Wendy Ann & Little Betty) ....$1,400.00 up

Mother Goose — 8" straight leg, #427, #459, 1986 – 1992, Storybook Series
(Wendy Ann)..$70.00

8", #11620, 1997 – 1999, with goose and book of rhymes....................................$70.00

Mother Gothel and Rapunzel — 8" & 14", #1539, 1993 – 1994, limited to
3,000 sets..$250.00 set

Mother Hubbard — 8", #439, #459, 1988 – 1989, Storyland Series (Wendy) $65.00

Mother's Day — 8", #10380 – 10382, 1995, three hair colors, Special Occasions.....$60.00

8", #30265, 201, pink, white dress with porcelain flower box $90.00

Mouseketeer — 8" (see Disney under Special Events/Exclusives)

Mr. and Mrs. Frankenstein Set — 8", 1996 ....$160.00

Mr. Monopoly — 8", #25260, 2000, tails, top hat, comes with game $75.00

Mr. O'Hara — 8", #638, 1993 only, Scarlett Series (Wendy) $125.00

Mrs. Buck Rabbit — cloth/felt, mid-1930s $625.00

Mother Goose, 8", #427, 1986 – 1990, (Wendy). Storyland Series.

Mrs. Claus — (see mid-year specials for Madame Alexander Co. under Special Events/Exclusives)

14", #24607, 1995, Christmas Series $100.00

Mrs. Darling — 10", 1993 – 1994, Peter Pan Series (Cissette) $125.00

Mrs. Fezziwig — 8", #18005, 1996, Dickens, moiré gown................................$60.00

Mrs. March Hare — cloth/felt, mid-1930s...$625.00

Mrs. Malloy's Millinery Shop — 10" Portrette, #201167, 1995 only, trunk set with wardrobe and hats $250.00

Mrs. O'Hara — 8", #638, 1992 – 1993 only, Scarlett Series (Wendy).................$150.00

Mrs. Quack-a-Field — cloth/felt, mid-1930s...$625.00

Mrs. Snoopie — cloth/felt, 1940s...$625.00

Muffin — 19" cloth, 1966 only $125.00

14", 1963 – 1977 ....$95.00

14" cloth, 1965 only, sapphire eyes $95.00

14" black cloth, 1965 – 1966 only...$125.00

14" cloth, 1966 – 1970, cut slanted blue eyes...$100.00

14" cloth, eyes like sideways commas..$75.00

12" all vinyl, 1989 – 1990 (Janie) $75.00

12", 1990 – 1992, in trunk/wardrobe $150.00

Munchkin Peasant — 8", #140444, 1993 – 1995, Wizard of Oz Series...............$100.00

Daisy, 8", #28770, 2001, daisies on costume $65.00

Flower Basket, 8", #28775, 2001, blue, white costume $70.00

Herald, 8" #140445, 1994 – 1995, Wizard of Oz Series..................................$100.00

Mayor, 8", #140443, 1993 – 1995, Wizard of Oz Series $125.00

Lollipop, 8", #14513, 1995, Wizard of Oz Series, pink/white striped outfit......$125.00

Lullaby, 8", #14512, 1995, Wizard of Oz Series, white gown $85.00

Lullaby, 8", #13300, 1999 – 2001, pink dress and hat $80.00

Lullaby Munchkin, 5", #27070, porcelain, 2000 – 2001, pink costume $80.00

My Doll House — (see Special Events/Exclusives)

My Favorite Ballerina — 14", #25485, 2000, lilac, ballet outfit $75.00

14", #25480, 2000, pink, ballet outfit $75.00

My Little Sweetheart — (see Child At Heart under Special Events/Exclusives)

Mystery Dance 1951 — 14", #26035, 2000, pink lace and tulle long gown $170.00

Nan McDare — cloth/felt, 1940s $625.00

Nana — 6" dog with bonnet, #441, 1993 only, Peter Pan Series........................$55.00

Nana/Governess — 8" h.p., #433, 1957 only (Wendy Ann)...........................$2,000.00 up

Nancy Ann — 17 – 18" h.p., 1950 only (tagged Nancy Ann) ....$975.00 up

Nancy Dawson — 8", #441, 1988 – 1989, Storybook Series (Maggie) $70.00

Nancy Drew — 12" plastic/vinyl, 1967 only, Literature Series ....$400.00 up

Nancy Jean — 8" (see Belks & Leggett under Special Events/Exclusives)

Napoleon — 12", #1330, 1980 – 1986, Portraits of History (Nancy Drew) $75.00

Nat (Little Men) — 15" h.p., 1952 (Maggie)...$850.00 up

Natasha — 21", #2255, 1989 – 1990, brown & paisley brocade (Jacqueline).........$350.00

Nativity Set — 1997 – 2000, #19460, Mary, Joseph, Jesus, Angel, creche, Three Wise Men, Shepherd, Drummer..$950.00

Nashville Goes Country — 8" (1995, see C.U. under Special Events/Exclusives)

Nashville Skater — #1 (see Collectors United under Special Events/Exclusives)

#2 (see Collectors United under Special Events/Exclusives)

National Velvet — 12", 1991 only, Romance Series, no riding crop (Nancy Drew) $85.00

8", #10409, 1996, riding habit $95.00

Neiman-Marcus — (see Special Events/Exclusives)

Nelson, Lord — 12" vinyl, #1336, 1984 – 1986, Portraits of History (Nancy Drew) $75.00

Netherlands Boy — Formerly "Dutch" (Wendy)

8" h.p., straight leg, #577, 1974 – 1975, marked "Alex" $75.00

8" h.p., straight leg, #577, 1976 – 1989, marked "Alexander" (1985 – 1987)............$65.00

Netherlands Girl — 8" h.p., #591, #525, 1974 – 1992 (Wendy)........................$65.00

New Arrival — 19", #30290, 2001, stork with Baby Kisses 8" doll.....................$50.00

New England Collector Society — (see Special Events/Exclusives)

Nicole — 10", #1139, 1989 – 1990, Portrette, black/off white outfit (Cissette) $85.00

Nigeria — 8", #11552, 1995 only (also in 1994 Neiman-Marcus trunk set as Kenya)............$60.00

Nightingale, Florence — 14", #1598, 1986 – 1987, Classic Series....................$100.00

Nina Ballerina — 7" compo., 1940 (Tiny Betty)..$325.00

9" compo., 1939 – 1941 (Little Betty) $350.00

14" h.p., 1949 – 1951 (Margaret) ....$575.00 up

Nina Ballerina, continued

17", 1949 – 1951 ....$550.00

15" h.p., 1951, came in various colors, all years (Margaret) $700.00

19", 1949 – 1950 ....$850.00 up

23", 1951 ....$850.00

Nixon, Pat — (see Presidents' Ladies/First Ladies Series) 14", 1994 only ....$135.00 up

Nod — (see Dutch Lullaby)

Noel — 12" (see New England Collector Society under Special Events/Exclusives)

Normandy — 7" compo., 1935 – 1938 (Tiny Betty) $300.00

Norway — 8" h.p., BK, #584, 1968 – 1972 (Wendy Ann) $100.00

8" straight leg, #584, 1973 – 1975, marked "Alex" $75.00

8" straight leg, #584, 1976 – 1987, marked "Alexander" (1985 – 1987 white face) $65.00

8" straight leg, #11566, 1996 International Viking costume $75.00

Norwegian — 7 – 8" compo., 1936 – 1940 (Tiny Betty) $300.00

9" compo., 1938 – 1939 (Little Betty) $325.00

Now I Lay Me Down to Sleep — 8", #28380, 2001, white gown, bonnet $80.00

Nurse — 16", 1930s, cloth and felt $675.00

7" compo., 1937, 1941 – 1943 (Tiny Betty) $325.00

9" compo., 1939, 1942 – 1943 ....$350.00

13 – 15" compo., 1936 – 1937 (Betty) all white outfit, Dionne nurse, mint in box ....$950.00 up

15" compo., 1939, 1943 (Princess Elizabeth) $550.00

14" h.p., 1948 (Maggie & Margaret) $850.00

8" h.p., #563, 1956 only, all white dress (Wendy Ann) ....$600.00 up

8", #429, 1961, all white dress, comes with baby ....$650.00 up

8" BKW, BK, #329, #460, #660, #624, 1962 – 1965, wears striped dress, comes with baby....$475.00

8", #308, all white uniform, Americana Series, 1991 ....$75.00

8", #17620, 1999, World War II, brown, white costume with medicine bag $70.00

Nutcracker — 16", #21700, 1998 – 1999, Clara in rose embroidered costume $195.00

8", 2001, #27560, silver pants, red jacket, black hat $90.00

Nutcracker Prince — 8", #14571, 1995, Nutcracker Series, has mask $70.00

O'Brien, Margaret — 14½" compo., 1946 – 1948 ....$750.00 up

17", 18", 19" compo., 1946 – 1948 ....$850.00 – 1,200.00

21 – 24" compo., 1946 – 1948 ....$1,000.00 – 1,500.00

14½" h.p., 1949 – 1951 ....$900.00 up

17 – 18" h.p., 1949 – 1951 ....$975.00 up

21 – 22" h.p., 1949 – 1951 ....$1,200.00 up

15", porcelain, #90100, white blouse, blue pinafore $133.00

Off to the North Pole – Coca-Cola — 8", #25245, 2000, fur costume with white bear $100.00

Oktoberfest — 8" (see Collectors United under Special Events/Exclusives)

Old Fashioned Girl — 13" compo., 1945 – 1947 (Betty) ....$550.00 up

20" compo. (Betty) $700.00

20" h.p., 1948 only (Margaret) ....$850.00 up

14" h.p., 1948 only (Margaret) $650.00

Old McDonald — 8", #30785, 2001, red check dress $90.00

Olive Oyl — 10", #20126, 1996, Timeless Legends $90.00

Oliver Twist — 16" cloth, 1934, Dickens character $650.00

7" compo., 1935 – 1936 (Tiny Betty) $300.00

8", #472, 1992 only, Storyland Series (Wendy Ann) $70.00

Oliver Twistail — Cloth/felt, 1930s $650.00

One, Two, Buckle My Shoe — 14", #24640, Nursery Rhymes (Louisa) $95.00

Onyx Velvet and Lace Gala Gown and Coat — 10", h.p.,
#22170, 1997 – 1998 (Cissette) $125.00

Opening Night — 10", #1126, 1989 only, Portrette, gold sheath and overshirt (Cissette) $85.00

Ophelia — 12", 1992, Romance Collection (Nancy Drew) $100.00

12", 1993 only (Lissy) $150.00

Orchard Princess — 21" compo., 1939, 1946 – 1947, has extra make-up (Wendy Ann).......$2,400.00 up

Orphan Annie — 14" plastic/vinyl, #1480, 1965 – 1966 only, Literature Series (Mary Ann) ..$325.00

#1485, 1965 only, in window box with wardrobe ....$500.00 up

Out for a Stroll — 10", #27815, 2001, pink long dress trimmed in lace $120.00

Oz Flower Munchkin — 8", #27035, 2000 – 2001, Wizard of Oz series.........$50.00

Pakistan — 8" h.p., #532, 1993 only $65.00

Pamela — 12" h.p., 1962 – 1963 only, takes wigs, excellent condition, doll only (Lissy)............$375.00 up

12" h.p. in case, 1962 – 1963 ....$1,000.00 up

12" h.p. in window box, 1962 – 1963 ....$1,000.00 up

Pamela, continued

    12" plastic/vinyl, 1969 – 1971, doll only (Nancy Drew) $225.00

    12" plastic/vinyl in case, 1969 ....$625.00 up

Pamela Plays Dress Up — 12" (see Horchow under Special Events/Exclusives)

Pan American – (Pollera) — 7" compo., 1936 – 1938 (Tiny Betty) $300.00

Panama — 8", #555, 1985 – 1987 ....$65.00

Pandora — 8" (see Dolls 'n Bearland under Special Events/Exclusives)

Parisian Chic 1940 — 10", #17770, 1999, dress, coat, hat, purse $125.00

Park Avenue Alex the Bellhop — 8", h.p., #31180, 1997 – 1999, burgundy uniform.............$80.00

Park Avenue Wendy — 8", h.p., #31060, 1997 – 1999, black and white ensemble...................$80.00

Parlour Maid — 8" h.p., #579, 1956 only (Wendy Ann) ....$950.00 up

Party Sun Dress — 8", h.p., #344, 1957, BKW, blue or red dress with gold accents

    (Wendy Ann)..$525.00 up

Pat-A-Cake — 8", #12812, 1995, floral dress with white apron and chef's hat,

    Nursery Rhymes Series $65.00

Patchity Pam & Pepper — 15" cloth, 1965 – 1966 ....$175.00

Patterson, Martha Johnson — 1982 – 1984, 3rd set Presidents' Ladies/First

    Ladies Series (Martha)...$125.00

Patty — 18" plastic/vinyl, 1965 only $275.00

Patty Pigtails — 14" h.p., 1949 only (Margaret)...$675.00 up

Paulette — 10", #1128, 1989 – 1990 only, Portrette, dressed in pink velvet (Cissette) $125.00

Peachtree Lane — 8" in blue and 14" Scarlett in green/white stripes, #16551,

    limited to 2,500..$275.00 set

Pearl (June) — 10", #1150, 1992 only, Birthstone Collection, white/silver flapper doll............$75.00

Pearl of the 1920s — 10", #79700 ....$185.00

Peasant — 7" compo., 1936 – 1937 (Tiny Betty)...$275.00

    9" compo., 1938 – 1939 (Little Betty)..$300.00

Peggy Bride — 14 – 18" h.p., 1950 – 1951, very blonde hair (Margaret).................$900.00 – 1,300.00

    21" h.p., 1950...$1,400.00 up

Penny — 34" cloth/vinyl, 1951 only ....$500.00 up

    42", 1951 only $800.00

    7" compo., 1938 – 1940 (Tiny Betty)...$275.00

Peppermint Twist — 8", #14591, 1995, pink skirt and jacket in 1950s style, Nostalgia Series....$60.00

Persia — 7" compo., 1936 – 1938 (Tiny Betty)..$300.00

Peru — 8", #556, 1986 – 1987..$80.00

    8" h.p., #531, 1993 only (Wendy Ann) $70.00

Peruvian Boy — 8" h.p., BK, #770, 1965 – 1966 (Wendy Ann)..$450.00

    8" h.p., BKW, #770 ....$450.00

Peter Pan — 15" h.p., 1953 – 1954 (Margaret) ....$750.00 up

    8" h.p., #310, 1953 – 1954 (Wendy Ann) Quiz-Kin..$850.00 up

    8" h.p., #465, reintroduced 1991 – 1993, #140465 in 1994, Storyland Series (Wendy Ann).....$75.00

    8" h.p., #13660, 1999 – 2000, green costume with Tinker Bell pin and sword $75.00

    14" plastic/vinyl, #1410, 1969 only (Mary Ann)..$250.00

    1969 only, complete set of 4 dolls – Peter, Michael (12" Jamie),

        Wendy (14" Mary Ann), Tinker Bell (10" Cissette) ....$1,000.00 up

Peter Pan's Wendy — 8", #13670, 1999 – 2001, blue gown and fuzzy shoes $70.00

Philippines — 8" straight leg, #554, 1986 – 1987 (blue gown)..$100.00

    1987, #531, dressed in yellow gown..$175.00

Picnic Day — 18" h.p., #2001C, 1953 only, Glamour Girl Series, leaves on pink or

    blue print dress (Margaret) ....$1,800.00 up

Pierce, Jane — 1982 – 1984, 3rd set Presidents' Ladies/First Ladies Series (Mary Ann) $125.00

Pierrot Clown — (see Clowns, 8" and 14")

Pilgrim — 7" compo., 1935 – 1938 (Tiny Betty)..$275.00

    8" h.p., #100349, 1994, Americana Series $60.00

    8", #10349, 1995, Special Occasions Series $60.00

Pink Butterfly Princess — 8", #25675, 2000 – 2001, pink wings...$75.00

Pink Carnation — 10", #25615, 2000, (Cissette), pink tiered gown $130.00

Pink Champagne (Arlene Dahl) — 18" h.p., red hair/pink lace/rhinestone bodice gown ..$5,500.00 up

Pink Pristine Angel — 10", #10700, 1997 – 2000, pink feather wings $130.00

Pink Sparkle Princess — 15", #22670, 1999, porcelain, pink gown $170.00

Pinkie — 12" plastic/vinyl, 1975 – 1987, Portrait Children Series (Nancy Drew)........................$75.00

    8", 1997 – 1998, #22120, chiffon gown, pink hat...$70.00

Pinky — 16" cloth, 1940s ....$475.00 up

    23" compo./cloth baby, 1937 – 1939 ....$300.00

13 – 19" vinyl baby, #3561, #5461, 1954 only, one-piece vinyl body and legs ....$100.00 – 150.00

Pinocchio — 8", #477, 1992 – 1993, Storyland Series
(Wendy Ann) #140477, 1994...$80.00

Pip — All cloth, early 1930s, Dickens character $800.00
7" compo., 1935 – 1936 (Tiny Betty)...$300.00

Pippi Longstocking — 18", #16003, 1996, Rag Dolls (cloth doll)......................not available for sale
8", #25975, 2000 – 2001, (Maggie) with monkey...$60.00
14", #28780, 2001, cloth...$35.00

Pisces — 8", #21320, 1998, blue fish costume..$90.00

Pitty Pat — 16" cloth, 1950s...$475.00

Pitty Pat Clown — 1950s...$450.00

Place in the Sun, A — 10", #24624, lavender ball gown.....................................$110.00

Playmates — 29" cloth, 1940s...$450.00 up

Pocahontas — 8" h.p., BK, #721, 1967 – 1970, Americana & Storyland Series,
has baby (Wendy Ann) $450.00
8" h.p., #318, 1991 – 1992, Americana Series (Wendy Ann).............................$70.00
8" h.p., #100350, 1994 – 1995, Americana & Favorite Book Series (Wendy Ann) $60.00
14", #24613, 1995, first dark skin doll this size, Favorite Books Series (Louisa) $90.00

Polish (Poland) — 7" compo., 1935 – 1936 (Tiny Betty)......................................$300.00
8" h.p., BKW, #780, 1964 – 1965 (Wendy Ann)..$150.00
8" BKW, #780, 1965 only (Maggie Mixup)...$175.00
8" h.p., BK, #780, 1965 – 1972 ....$100.00
8" h.p., straight leg, #0780, #580, 1973 – 1975, marked "ALEX".........................$75.00
8" straight leg, #580, 1976 – 1988 (1985 – 1987 white face), marked "Alexander" $65.00
8", #523, reintroduced 1992 – 1993 (Maggie Mixup) 1994, #110523 ....$65.00

Polk, Sarah — 1979 – 1981, 2nd set Presidents' Ladies/First Ladies Series (Martha)..............$135.00

Pollera (Pan American) — 7" compo., 1936 – 1938 (Tiny Betty) $275.00

Polly — 17" plastic/vinyl, 1965 only, dressed in ball gown $375.00
Dressed in street dress...$275.00
Dressed as ballerina..$275.00
Dressed as bride $300.00
1965 only, came in trunk with wardrobe ....$750.00 up

Polly Flinders — 8", #443, 1988 – 1989, Storybook Series (Maggie) $75.00

Polly Pigtails — 14½" h.p., 1949 – 1951 (Maggie) $500.00
17 – 17½", 1949 – 1951...$625.00
8" (see M.A.D.C. under Special Events/Exclusives)

Polly Put Kettle On — 7" compo., 1937 – 1939 (Tiny Betty)..............................$300.00
8", h.p., #11640, 1998 – 1999, teacup print dress, kettle $75.00

Pollyana — 16" rigid vinyl, 1960 – 1961, marked "1958," (Mary-Bel)....................$425.00
16", dressed in formal...$450.00
22", 1960 – 1961 ....$500.00
14", #1588, 1987 – 1988, Classic Series (Mary Ann) $90.00
14", reintroduced 1994 only, #24159 ....$100.00
8", #474, 1992 – 1993 only, Storyland Series (Wendy) $85.00
8", #25210, 2000 – 2001, (Wendy), pink dress, straw hat $80.00

Poodles — 14 – 17", early 1950s, standing or sitting, named Ivy, Pierre,
Fifi, and Inky ....$450.00 up

Poor Cinderella — (see Cinderella)

Popeye — 8", #10428, 1996, Timeless Legends $85.00

Popeye, Olive Oyl, and Sweet Pea — #20127, 1996 ....$175.00 set

Poppy — 9" early vinyl, 1953 only, orange organdy dress & bonnet..................$95.00

Portrait Elise — 17" plastic/vinyl, 1972 – 1973 ....$225.00

Portugal — 8" h.p., BK, #785, 1968 – 1972 (Wendy Ann)..............................$100.00
8" straight leg, #0785, #585, 1973 – 1975, marked "Alex"..............................$75.00
8" straight leg, #585, #537, 1976 – 1987, marked "Alexander".........................$65.00
8", #537, 1986, white face $60.00
8" h.p., #535, 1993, #110535, 1994 ....$60.00

Posey Pet — 15" cloth, 1940s, plush rabbit or other animals, must be clean...$450.00 up

Precious — 12" compo./cloth baby, 1937 – 1940 ....$275.00
12" all h.p. toddler, 1948 – 1951...$350.00

Premier Dolls — 8" (see M.A.D.C. under Special Events/Exclusives)

Presidents' Ladies/First Ladies —
1st set, 1976 – 1978 ....$150.00 – 175.00 singles, 1,000.00 set

Poodles. Early 1950s. Made in 14" and 17".

2nd set, 1979 – 1981 ....$125.00 singles, 800.00 set
3rd set, 1982 – 1984 ....$125.00 singles, 800.00 set
4th set, 1985 – 1987 ....$115.00 singles, 700.00 set
5th set, 1988 ....$115.00 singles, 700.00 set
6th set, 1989 – 1990 ....$115.00 singles, 700.00 set
Pretty Pals — 8", #26770, pink; #26835, ivory; 2001, smocked dresses ....$95.00 ea.
Prince Charles — 8" h.p., #397, 1957 only (Wendy Ann)..$750.00 up
Prince Charming — 16 – 17" compo., 1947 (Margaret) $800.00
   14 – 15" h.p., 1948 – 1950 (Margaret) $700.00
   17 – 18" h.p., 1948 – 1950 (Margaret) $850.00
   21" h.p., 1949 – 1951 (Margaret) ....$1,000.00 up
   12", 1990 – 1991, Romance Collection (Nancy Drew)...$90.00
   8", #479, 1993, Storybook Series, royal blue/gold outfit..$80.00
   8", #14541, 1995, Brothers Grimm Series, braid trimmed jacket with brocade vest $70.00
Prince Phillip — 17 – 18" h.p., 1953 only, Beaux Arts Series (Margaret)...................................$900.00 up
   21", 1953 only ....$1,000.00 up
Princess — 12", 1990 – 1991 only, Romance Collection (Nancy Drew) $95.00
   14", #1537, 1990 - Mary Ann; 1991 - Jennifer, Classic Series $100.00
Princess Alexandria — 24" cloth/compo., 1937 only ....$300.00 up
Princess Ann — 8" h.p., #396, 1957 only (Wendy Ann)..$800.0 up
Princess and the Pea — 8", #27745, 2001, (Maggie), includes mattress and pea $110.00
Princess and the Dragon — pink and purple costume, silver dragon $130.00
Princess Budir Al-Budor — 8", #483, 1993 – 1994 only, Storybook Series...........................$65.00
Princess Diana Birthday — 10", white satin and gold gown..$170.00
Princess Doll — 13 – 15" compo., 1940 – 1942 (Princess Elizabeth) ....$550.00 up
   24" compo., 1940 – 1942 (Princess Elizabeth) ....$850.00 up
Princess Elizabeth — 7" compo., 1937 – 1939 (Tiny Betty)...$375.00
   8", 1937, with Dionne head (rare) $400.00
   9 – 11" compo., 1937 – 1941 (Little Betty) ....$375.00 – 425.00
   13" compo., 1937 – 1941, with closed mouth (Betty)..$625.00 up
   14" compo., 1937 – 1941 ....$600.00 up
   15" compo., open mouth...$600.00
   18 – 19" compo., 1937 – 1941, open mouth...$750.00 up
   24" compo., 1938 – 1939, open mouth...$900.00 up
   28" compo., 1938 – 1939, open mouth..$1,000.00 up
Princess Diana — 10", #22500, 1998 (Cissette), white satin gown................................$175.00
Princess Flavia (also Victoria) — 21" compo., 1939, 1946 – 1947 (Wendy Ann)..............$2,000.00 up

Sarah Jackson, 14", #1507, 1979 – 1981, (Louisa). Represents daughter-in-law of Andrew Jackson.

Martha Randolph, 14", #1503, 1976 – 1978. Represents daughter of Thomas Jefferson.

Julia Tyler, 14", #1510, 1979 – 1981, (Martha). Represents wife of John Tyler.

Princess Margaret Rose — 15 – 18" compo., 1937 – 1938 (Princess Elizabeth) ....$800.00 up
   21" compo., 1938..$975.00
   14 – 18" h.p., 1949 – 1953 (Margaret)..$650.00 – 975.00
   18" h.p. #2020B, 1953 only, Beaux Arts Series, pink taffeta gown w/red ribbon,
      tiara (Margaret) ....$1,800.00 up
Princess of Quite A Lot — 8", #25275, 2000 – 2001, (Maggie), Mary Engelbreit,
   yellow dress, crown, limited to 2,800 ....$80.00
Princess of Storyland — 8", #25990, 2000, long pink gown...$80.00
Princess Rosetta — 21" compo., 1939, 1946 – 1947 (Wendy Ann) $2,300.00
Pristine Angel — 10", #10604, 100th Anniversary, second in series, white/gold $95.00
Priscilla — 18" cloth, mid-1930s $625.00
   7" compo., 1935 – 1938 (Tiny Betty) $275.00
   8" h.p., BK, #729, 1965 – 1970, Americana & Storybook Series (Wendy Ann) $325.00
Prissy — 8", #630, 1990 only, Scarlett Series (Wendy Ann) $125.00
   8", #637, reintroduced 1992 – 1993 ....$125.00
   8", #16650, 1995, Scarlett Series, floral gown $85.00
Prom Queen (Memories) — 8" (see M.A.D.C. under Special Events/Exclusives)
Psycho — 10", #14810, doll in shower, pictured 1998 catalog ....not available for sale
Puddin' — 14 – 21" cloth/vinyl, 1966 – 1975 ....$85.00
   14 – 18", 1987 ....$75.00 – 100.00
   14 – 21", 1990 – 1993 ....$75.00 – 125.00
   14" only, 1994 – 1995 ....$85.00
   21", 1995 ....$125.00
Puerto Rico — 8", 1998 – 1999, #24120, red outfit, carries flag and frog $75.00
Pumpkin — 22" cloth/vinyl, 1967 – 1976 ....$125.00
   22", 1976 only, with rooted hair $150.00
Pumpkin Patch Treats — 8", #26350, 2001, one doll with three Halloween costumes $190.00
Puppet, Hand (also see Marionettes) — Compo. head, cloth hand mitt body,
   by Tony Sarg, ca. 1936 ....$475.00 up
Puss 'n Boots — 8", #14552, Fairy Tales Series $65.00
Pussy Cat — cloth/vinyl
  White dolls:
   14", 1965 – 1985 (20-year production) $65.00
   14", 1987 – 1995 ....$65.00
   14", 1966, 1968, in trunk/trousseau ....$250.00 up
   18", 1989 – 1995 ....$100.00
   20", 1965 – 1984, 1987 – 1988 (20+ year production) $100.00
   24", 1965 – 1985 (20-year production) $125.00
   14", 1998, variety of outfits ....$75.00 – 90.00
   14", 2000, #25510, pink knit layette, pink outfit $120.00
  Black dolls:
   14", 1970 – 1976 ....$75.00
   14", 1984 – 1995 (12-year production) $75.00
   20", 1976 – 1983 ....$125.00
Pussy Cat, Lively — 14", 20", 24", 1966 – 1969 only, knob makes head
   & limbs move ....$75.00 – 175.00
Queen — 18" h.p., #2025, 1953 only, Beaux Arts Series, white gown, long velvet
   cape trimmed with fur (Margaret) ....$1,800.00 up
   18" h.p., 1953 only, Glamour Girl Series, same gown/tiara as above
      but no cape (Margaret) ....$1,500.00 up
   18" h.p., 1954 only, Me & My Shadow Series, white gown, short Orlon cape (Margaret)...$1,200.00 up
   8" h.p., 1954, #0030C, #597, Me & My Shadow Series, Orlon cape attached
      to purple robe (Wendy Ann) ....$1,000.00 up
   8", #499, 1955 only, scarlet velvet robe $800.00
   10" h.p., #971, #879, #842, #763, 1957 – 1958, 1960 – 1961, gold gown with blue ribbon.....$450.00
   #742, #765, 1959, 1963, white gown with blue ribbon $425.00
   #1186, #1187, 1972 – 1973, white gown with red ribbon $350.00
   1959, in trunk with wardrobe, must be mint ....$950.00 up
   14", #1536, 1990 only, Classic Series (Louisa, Jennifer) $90.00
   20" h.p./vinyl arms, 1955, Dreams Come True Series, white brocade gown (Cissy)............$1,200.00 up
   1957, Fashion Parade Series, white gown ....$950.00 up
   1958, 1961 – 1963 (1958 - Dolls To Remember Series), gold gown.................................$900.00 up
   18", 1963 only, white gown with red ribbon (Elise) $750.00
   With vinyl head (Mary-Bel) $875.00

    18" vinyl, same as 1965 (21" with rooted hair, 1966 only), gold brocade gown,
        rare doll (Elise)..$975.00
    #2150, 21" h.p./vinyl arms, 1965, white brocade gown (Jacqueline)......................$750.00
    1968, gold gown $750.00
Queen Alexandrine — 21" compo., 1939 – 1941 (Wendy Ann) ....$1,975.00 up
Queen Charlotte — 10" (see M.A.D.C. under Special Events/Exclusives)
Queen Elizabeth I — 10" (see My Doll House under Special Events/Exclusives)
    8", #12610, 1999, red velvet trimmed in gold..$100.00
Queen Elizabeth II — 8", 1992 only (mid-year issue), commemorating
    reign's 40th anniversary..$175.00
Queen Esther — 8", #14584, 1995 only, Bible Series $100.00
Queen of Hearts — 8" straight leg, #424, 1987 – 1990, Storybook Series (Wendy Ann) $70.00
    8", #14511, 1995, Alice in Wonderland Series $80.00
    10" (see Disney under Special Events/Exclusives)
Queen Isabella — 8" h.p., #329, 1992 only, Americana Series $125.00
Queen of the Roses — 10", #22660, 1999, yellow satin long dress, limited to 1,500 ....$110.00
Queen of Storyland — 10", #26025, 2000, long white gown, limited to 2,600 ....$120.00
Quintuplets (Fischer Quints) — 7", h.p. & vinyl 1964 (Genius), with original box ....$550.00 set
Quiz-Kins — 8" h.p., 1953, bald head, in romper only (Wendy Ann) ....$475.00 up
    1953 Peter Pan, caracul wig...$850.00
    1953 – 1954, as groom..$600.00 up
    1953 – 1954, as bride ....$650.00 up
    1953 – 1954, girl with wig ....$650.00 up
    1953, girl without wig, in romper suit $550.00
Rachel/Rachael — 8", 1989 (see Belks & Leggett under Special Events/Exclusives)
Randolph, Martha — 1976 – 1978, 1st set Presidents' Ladies/First Ladies Series (Louisa) $150.00
Rapunzel — 10", #M31, 1989 – 1992 only, Portrette, gold velvet (Cissette).....................$125.00
    14", #1539, 1993 – 1994, Doll Classics, limited to 3,000, comes with 8" Mother Gothel ....$250.00 set
    14", #87005, 1996, purple gown (Louisa)..$125.00
    8", #14542, 1995, Brothers Grimm Series, pink gown with gold scallops,
        #13980, 1997 – 2001 ....$75.00
    14", #25460, 2000 – 2001, lavender dress, cone hat with tulle (Margaret) $140.00
Really Ugly Stepsister — 8" h.p., #13450, 1997 – 1998, Cinderella Series $85.00
Rebecca — 14 – 17", 21" compo., 1940 – 1941 (Wendy Ann)................................$600.00 – 1,000.00
    14" h.p., 1948 – 1949 (Margaret) ....$850.00 up

Queen Elizabeth, 8", #499, 1955, SLW, (Wendy Ann).
All original. Tag: Alexander-Kin.

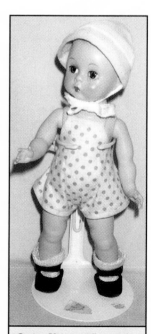

Quiz-Kins, 8", 1953, SLNW. Yes/no push buttons on back make the head move. All original.

14" plastic/vinyl, #1485, 1968 – 1969, Classic Series, two-tiered skirt
    in pink (Mary Ann) $165.00
    #1485, #1515, #1585, 1970 – 1985, one-piece skirt, pink pindot or check dress......................$80.00
    #1586, 1986 – 1987, blue dress with striped pinafore $80.00
    8", #14647, 1996 ....$65.00
Record Album — "Madame Alexander Collector's Album," 1978, children's stories
    told by Madame, cover is like Alexander box $35.00
Red Boy — 8" h.p., BK, #740, 1972 (Wendy) $125.00
    #0740, 1973 – 1975, marked "Alex" $75.00
    #440, 1976 – 1988, marked "Alexander" $65.00
Red Cross Nurse — 18", #16002, Rag Doll Series ....not available for sale
Red Riding Hood — 7" compo., 1936 – 1942 (Tiny Betty) $300.00
    9" compo., 1939 – 1940 (Little Betty) $325.00
    8" h.p., SLW, #608, 1955, cape sewn under arms (Wendy Ann) $625.00
    8" h.p., BKW, #382, 1962 – 1965, Storybook Series (Wendy Ann) $275.00
    8" h.p., BK, #782, 1965 – 1972 ....$125.00
    8" h.p., straight leg, #0782, #482, 1973 – 1975, marked "Alex" $75.00
    8" h.p., straight leg, #482, 1976 – 1986 (1985 – 1987 white face), marked "Alexander" $65.00
    8", #485, #463, 1987 – 1991 (Maggie), 1992 – 1993 (Wendy Ann), #140463, 1994,
        #13970, 1998 – 1999 ....$70.00
    14", #24617, 1995, patchwork dress with red cape (Mary Ann) $100.00
    14", #87004, plaid dress with red cape (Mary Ann) $75.00
    8", #25970, 2000 – 2001, print dress, red cape, braided hair $70.00
    14", #28620, 2001 (Margaret) print dress, red cape $150.00
Red Shoes — 8", #14533, 1995, ballerina with same head as Spain $70.00
Red Queen — 8", h.p., 1997 – 1999, #13010, red and gold gown $125.00
Red Queen and White King Set — 8" pair, #13030, 1997 ....$225.00
Red Sequin — 10", #19974, 1998 (Cissette), long red velvet gown $160.00
Renaissance Bride — 10", #25000, 2000 (Cissette) $140.00
Renoir — 21" compo., 1945 – 1946, extra make-up, must be excellent condition
    (Wendy Ann) ....$2,000.00 up
    14" h.p., 1950 only (Margaret) ....$875.00 up
    21" h.p./vinyl arms, 1961 only (Cissy) ....$825.00 up
    18" h.p./vinyl arms, vinyl head, 1963 only (Elise) ....$575.00 up
    21" h.p./vinyl arms, #2154, 1965, pink gown (Jacqueline) $700.00
    14", #28620, 2001, (Margaret), print dress, red cape $150.00
    #2062, 1966, blue gown with black trim (Coco) ....$2,200.00 up
    #2175, 1967, navy blue gown, red hat $750.00
    #2194, #2184, 1969 – 1970, blue gown, full lace over dress $650.00
    #2163, 1971, all yellow gown $650.00
    #2190, 1972, pink gown with black jacket & trim $550.00
    #2190, 1973, yellow gold gown, black ribbon $550.00
    10" h.p., #1175, 1968, all navy with red hat (Cissette) $475.00
    #1175, 1969, pale blue gown, short jacket, striped or dotted skirt $475.00
    #1180, 1970, all aqua satin $425.00
Renoir Child — 12" plastic/vinyl, #1274, 1967 only, Portrait Children Series (Nancy Drew)...$175.00
    14", #1474, 1968 only (Mary Ann) $175.00
Renoir Girl — 14" plastic/vinyl, #1469, #1475, 1967 – 1968,
    Portrait Children Series, white dress with red ribbon trim (Mary Ann) $175.00
    #1477, 1969 – 1971, pink dress, white pinafore $100.00
    #1477, #1478, #1578, 1972 – 1986 (14-year production), pink multi-tiered lace gown $85.00
    #1572, 1986 only, pink pleated nylon dress $75.00
Renoir Girl with watering can — #1577, 1985 – 1987, Classic & Fine Arts Series $100.00
    8", h.p., #22150, 1997, navy taffeta dress..$75.00
Renoir Girl with hoop — #1574, 1986 – 1987, Classic & Fine Arts Series $100.00
Renoir Mother — 21" h.p./vinyl arms, 1967 only, navy blue, red hat (Jacqueline) ....$900.00 up
Renoir's on the Terrace — 8", 1999 (Wendy) blue dress with white overdress........................$80.00
Rhett — 12", #1380, 1981 – 1985, Portrait Children Series, black jacket/grey
    pants (Nancy Drew) $85.00
    8", #401, 1989 only, Jubilee II (Wendy Ann) $100.00
    8", #632, #642, 1991 – 1992 only, Scarlett Series, all white/blue vest $85.00
    8", #642, 1993, #160642, 1994, tan pants/vest/tie with white jacket........................$80.00
    10", h.p., #15050, 1997, *Gone with the Wind* Series $95.00

Riding Habit — 8", 1990 only, Americana Series (Wendy Ann) $75.00
    #571, 1956 ....$500.00
    #373G, 1957 ....$475.00
    #541, 1958 ....$550.00
    #355, 1962 ....$385.00
    #623, 1965 ....$350.00
Riley's Little Annie — 14" plastic/vinyl, #1481, 1967 only, Literature Series (Mary Ann).......$250.00
Ring Around the Rosey — 8", #12813, Nursery Rhymes Series $60.00
    8", #13520, 1998 – 2000, pink and white lacy dress $80.00
Ringbearer — 14" h.p., 1951 only, must be near mint (Lovey Dove) ....$550.00 up
    8", #28655, 2001, white jacket, black pants $80.00
Ringmaster — 8" (see Collectors United under Special Events/Exclusives)
Riverboat Queen (Lena) — (see M.A.D.C. under Special Events/Exclusives)
Riviera Night — 16", print dress, matching hat $170.00
Roaring 20's Bride — 10", #22630, 1999, white lace, pink roses, limited to 2,500...................$150.00
Roaring 20's Catherine — 16", porcelain, blue satin fringed costume $215.00
Robin Hood — 8", #446, 1988 – 1990, Storybook Series (Wendy Ann) $65.00
Rock and Roll Group — #22110, 1997, four 8" dolls, mod costumes $300.00
Rococo Bride — 10", pink satin and lace gown, #22460, 1999 – 2000.................................$160.00
Rococo Catherine — 16", porcelain, elaborate pink satin gown $300.00
Rodeo — 8" h.p., #483, 1955 only (Wendy Ann) ....$850.00 up
Rodeo Rosie — 14", #87012, 1996, red checked western costume $125.00
Rogers, Ginger — 14 – 21" compo., 1940 – 1945 (Wendy Ann) ....$2,500.00 up
Roller Blades — 8", "Throughly Modern Wendy" (see Disney under Special Events/Exclusives)
Roller Skating — 8" h.p., SL, SLW, BKW, #556, 1953 – 1956 (Wendy Ann) ....$600.00 up
Romance — 21" compo., 1945 – 1946, extra make-up, must be mint (Wendy Ann) ....$2,100.00 up
Romeo — 18" compo., 1949 (Wendy Ann) ....$1,500.00 up
    8" h.p., #474, 1955 only (Wendy Ann) ....$950.00 up
    12" plastic/vinyl, #1370, 1978 – 1987, Portrait Children Series (Nancy Drew) $75.00
    12", reintroduced 1991 – 1992 only, Romance Collection (Nancy Drew)............................$80.00
    8", 1994, mid-year introduction (see M.A.D.C. under Special Events/Exclusives)
Roosevelt, Edith — 1988, 5th set Presidents' Ladies/First Ladies Series (Louisa)....................$125.00
Roosevelt, Eleanor — 14", 1989 – 1990, 6th set Presidents' Ladies/First
Ladies Series (Louisa)..$135.00
Rosamund Bridesmaid — 15" h.p., 1951 only (Margaret, Maggie) ....$500.00 up
    17 – 18" h.p., 1951 only (Margaret, Maggie) ....$650.00 up
Rose — 9" early vinyl toddler, 1953 only, pink organdy dress & bonnet................................$125.00
Rosebud — 16 – 19" cloth/vinyl, 1952 – 1953 ....$150.00
    13", 1953 only..$175.00

Romeo #474, and Juliet #473, 8" straight leg walkers, 1955. Juliet has a very unique hairdo. Very mint dolls.

Rosebud, continued

23 – 25", 1953 only	$175.00
Rosebud (Pussy Cat) — 14" – 20", 1986 only, white	$50.00
14", black	$75.00
Rose Bouquet — 10", #28880, 2001, white and red dress with red roses	$120.00
Rose Fairy — 8" h.p., #622, 1956 only (Wendy Ann)	$1,400.00 up
8", #22640, 1999, yellow and rose costume with wings, limited to 1,500	$80.00
Rosette — 10", #1115, 1987 – 1989, Portrette, pink/rose gown (Cissette)	$90.00
Rosey Posey — 14" cloth/vinyl, 1976 only	$75.00
21" cloth/vinyl, 1976 only	$100.00
Rosie the Riveter — 8", #17530, 1999, overalls, lunch bucket	$80.00
Ross, Betsy — 8" h.p., Americana Series, 1967 – 1972, (Wendy Ann), bent knees, #731	$125.00
Straight legs, #0731, #431, 1973 – 1975, Storybook Series, marked "Alex"	$75.00
Straight legs, #431, 1976 – 1987 (1985 – 1987 white face)	$70.00
8", #312, reintroduced 1991 – 1992 only, Americana Series	$60.00
#312, 1976 Bicentennial gown (star print)	$125.00
Rosy — 14", #1562, 1988 – 1990, Classic Series, all pink dress with cream lace trim (Mary Ann)	$85.00
Round Up Cowgirl — 8" (see Disney under Special Events/Exclusives)	
Row, Row, Row Your Boat — 8", #13510, 1998 – 1999, comes with boat	$100.00
Roxanne — 8" h.p., #140504, 1994 only, Storyland Series	$75.00
Royal Bouquet — 8", #28895, 2001, white dress, pink sash	$120.00
Royal Evening — 18" h.p., 1953 only, cream/royal blue gown (Margaret)	$2,400.00 up
Royal Wedding — 21" compo., 1947, full circles trimmed in lace on lower skirt (Wendy Ann)	$3,250.00 up
Rozy — 12" plastic/vinyl, #1130, 1969 only (Janie)	$375.00
Ruby (July) — 10", #1151, 1992 only, Birthstone Collection, all red/gold (Cissette)	$100.00
Ruffles Clown — 21", 1954 only	$425.00
Rumania — 8" h.p., BK, #786, 1968 – 1972 (Wendy)	$100.00
8" straight leg, #0786, #586, 1973 – 1975, marked "Alex"	$75.00
8" straight leg, #586, #538, 1976 – 1987, marked "Alexander"	$65.00
8", #538, 1986 – 1987	$55.00
Rumbera/Rumbero — 7" compo., 1938 – 1943 (Tiny Betty)	$350.00 ea.
9" compo., 1939 – 1941 (Little Betty)	$375.00 ea.
Rumpelstiltskin & Miller's Daughter — 8" & 14", #1569, 1992 only, limited to 3,000 sets	$300.00 set
8" & 5", porcelain, #27750, 2001	$200.00 set
Russia — 8" h.p., BK, #774, 1968 – 1972 (Wendy Ann)	$100.00
8" straight leg, #0774, 1973 – 1975, marked "Alex"	$75.00
8" straight leg, #574, #548, 1976 – 1988 (1985 – 1987 white face), marked "Alexander"	$60.00
8", #548, 1985 – 1987, white face	$60.00
8", #581, 1991 – 1992 only	$60.00
8", #110540, 1994 only, long blue gown with gold trim	$60.00
8", #24150, 1999 – 2001, comes with painted stacking doll and miniature doll	$150.00
Russian — 7" compo., 1935 – 1938 (Tiny Betty)	$285.00
9" compo., 1938 – 1942 (Little Betty)	$300.00
Rusty — 20" cloth/vinyl, 1967 – 1968 only	$300.00
Sagittarius — 8", #21410, 1998 (Maggie), horse costume	$90.00
Sailor — 14" compo., 1942 – 1945 (Wendy Ann)	$750.00
17" compo., 1943 – 1944	$875.00
8" boy, 1990 (see U.F.D.C. under Special Events/Exclusives)	
8" boy, 1991 (see FAO Schwarz under Special Events/Exclusives)	
Sailor, Columbian — (see U.F.D.C. under Special Events/Exclusives)	
Sailorette — 10" h.p., #1119, 1988 only, Portrette Series, red/white/blue outfit (Cissette)	$75.00
Sally — 10", #26430, 2001, Peanuts Gang, red dress	$35.00
Sally Bride — 14" compo., 1938 – 1939 (Wendy Ann)	$475.00 up
18 – 21" compo., 1938 – 1939	$475.00 – 650.00
Salome — 14", #1412, 1984 – 1986, Opera Series (Mary Ann)	$90.00
Salute to the Century — 8", #17630, 1999, white chiffon long gown, limited to 4,000	$100.00
Samantha — 14" 1989 (see FAO Schwarz under Special Events/Exclusives)	
14", #1561, 1991 – 1992 only, Classic Series, gold ruffled gown (Mary Ann)	$175.00
10", h.p., #15300, from the *Bewitched* TV series	$105.00
Samson — 8", #14582, 1995 only, Bible Series	$100.00
Sandy McHare — cloth/felt, 1930s	$675.00

Santa Claus — 14", #24608, 1995, Christmas Series..$125.00
Santa and Mrs. Claus — 8", mid-year issue (see Madame Alexander Doll Co.
    under Special Events/Exclusives)
Santa's Little Helper — 8", #19660, 1998 – 1999, elf with candy cane trim............................$105.00
Sapphire (September) — 10", 1992 only, Birthstone Collection $100.00
Sardinia — 8", #509, 1989 – 1991 only (Wendy Ann)..$65.00
Sargent — 14", #1576, 1984 – 1985, Fine Arts Series, dressed in lavender (Mary Ann).............$85.00
Sargent's Girl — 14", #1579, 1986 only, Fine Arts Series, dressed in pink (Mary Ann) $85.00
Saturday's Child — 8", #27795, 2001, watering can $110.00
Scarecrow — 8", #430, 1993, #140430, 1994 – 1996, Wizard of Oz Series,
    #13230, 1997 – 2001 ....$70.00
    5", #28690, 2001, porcelain $70.00
Scarlett O'Hara — (Before movie, 1937 – 1938)
    7" compo., 1937 – 1942 (Tiny Betty) $475.00
    9" compo., 1938 – 1941 (Little Betty) $500.00
    11", 1937 – 1942 (Wendy Ann) $675.00
    14 – 15" compo., 1941 – 1943 (Wendy Ann) $750.00
    18" compo., 1939 – 1946 (Wendy Ann)...$1,200.00
    21" compo., 1945, 1947 (Wendy Ann)...$1,500.00
    14 – 16" h.p., 1950s (Margaret)...$1,600.00
    14 – 16" h.p., 1950s (Maggie)...$1,650.00
    20" h.p., 1950s (Margaret)..$1,800.00 up
    21", 1955, blue taffeta gown w/black looped braid trim, short jacket (Cissy) ......$1,500.00 up
      1958, jointed arms, green velvet jacket and bonnet trimmed in light green net, *rare*.......$2,000.00 up
      1961 – 1962, straight arms, white organdy, green ribbon inserted into tiers of
        lace on skirt, white picture hat, *rare* ....$2,000.00 up
    18" h.p./vinyl arms, 1963 only, pale blue organdy w/rose buds, straw hat (Elise)....................$950.00 up
    12" h.p., 1963 only, green taffeta gown and bonnet (Lissy)...................................$1,500.00
    7½ – 8", 1953 – 1954, white gown w/red rosebuds, white lace hat (Wendy Ann) ....$1,400.00 up
    7½ – 8" h.p., #485, 1955, two layer gown, white/yellow/green trim (Wendy Ann).............$1,500.00 up
    8" h.p., BKW, 1956, pink, blue, or yellow floral gown ....$1,400.00 up
    8" h.p., BKW, #431, 1957, white, lace and ribbon trim (dress must be mint)......................$1,400.00 up
    8" h.p., BK, #760, 1963 ....$650.00 up
    8", BK, 1965, in white or cream gown (Wendy Ann) ....$750.00 up
    8", BK, 1971 only, bright pink floral print..$650.00
    8", BK, #725, 1966 – 1972, Americana & Storybook Series, floral gown $375.00

Scarlett, 21", #2180, 1968, (Jacqueline).

Scarlett, 21", (Coco). Made in 1966 only. Body has a swivel waist and lower torso is one piece with one knee bent.

8", #0725, #425, 1973 – 1991 (18-year production), white gown (Wendy Ann) $100.00

    Straight leg, #425, #426, 1976 – 1986, marked "Alexander" $75.00

    #426, 1987, white face, blue dot gown $225.00

Straight leg, #426, 1988 – 1989, floral gown $100.00

1986 (see M.A.D.C. under Special Events/Exclusives)

1989, #400, Jubilee II, green velvet/gold trim...$150.00

Straight leg, #626, 1990 only, tiny floral print $100.00

    #631, 1991 only, 3-tier white gown, curly hair $90.00

    #627, 1992 only, rose floral print, oversized bonnet $100.00

    #641, 1993, white gown with green stripes and trim $90.00

    #643, 1993, #160643, 1994 (Honeymoon in New Orleans), trunk with wardrobe $275.00

    #160644, 1994 only, Scarlett Bride $100.00

    #160647, 1994 only, Scarlett Picnic, green/red floral on white, large ruffle at hem...........$100.00

    #16648, 1995 – 1996, white, four-tiered organdy gown with red trim..........................$85.00

    #16652, 1995 only, floral print picnic outfit with organdy overskirt................................$100.00

    #16553, green drapery gown, 100th Anniversary..$100.00

    #16653, 1996, Ashley's Farewell, maroon taffeta skirt..$75.00

    #17025, 1996, Tomorrow is Another Day, floral gown $85.00

    #86004, 1996, Ashley's Birthday, red velvet gown..$100.00

    #15030, 1997 – 1998, Shadow, rose picnic dress $80.00

    #14970, 1998 – 1999, Poor Scarlett, floral calico, straw hat $95.00

    #15180, 1999 – 2000, Sweet Sixteen, white dress, red ribbons......................................$90.00

    #26860, 2000, Picnic, print dress, straw hat $90.00

    #27825, 2001, green drapery gown and hat $85.00

    #28750, 2001, Honeymoon Scarlett, white dress, hat, black trim....................................$95.00

8" h.p., 1990, M.A.D.C. Symposium (see M.A.D.C. under Special Events/Exclusives)

8", 1993, mid-year issue (see Madame Alexander Doll Co. under Special Events/Exclusives)

21" h.p./vinyl arms, #2153, 1963 – 1964 (became "Godey" in 1965 with blonde hair) ....$1,500.00 up

21" h.p./vinyl arms, 1965, #2152, green satin gown (Jacqueline)...$1,900.00 up

    #2061, 1966, all white gown, red sash, & roses (also with plain wide lace hem;

        also inverted "V" scalloped lace hem – allow more for this gown) (Coco) ....$2,800.00 up

    #2174, 1967, green satin gown with black trim $675.00

    #2180, 1968, floral print gown with wide white hem ....$1,000.00 up

    #2190, 1969, red gown with white lace...$650.00

    #2180, 1970, green satin, white trim on jacket $575.00

    #2292, 2295, 2296, 1975 – 1977, all green satin, white lace at cuffs..................................$450.00

    #2110, 1978, silk floral gown, green parasol, white lace $500.00

    #2240, 1979 – 1985, green velvet..$375.00

Scarlett, 8", SLW, #485, 1955, (Wendy Ann). All original. Tag: Alexander-Kin.

Scarlett, 8", BKW, 1965, (Wendy Ann). Taffeta dress with roses. Mint and all original.

#2255, 1986 only, floral gown, green parasol, white lace $375.00

#2247, 1987 – 1988, layered all over white gown $350.00

#2253, 1989, doll has full bangs, all red gown (Birthday Party gown)............................$400.00

#2258, 1990 – 1993 only, Scarlett Bride, Scarlett Series..$375.00

#2259, 1991 – 1992 only, green on white, three ruffles around skirt $350.00

21" #162276, 1994 (Jacqueline) tight green gown, three-layered bustle $300.00

#009, porcelain, 1991 only, green velvet, gold trim...$550.00

#50001, Scarlett Picnic (Jacqueline), floral gown..$325.00

#15020, 1997, rose picnic dress, carries garden basket..$375.00

#15170, Black Mourning Scarlett, 1999 ....$500.00

#25765, 2000, Atlanta Stroll Scarlett, striped bodice...$450.00

#28760, 2001, Peachtree Promenade, limited to 500, blue dress, black trim.....................$550.00

10" h.p., #1174, 1968 only, lace in bonnet, green satin gown with black braid trim (Cissette) $475.00

#1174, 1969, green satin gown with white & gold braid $450.00

#1181, #1180, 1970 – 1973, green satin gown with gold braid trim.....................................$400.00

#1100, 1989 only, Jubilee II, burgundy and white $125.00

#1102, 1990 – 1991 only, Scarlett Series, floral print gown..$150.00

#1105, 1992 only, Scarlett at Ball, all in black $140.00

1993, #161105, 1994, green velvet drapes/gold trim $150.00

1994 – 1995, Scarlett in red dress with red boa $150.00

#16107, 1995 only, white sheath with dark blue jacket..$140.00

#16654, 1996, mourning dress...$125.00

#16656, 1996, Scarlett and Rhett, limited set $200.00

#15000, 1997 – 1998, Hoop-Petti outfit $125.00

#15040, 1997, mourning outfit...$115.00

#14980, 1998 – 2000, blue satin gown, lace shawl (Cissette), Portrait Scarlett $140.00

#25770, 2000, Sewing Circle Scarlett, white top, lavender skirt $120.00

#28755, 2001, Atlanta Stroll Scarlett, red, white striped dress $150.00

12", 1981 – 1985, green gown with braid trim (Nancy Drew)...$125.00

14" plastic/vinyl, #1495, 1968 only, floral gown (Mary Ann)...$450.00

#1490, #7590, 1969 – 1986 (18-year production), white gown, tagged "Gone With
        The Wind" (Mary Ann)..$100.00

#1590, #1591, 1987 – 1989, blue or green floral print on beige..$140.00

#1590, 1990, Scarlett Series, tiny floral print gown $150.00

#1595, 1991 – 1992 only, Scarlett Series, white ruffles, green ribbon (Louisa, Jennifer)....$140.00

#16551, 1995 (see Peachtree Lane)

#1500, 14", 1986 only, Jubilee #1, all green velvet (Mary Ann)..$175.00

#1300, 14", 1989 only, Jubilee #2, green floral print gown (Mary Ann)............................$150.00

Scarlett, Miss —14" (see Belks & Leggett under Special Events/Exclusives)

School Girl — 7" compo., 1936 – 1943 (Tiny Betty) $300.00

Scotch — 7" compo., 1936 – 1939 (Tiny Betty) $275.00

9" compo., 1939 – 1940 (Little Betty) $350.00

10" h.p., 1962 – 1963 (Cissette) ....$900.00 up

Scots Lass — 8" h.p., BKW, #396, 1963 only (Maggie Mixup, Wendy Ann)...........................$275.00 up

Scorpio — 8", #21400, 1998, Scorpion costume, golden spear $90.00

Scottish (Scotland) — 8" h.p., BKW, #796, 1964 – 1965 (Wendy Ann) $150.00

8" h.p., BK, #796, 1965 – 1972 ....$125.00

8" straight leg, #0796-596, 1973 – 1975, marked "ALEX"..$85.00

8" straight leg, #596, #529, 1976 – 1993 (1985 – 1987 white face), marked "Alexander" $70.00

8" redressed, Scot outfit with English guard hat, 1994..$70.00

8", #28550, 2001, Scot costume, blue plaid, bag pipes $85.00

Scouting — 8", #317, 1991 – 1992 only, Americana Series..$100.00

Scrooge — 14", #18401, 1996, Dickens (Mary Ann) $125.00

Sears Roebuck — (see Special Events/Exclusives)

Season's Greetings Maggie — 8", #26840, 2001, green smocked dress.................................$100.00

Season's Greetings Wendy — 8", #26845, 2001, red smocked dress $100.00

Secret Garden, My — 8" (see FAO Schwarz under Special Events/Exclusives)

14", #24616, 1995, has trunk and wardrobe (Louisa) $250.00

Sense and Sensibility — 10", #25340, 2000, long white gown with embroidery $120.00

September — 14", #1527, 1989 only, Classic Series (Mary Ann) $85.00

10", #1152, 1992, Portrette, royal blue/gold flapper $100.00

Seven Dwarfs — compo., 1937 only, must be mint ....$475.00 ea.

Seventy-Fifth Anniversary Wendy — 8", #22420, 1998, pink outfit $110.00

Shadow of Madame — (see Doll & Teddy Bear Expo under Special Events/Exclusives)
Shadow Stepmother — 8", #14638, 1996 ....$100.00
Shaharazad — 10", #1144, 1992 – 1993 only, Portrette (Cissette) $90.00
She Sells Seashells — 8", #14629, 1996, Nursery Rhymes Series (Maggie)..........$75.00
Shea Elf — 8" (see Collectors United under Special Events/Exclusives)
Shepherd and Drummer Boy Set — 8", #19490, 1997 – 2000, Nativity Set..........$190.00
Shepherdess with Lamb — 8", #20010, 1999 – 2000, red robe, headdress $85.00
Shimmering Dance — 8", #30645, 2001, ballerina..$60.00
Shimmering 1930s Catherine — porcelain, 16", long white gown $200.00
Shirley's Doll House — (see Special Events/Exclusives)
Shoemaker's Elf Boy — 8", #14637, 1996..$65.00
Shoemaker's Elf Girl — 8", #14636, 1996..$65.00
Sicily — 8", #513, 1989 – 1990 (Wendy Ann)..$75.00
Silver Star — 8", #28875, 2001, silver satin and tulle.......................................$85.00
Simone — 21" h.p./vinyl arms, 1968 only, in trunk (Jacqueline) ....$2,150.00 up
Sir Lapin Hare — cloth/felt, 1930s $700.00
Sister Brenda — (see FAO Schwarz under Special Events/Exclusives)
Sitting Pretty — 18" foam body, 1965 only, *rare* $400.00
Skater's Waltz — 15" – 18", 1955 – 1956 (Cissy)..$650.00
Skating Doll — 16", 1947 – 1950 (untagged "Sonja Henie" after contract expired) $700.00
Sleeping Beauty — 7 – 9" compo., 1941 – 1944 (Tiny Betty & Little Betty) ....$325.00 – 425.00
   15 – 16" compo., 1938 – 1940 (Princess Elizabeth) $475.00
   18 – 21" compo., 1941 – 1944 (Wendy Ann) ....$650.00 – 950.00
   10", #1141, 1991 – 1992 only, Portrette, blue/white gown $90.00
   21", #2195, 1959 only year this head used, authorized by Disney,
      blue satin brocade, net cape, gold tiara....................................$850.00 up
   16" #1895, same head as 21" on Elise body, authorized by Disney $650.00
   10" h.p., 1959 only, authorized by Disney, blue gown (Cissette) $325.00
   14" plastic/vinyl, #1495, #1595, 1971 – 1985 (14-year production),
      Classic Series, gold gown (Mary Ann)..$85.00
   14", #1596, 1986 – 1990, Classic Series, blue gown (Mary Ann)........$120.00
   14", #87010, 1996, pink and gold ball gown (Mary Ann) $125.00
   8", #14543, 1995, Brothers Grimm Series, blue with silver crown $70.00
   8", #13600, 1997 – 2000, blue satin gown, spinning wheel $75.00
   16", #25325, 2000, gold and lilac long ballet costume $190.00
   8", #30680, 2001, blue gown, lace and rose trim $75.00
   16", #25325, 2001, lilac ballerina costume $190.00
Sleeping Beauty's Prince — 8", #13650, 1999 – 2000, (Wendy) bent knees, purple costume ...$80.00
Slumber Party Chloe — 14", #30065, 2001, pajamas, sleeping bag................$60.00
Slumbermate — 11 – 12" cloth/compo., 1940s ....$250.00 up
   21" compo./cloth, 1940s ....$475.00 up
   13" vinyl/cloth, 1951 only...$125.00 up
Smarty — 12" plastic/vinyl, #1160, #1136, 1962 – 1963 ....$325.00
   1963 only, "Smarty & Baby"...$375.00
   1963 only, with boy "Artie" in case with wardrobe $950.00
Smee — 8", #442, 1993, #140442, 1994, Storybook Series (Peter Pan), wears glasses.....$65.00
Smiley — 20" cloth/vinyl, 1971 only (Happy)..$250.00
Smokey Tail — cloth/felt, 1930s $650.00
Snap, Crackle & Pop Set — 8", #12120, 1998 – 1999, Rice Krispies Dolls set $250.00
Snips and Snails — 8", #31330, 2000, sweater, jeans, dog...............................$70.00
Snowflake — 10", #1167, 1993 only, Portrette, ballerina dressed in
  white/gold outfit (Cissette)..$90.00
Snowflake Symposium — (see M.A.D.C. under Special Events/Exclusives)
Snow Queen — 10", #1130, 1991 – 1992 only, Portrette, silver/white gown (Cissette)............$100.00
   8", #14548, Hans Christian Andersen Series, white with gold trim $70.00
   8", #32150, 2000, white gown, fur-trimmed robe $95.00
Snow White — 13" compo., 1937 – 1939, painted eyes (Princess Elizabeth)............$475.00
   12" compo., 1939 – 1940 (Princess Elizabeth) $450.00
   13" compo., 1939 – 1940, sleep eyes (Princess Elizabeth) $475.00
   16" compo., 1939 – 1942 (Princess Elizabeth) $500.00
   18" compo., 1939 – 1940 (Princess Elizabeth) $750.00
   14 – 15" h.p., 1952 only (Margaret) $750.00
   18 – 23", 1952 only ....$850.00 – 1,100.00
   21" h.p., *rare* (Margaret) $1,200.00

Snow White, continued

14", #1455, 1967 – 1977, Disney crest colors (Mary Ann) $350.00
8" h.p., 1972 – 1977, Disney crest colors (Wendy)...$425.00
8", #495, 1990 – 1992 only, Storyland Series (Wendy) $85.00
8", #14545, 1995, Brothers Grimm Series, crest colors but with red bodice,
   #13800, 1997 – 2001 ....$65.00
12", 1990 (see Disney under Special Events/Exclusives)
14" plastic/vinyl, #1455, #1555, 1970 – 1985 (15-year production), Classic Series,
   white gown (Mary Ann) $125.00
#1556, #1557, 1986 – 1992, ecru & gold gown, red cape (Mary Ann, Louisa) $125.00
14", #14300, 1995, crest colors but red bodice (Louisa) $200.00
14", #87013, 1996, Snow White's trunk set (Mary Ann) $325.00
10", Disney crest colors (see Disney under Special Events/Exclusives)
14", #28615, 2001, white gown, red cape $180.00
Snow White's Prince — 8", #14639, 1996 ....$65.00
Snow White Wedding — 8", #30460, 2001, white gown, red cape $90.00
So Big — 22" cloth/vinyl, 1968 – 1975, painted eyes $225.00
18", #30310, 2001, cloth, Mary Englebreit..$45.00
Soccer Boy — 8", #16350, sports outfit with soccer ball, 1997...$60.00
Soccer Girl — 8", #16341, sports outfit with soccer ball, 1997 – 1998 ....$60.00
Sock Hop 1950 — 8", #17780, 1999, poodle skirt..$75.00
So Lite Baby or Toddler — 20" cloth, 1930 – 1940s ....$375.00 up
Soldier — 14" compo., 1943 – 1944 (Wendy Ann) $375.00
17" compo., 1942 – 1945 (Wendy Ann) $850.00
Sound of Music
Sound of Music, large set, 1965 – 1970
   14", #1404, Louisa (Mary Ann)..$275.00
   10", #1107 Friedrich (Janie or Smarty)...$275.00
   14", #1403 Brigitta (Mary Ann) $225.00
   14", #1405 Liesl (Mary Ann)..$275.00
   10" Marta, 10" Gretl (Smarty or Janie) $225.00
   17", #1706 Maria (Elise or Polly) $300.00
   Full set of 7 dolls..$1,300.00
Sound of Music, small set, 1971 – 1973
   12" Maria (Nancy Drew) $350.00
   8" #801 Gretl (Wendy Ann) $175.00
   8" #802 Marta, #807 Friedrich (Wendy Ann) $225.00

Snow White, 18", #1835, (Margaret), all hard plastic. Made in 1952 only. All original.

Sound of Music Louisa, 10", 1971 – 1973, (Cissette). All original.

Sound of Music Liesl, 10", 1971 – 1973, (Cissette). All original.

Sound of Music, continued

10" Brigitta (Cissette) $175.00
10" Liesl (Cissette)..$250.00
10" Louisa (Cissette) $275.00
Set of 7 dolls $1,300.00

Sound of Music, dressed in sailor suits & tagged, date unknown

17" Maria (Elise or Polly)...$500.00
14" Louisa (Mary Ann)..$500.00
10" Friedrich (Smarty) $375.00
14" Brigitta (Mary Ann) $375.00
14" Liesl (Mary Ann)...$375.00
10" Gretl (Smarty) $350.00
10" Marta (Smarty) $375.00
Set of 7 dolls ....$2,700.00 up
12", 1965, in sailor suit (Lissy)...$750.00 up
12", 1965, in Alpine outfit (Lissy) $650.00

Sound of Music, all in same oufit: red skirt, white attached blouse, black vest that ties in
front with gold cord, *very rare* ....$400.00 – 600.00 ea.

Sound of Music, reintroduced 1992 – 1993

8", #390, #391, 1992 – 1993 only, Gretl and Kurt (boy in sailor suit) $125.00
8", #390, #392, 1992 – 1994, Brigitta $100.00
8", #394, 1993 only, Friedrich dressed in green/white playsuit...........$100.00
8", #393, 1993 only, Marta in sailor dress.....................................$200.00
10", 1992 – 1993 only, Maria (Cissette) $125.00
10", 1993 only, Liesl $125.00
12", 1992 only, Maria Bride (Nancy Drew) $125.00
10", Maria at Abbey, dressed in nun's outfit (Cissette), 1993 only $125.00

Sound of Music, reintroduced 1998

8", #14060, Gretl Von Trapp (Wendy), green, gray sailor suit $100.00
8", #14050, Marta Von Trapp (Maggie), sailor suit $100.00
9", #14040, Brigitta Von Trapp (Wendy), sailor outfit......................$100.00
10", #14030, Captain Von Trapp (Cissette), gray Tyrolean suit..........$125.00
10", #13890, Maria at the Abbey (Cissette), navy dress, guitar $125.00
10", #13870, Mother Superior (Cissette), black and white nun habit...........$115.00
10", #13880, Maria Travel Ensemble (Cissette), pleated skirt, bolero..........$125.00
9", #14020, Friedrich Von Trapp (Maggie), blue & gray sailor suit $100.00
10", #14160, Louisa Von Trapp (Wendy), blue, gray pleated sailor suit $100.00
10", #14090, Kurt Von Trapp (Wendy), sailor uniform $100.00
10", #14170, Liesl Von Trapp (Cissette), blue & gray sailor outfit $100.00

South American — 7" compo., 1938 – 1943 (Tiny Betty)....................$275.00
9" compo., 1939 – 1941 (Little Betty) $300.00

Southern Belle or Girl — 8" h.p., SLNW, 1953, white dress, straw hat w/pink silk roses ......$750.00 up
8" h.p., #370, 1954 (Wendy Ann) ....$1,000.00 up
8" h.p., #437, #410, 1956, pink or blue/white striped gown (Wendy Ann)..........$1,000.00 up
8" h.p., #385, 1963 only (Wendy Ann) $575.00
12" h.p., 1963 only (Lissy) $1,500.00
21" h.p./vinyl arms, #2155, 1965, blue gown with wide pleated hem (Jacqueline) $1,200.00
21", #2170, 1967, white gown with green ribbon trim $625.00
10" h.p., #1170, 1968, white gown with green ribbon through 3 rows of lace (Cissette) $450.00
1969, white gown with 4 rows of lace, pink sash, (Cissette) $475.00
#1185, 1970, white gown with red ribbon sash (Cissette) $400.00
#1185 (#1184 in 1973), 1971 – 1973, white gown with green ribbon sash..........$350.00
10" (see My Doll House under Special Events/Exclusives)

Southern Belle — 10", #25985, 2000, long white gown with lace, limited to 2,000 ....$150.00
Southern Flower Girl — 8", #25980, 2000, long pink gown, basket, limited to 2,800 ....$90.00
Southern Girl — 11 – 14" compo., 1940 – 1943 (Wendy Ann)................$350.00 – 500.00
17 – 21" compo., 1940 – 1943 (Wendy Ann) ....$650.00 – 900.00
Southern Symposium — (see M.A.D.C. under Special Events/Exclusives)
Spanish — 7 – 8" compo., 1935 – 1939 (Tiny Betty) $275.00
9" compo., 1936 – 1940 (Litte Betty) $300.00
Spanish Boy — 8" h.p., BK & BKW, #779, 1964 – 1968 (Wendy Ann) $365.00
Spanish Girl — 8" h.p., BKW, #795, #395, 1962 – 1965, three-tiered skirt (Wendy Ann) $150.00
8" h.p., BK, #795, 1965 – 1972, three-tiered skirt.............................$100.00
8" straight leg, #0795, #595, 1973 – 1975, three-tiered skirt, marked "ALEX" $75.00

    8" straight leg, #595, 1976 – 1982, three-tiered skirt, marked "Alexander"................................$65.00

    8" straight leg, #595, 1983 – 1985, two-tiered skirt..$60.00

    8" straight leg, #541, 1986 – 1990, white with red polka dots (1986 – 1987 white face)............$60.00

    8" straight leg, #541, 1990 – 1992, all-red tiered skirt...$60.00

    8" h.p., #110545, 1994 – 1995, red, two-tiered polka dot gown...$60.00

    8" h.p., #24160, 1999 – 2000, red rose and black gown...$90.00

Spanish Matador — 8", #530, 1992 – 1993 only (Wendy)..$65.00

Sparkling Sapphire — 10", #32080, 2000, red and blue long gown...$150.00

Special Girl — 23" – 24" cloth/comp., 1942 – 1946...$500.00

Spiegel's — (see Spiegel's under Special Events/Exclusives)

Spring — 14", 1993, Changing Seasons, doll and four outfits..$125.00

    5", #25850, 2000, porcelain, pink dress, straw hat...$65.00

Spring Angel — 10", #28370, 2001, long gown, feather wings..$110.00

Spring Bouquet — 8", #30890, 2001, white ballet outfit..$70.00

Spring Break — (see Metroplex Doll Club under Special Events/Exclusives)

Spring Promenade — 10", #27810, 2001, white long dress, straw hat...$125.00

Springtime — 8" (see M.A.D.C. under Special Events/Exclusives)

Starlight Angel — 10", #10790, 1999 – 2000, (Cissette) star-accented gown $130.00

Stepmother — 8", 1997, #13820, velvet cape, satin dress $80.00

Stick Piggy — 12", 1997, #10030, sailor outfit $95.00

Stilts — 8", #320, 1992 – 1993 only, clown on stilts $85.00

Straw Piggy — 12", 1997, #10020, plaid pants, straw hat $95.00

Story Princess — 15 – 18" h.p., 1954 – 1956 (Margaret, Cissy, Binnie)..................$550.00 – 900.00

    8" h.p., #892, 1956 only (Wendy Ann) ....$1,300.00 up

Stuffy (Boy) — h.p., 1952 – 1953 (Margaret) ....$850.00 up

Suellen — 14 – 17" compo., 1937 – 1938 (Wendy Ann)...$975.00 up

    12", 1990 only, yellow multi-tiered skirt, Scarlett Series (Nancy Drew)....................................$85.00

    8" pink bodice, floral skirt, apron, #160645, 1994 – 1995 ....$85.00

    Special for Jean's Doll Shop (see Special Events/Exclusives)

Suellen O'Hara — 8", #15200, 1999..$85.00

Suffragette 1910 — 10", #17730, 1999 ....$110.00

Sugar and Spice — 8", #13530, 1998 – 1999, pink and white lace dress...$90.00

    8", #32145, 2000, three rows of ribbon on skirt, lollipop...$50.00

Sugar Darlin' — 14 – 18" cloth/vinyl, 1964 only ....$75.00 – 125.00

    24", 1964 only $150.00

    Lively, 14", 18", 24", 1964 only, knob makes head & limbs move ....$125.00 – 200.00

Sugar Plum Fairy — 10", #1147, 1992 – 1993 only, Portrette, lavender ballerina....................$100.00

Sugar Plum Fairy — 8" (Wendy), 1999 – 2000, #12640, pink satin and tulle $75.00

    16", #80780, 2000, long ballet costume from The Nutcracker $180.00

Sugar Tears — 12" vinyl baby, 1964 only (Honeybea) $110.00

Sulky Sue — 8", #445, 1988 – 1990, marked "Alexander" (Wendy Ann) $75.00

Summer — 14", 1993, Changing Seasons, doll and four outfits...$135.00

    5", #25855, 2000, porcelain, blue dress, straw hat $65.00

Summer Angel — 8", #27640, 2001, multicolored tulle..$100.00

Sunbeam — 11", 16", 19", 1951 only, newborn infant, clean and in fair condition........$75.00 – 150.00

    16", 20", 24" cloth/vinyl, 1950, Divine-a-Lite Series (reg #573, 313), scowling expression $125.00

Sunbonnet Sue — 9" compo., 1937 – 1940 (Little Betty) $300.00

Sunday's Child — 8", #27800, 2001, angel costume $110.00

Sunflower Clown — 40" all cloth, 1951 only, flower eyes ....$850.00 up

Sun-Maid Raisin Girl — 8", #26190, 2000, red costume..$70.00

Sunny — 8" (see C.U. under Special Events/Exclusives)

Susannah Clogger — 8" (see Dolly Dears under Special Events/Exclusives)

Susie Q — cloth, 1940 – 1942 ....$650.00

    8", #14590, 1995, Toy Shelf Series, has yarn braids and pink polka dot dress

        with green jacket $75.00

Suzy — 12" plastic/vinyl, 1970 only (Janie) $325.00

Swan Princess — 10", #14106, 1995 only, Fairy Tales Series $85.00

Swan Lake — 16", #22040, 1998, Odette in white tutu...$200.00

Sweden (Swedish) — 8 h.p., BKW, #392, #792, 1961 – 1965 (Wendy Ann).........................$125.00

    8" h.p., BK, #792, 1965 – 1972 ....$100.00

    8" straight leg, #0792, #592, 1973 – 1975, marked "Alex" $75.00

    8" straight leg, #592, #539, #521, 1976 – 1989, marked "Alexander".......................................$65.00

    8", 1986...$60.00

Sweden (Swedish), continued

8", #580, reintroduced 1991 only..$60.00
BKW with Maggie smile face..$175.00
Swedish — 7" compo., 1936 – 1940 (Tiny Betty)...............................$300.00
9" compo., 1937 – 1941 (Little Betty)..$325.00
Sweet Baby — 18½" – 20" cloth/latex, 1948 only.................$50.00 – 100.00
Sweet Baby — 14", 1983 – 1984 (Sweet Tears)......................................$75.00
14", reissued 1987, 1987 – 1993 (1991 has no bottle), (Sweet Tears)......$85.00
14", 1990 – 1992 only (1991 has bottle), in carry case.....................$125.00
14", reintroduced 1993 only, pink striped jumper or dress...................$85.00
Sweet Sixteen — 14", #1554, 1991 – 1992 only, Classic Series (Louisa)......$125.00
10", #21060, 1997, pink silk dress, lace stole.......................................$95.00
Sweet Tears — 9" vinyl, 1965 – 1974..$85.00
9" with layette in box, 1965 – 1973..$175.00
14", 1967 – 1974, in trunk/trousseau...$200.00
14", 1965 – 1974, in window box..$175.00
14", 1979, with layette..$125.00
14", 1965 – 1982..$75.00
16", 1965 – 1971..$75.00
Sweet Violet — 18" h.p., 1951 – 1954 (Cissy).................................$875.00 up
Sweetie Baby — 22", 1962 only..$125.00
Sweetie Walker — 23", 1962 only...$275.00 up
Swiss — 7" compo., 1936 (Tiny Betty)..$300.00
9" compo., 1935 – 1938 (Little Betty)..$325.00
10" h.p., 1962 – 1963 (Cissette)...$825.00
Switzerland — 8" h.p., BKW, #394, #794, 1961 – 1965.....................$125.00
8" h.p., BK, #794, 1965 – 1972...$100.00
8" h.p., straight leg, #0794, #594, 1973 – 1975, marked "Alex"...........$75.00
8" h.p., straight leg, #594, #540, #518, 1976 – 1989, marked "Alexander"......$65.00
8", #546, 1986...$60.00
#518, 1988 – 1990, costume change...$60.00
8" BKW, Maggie smile face..$175.00
8", #25795, 2000, pink and white costume with watch..........................$90.00
Symposium — (see M.A.D.C. under Special Events/Exclusives)
Taft, Helen — 1988, 5th set Presidents' Ladies/First Ladies Series (Louisa)......$125.00
Tara — #14990, 1998, 2-sided home of Scarlett...................................$200.00
Taurus — 8", #21340, 1998 – brown and white bull costume................$90.00
Tea Rose Cissette — 10", #22370 – 1998, floral silk cocktail dress......$150.00
Team Canada — 8", #24130, 1998 – 1999, hockey skater........................$80.00
Teeny Twinkle — 1946 only, cloth with flirty eyes..............................$525.00
Tennis — 8" h.p., BKW, #415, #632 (Wendy Ann).............................$450.00
Tennis Boy — 8", #16331, 1997..$60.00
Tennis Girl — 8", #16320, 1997...$60.00
Tess — 10", #28405, 2001, green, pink vintage gown...........................$125.00
Texas — 8", #313, 1991 only, Americana...$85.00
Texas Shriner — (see Shriner's under Special Events/Exclusives)
Thailand — 8" h.p., BK, #767, 1966 – 1972 (Wendy)..........................$100.00
8" straight leg, #0767, #567, 1973 – 1975, marked "Alex".....................$75.00
8" straight leg, #567, 1976 – 1989, marked "Alexander"........................$65.00
Thank You — 8", #21110, 1997 – 1998, comes with a thank-you card......$60.00
That Girl — 10", #26345, 2000, (Cissette), navy blue suit.....................$90.00
There Was A Little Girl — 14", #24611, 1995, Nursery Rhymes Series (Mary Ann)......$90.00
"There's No Place Like Home" Doll House — trunk set, #13260, 1997 – 1999......$150.00
Thinking of You — 8", #21500, 1998 – 1999, print dress, straw hat......$80.00
Thomas, Marlo — 17" plastic/vinyl, 1967 only (Polly)...................$600.00 up
Three Little Kittens — 8", #26970, 2000 – 2001, blue plaid dress, 3 kittens......$90.00
Three Little Pigs Set — 12", #10000, brick, straw, and stick Piggy......$325.00
Three Little Pigs & Wolf — compo., 1938 – 1939, must be mint.....$675.00 up ea.
Three Wise Men Set — 8", #19480, 1997 – 1999, Nativity Set.............$340.00
Thumbelina & Her Lady — 8" & 21" porcelain, 1992 – 1993, limited to 2,500 sets......$500.00
Thursday's Child — 8", #27785, 2001, comes with suitcase.................$110.00
Tierney, Gene — 14 – 17" compo., 1945, must be mint (Wendy Ann)......$3,300.00 up
Tibet — 8" h.p., #534, 1993 only...$75.00
Tiger Lily — 8", #469, 1992 – 1993 only, Storybook Series (Peter Pan) (Wendy Ann)......$95.00

Time Out for Coca-Cola Sock Hop — 10", #26225, 2000 ....$115.00
Timmy Toddler — 23" plastic/vinyl, 1960 – 1961 ....$150.00
   30", 1960 only...$250.00
Tinker Bell — 11" h.p., #1110, 1969 only, Peter Pan Series, (Cissette) ....$475.00 up
   magic wand and wings, #13960 in 1998 – 2000 ....$75.00
   14", #87009, 1996 (Mary Ann)..$100.00
   8", #30675, 2001, pink, blue costume, lace wings, limited to 2,500 pieces $75.00
Tinkles — 8", #10400, 1995, Christmas Series $60.00
Tin Man — 8", #13210, 1998 – 2001, Wizard of Oz Series $70.00
   5", #28685, 2001, porcelain $70.00
Tin Woodsman — 8", #432 in 1993, #140432 in 1994 – 1995 ....$70.00
Tiny Betty — 7" compo., 1935 – 1942 ....$275.00 up
Tiny Tim — 7" compo., 1934 – 1937 (Tiny Betty) $325.00
   14" compo., 1938 – 1940 (Wendy Ann)...$625.00
   cloth, early 1930s ....$700.00 up
   8", #18001, 1996, Dickens (Wendy Ann) $65.00
Tippi Ballerina — 8" (see Collectors United under Special Events/Exclusives)
Tippy Toe — 16" cloth, 1940s $600.00
Today I Feel Silly — 12", #80710, 2000 – 2001, dressed cloth doll with 4 interchangeable faces$45.00
Tom Sawyer — 8" h.p., #491, 1989 – 1990, Storybook Series (Maggie Mixup)......$90.00
Tommy — 12" h.p., 1962 only (Lissy) $1,000.00
Tommy Bangs — h.p., 1952 only, Little Men Series (Maggie, Margaret) $875.00
Tommy Snooks — 8", #447, 1988 – 1991, Storybook Series $75.00
Tommy Tittlemouse — 8", #444, 1988 – 1991, Storybook Series (Maggie)..........$70.00
Tooth Fairy — 10" Portrette, 1994 only..$90.00
   8", #10389 – 10391, 1995 only, Special Occasions Series, three hair colors $65.00
   8", #21550, 1999 – 2000, pink sparkling outfit, satin pillow $80.00
   8", #30660, 2001, lavender costume, silver bag......................................$90.00
Tony Sarg Marionettes — (see Marionettes)
Topsy-Turvy — compo. with Tiny Betty heads, 1935 only ....$275.00 up
   With Dionne Quint head, 1936 only..$350.00
   Cinderella — #14587, 1995 only, two head, one side gown; other side dress with apron $125.00
   Red Riding Hood — 8", #14555 (3-way) Red Riding Hood, Grandma, Wolf......................$125.00
   Wicked Stepmother — 8", #14640, 1996, evil witch, stepmother................$160.00
Toulouse-Lautrec — 21", #2250, 1986 – 1987 only, black/pink outfit $300.00
Toy Soldier — 8", #481, 1993, #140481, 1994, #13210 – 1998, white face, red dots on cheeks...$75.00
Train Journey — 8", h.p., #486, 1955, white wool jacket, hat, red plaid dress $450.00
Trapeze Artist — 10", #1133, 1990 – 1991, Portrette (Cissette)........................$100.00
Tree Topper — 8" (½ doll only), #850, 1992 only, red/gold dress....................$100.00
   8" (½ doll only), #852, 1992 – 1994, Angel Lace with multi-tiered
     ivory lace skirt (Wendy) $110.00
   8" (½ doll only), #853, 1993 – 1994, red velvet/gold & green (Wendy) $100.00
   10" (½ doll only), #854, 1993 – 1994; #54854, 1995, pink Victorian (Cissette).$125.00
   8" (½ doll only), #540855, 1994; #540855 – 1995, all antique white (Wendy)$110.00
   8", #84857, 1995 – 1996, Yuletide Angel dressed in red and gold (Wendy),
     #19600, 1997 ....$100.00
   8", #84859, 1995 – 1996, Christmas Angel dressed in white and gold (Wendy) ..$100.00
   10", #54860, Glorious Angel dressed in red and white, gold crown, #19590,
     1997 – 1998 (Cissette) $110.00
   10", #19610, 1997 – 1998, Heavenly Angel, gold and ivory costume (Wendy) ..$110.00
   10", Glistening Angel, 1998 – 1999, #19700 (Wendy), silver brocade $125.00
   10", Winter Lights — #20000, 1999 – 2000 (Wendy), AC illuminated.........$135.00
   10", Holiday Trimmings, 2000 – 2001, #27040, (Wendy), red plaid gown $100.00
   10", Golden Dream, 2000, #27055, gold and white gown $100.00
   10", Caroler Tree Topper, 2000, #27045, red jacket, fur muff........................$100.00
   10", Star Tree Topper, 2000, #26100, gold star, tassels $60.00
   Shining Bright Angel Fiber-optic Tree Topper, 8", #28265, 2001,
     white, gold, (Wendy) $140.00
   Starburst Angel Tree Topper, 10", #28535, 2001, red, gold gown (Wendy) ...$100.00
Treena Ballerina — 15" h.p., 1952 only, must be near mint (Margaret)..........$700.00 up
   18 – 21", 1952 only...$650.00 – 875.00
Trellis Rose Flower Girl — 8", 2001, long dress................................$90.00
Trick and Treat — (see Child at Heart under Special Events/Exclusives)
Triumphant Topaz — 10", #32165, 2000, black and gold ball gown $150.00

Tiny Betty Bride, 7" composition, 1935 – 1939.

Truman, Bess — 14", 1989 – 1990, 6th set Presidents' Ladies/First Ladies Series (Mary Ann) $125.00
Tuesday's Child — 8", #27775, 2001, white dress, blue ribbon $110.00
Tunisia — 8", #514, 1989 only, marked "Alexander" (Wendy)..$70.00
Turkey — 8" h.p., BK, #787, 1968 – 1972 (Wendy)...$125.00
    8" straight leg, #0787, #587, 1973 – 1975, marked "Alex" $75.00
    8" straight leg, #587, 1976 – 1986, marked "Alexander" $65.00
'Twas the Night Before Christmas — 8", #27305, 2001, white long gown $90.00
Tweedledee & Tweedledum — 14" cloth, 1930 – 1931 ....$725.00 ea.
    8" h.p., #13080, 1998 – 1999, checked pants, red jackets, propeller caps $165.00
       (see Disney under Special Events/Exclusives)
Twilight Angel — 8", #10780, (Wendy) 1999 – 2000, white organza gown $105.00
Twinkle, Twinkle Little Star — 8", #11630, 1997 ....$65.00
20's Bride — #14103, 1995, Nostalgia Series $100.00
20's Traveler — 10", #1139, 1991 – 1992 only, Portrette, M.A. signature logo on box (Cissette)...$125.00
25th Anniversary — 1982 (see Enchanted Doll House under Special Events/Exclusives)
Tyler, Julia — 1979 – 1981, 2nd set Presidents' Ladies/First Ladies Series (Martha)................$125.00
Tyrolean Boy & Girl* — 8" h.p., BKW (girl - #398, #798; boy - #399, #799),
    1962 – 1965 (Wendy Ann)..$150.00 ea.
    8" h.p., BK (girl - #798; boy - #799), 1965 – 1972 ....$100.00 ea.
    8" straight leg (girl - #0798; boy - #0799), 1973, marked "ALEX"....................................$75.00 ea.
    8" BKW (Maggie Mixup)..$165.00 ea.
Ugly Stepsister — 10", h.p., #13340, 1997 – 1998, Cinderella series....................................$85.00
Ultimate Angel — 21", #10770, 1999, blue silk and lace gown $550.00
U.F.D.C. Sailor Boy — 1990 (see Special Events/Exclusives)
U.S.A. — 8" h.p., #536, 1993 – 1994 (#110536) (also see Neiman-Marcus trunk set, 1994)........$75.00
    Las Vegas, 8", #28565, 2001, silver costume $110.00
    Sacajawea, 8", #28575, 2001, includes papoose $75.00
Uncle Sam — 8", #10353, 1995 only (Wendy) $70.00
    8", h.p., #24170, 1999 – 2000, astronaut costume, United States of America $90.00
United States — 8" h.p., #559, straight leg, 1974 – 1975, marked "Alex" $75.00
    8" #559 Alex. mold, misspelled "Untied States" $100.00
    straight leg, #559, 1976 – 1987, marked "Alexander" $65.00
    #559, #516, 1988 – 1992 (Maggie face)...$60.00
    8", #11562, 1996, Statue of Liberty costume, #24000, 1997 – 1998 ....$80.00
United States Armed Forces Set — 4 dolls, 5 flags, and flag stand....................................$350.00
United States Air Force — 8", #12000, 1998 (Wendy), uniform and flag.........................$80.00
United States Army — 8", #12010, 1998 (Wendy) $80.00
United States Marines — 8", #12030, 1998 (Wendy) $80.00
United States Navy — 8", #12020, 1998 (Wendy) $80.00
Union Officer — 12", #634, 1990 – 1991, Scarlett Series (Nancy Drew)..............................$85.00
    Soldier, 8", #634, 1991 only, Scarlett Series $125.00
Valentine — (see Lady Valentine & Lord Valentine)
Valentine Kisses — 8", #27050, 2000 – 2001, red and silver outfit $70.00
Van Buren, Angelica — 1979 – 1981, 2nd set Presidents'
    Ladies/First Ladies Series (Louisa) $125.00
Velvet Party Dress — 8", h.p., #389, 1957 only, very rare (Wendy Ann) ....$2,000.00 up
Vermont Maid — 8" (see Enchanted Doll House under Special
    Events/Exclusives)
Victoria — 21" compo., 1939, 1941, 1945 – 1946 (also see Flavia)
    (Wendy Ann) ....$2,000.00 up
    20" h.p., 1954 only, Me & My Shadow Series (Cissy) ....$2,000.00 up
    14" h.p., 1950 – 1951 (Margaret) $875.00
    18" h.p., 1954 only, Me & My Shadow Series, slate blue gown (Maggie)........$1,800.00 up
    8" h.p., #0030C, 1954 only, matches 18" doll (Wendy Ann)..........................$1,200.00 up
    14" baby, 1975 – 1988, 1990 – 1997 ....$95.00
    18" baby, 1966 only $75.00
    18" reintroduced, 1991 – 1993, 1997 ....$65.00 – 125.00
    20" baby, 1967 – 1989 ....$100.00
    20" 1986 only, in dress/jacket/bonnet $100.00
    18", vinyl, 1998, velour romper, #29420 white, #29423 African-American........$110.00
    14", "Mozart Music" Concertina, #26915, 2000, plays Mozart music $90.00
    18", "Mozart Music" Symphony, #26900, 2000, plays Mozart music $135.00
Victorian — 18" h.p., 1953 only, pink taffeta/black velvet gown,
    Glamour Girl Series (Margaret)...$1,500.00 up

*Became Austria in 1974.

Victoria, 14", 1975 – 1988. Original clothes.

Victorian Bride — 10", #1148, #1118, 1992 only, Portrette $110.00
    10", blue satin and lace gown $135.00
Victorian Bride — (see Debra)
Victorian Catherine — 16", #90010, porcelain, elaborate gown $300.00
Victorian Christmas — 8", #19970, red velvet and lace.......................................$95.00
Victorian Countess — 10", #28885, 2001, white long dress with lace $150.00
Victorian Girl 1954 — 10", h.p., 2000, (Cissette) remake of 1954 Victoria........$110.00
Victorian Skater — 10", #1155, 1993 – 1994, Portrette, red/gold/black outfit (Cissette) $175.00
Victorian Valentine — 8", #30615, 2000, red pleated dress, hat $85.00
Victorians — 8", Adorable silk, #26875, 2000, flower adorned dress..................$95.00
    8", Charming silk, #25035, 2000 – 2001, white silk dress $95.00
    8", Innocent silk, #25045, 2000 – 2001, white lace trimmed silk dress $95.00
    8", Sophisticated silk, #26780, 2000 – 2001, lilac silk costume $95.00
    8", Sweet silk, #25040, 2000 – 2001, pink silk dress..$95.00
    8", Marigold, #27805, 2001, short yellow dress, hat with lace $80.00
Vietnam — 8" h.p., #788, 1968 – 1969 (Wendy Ann) $275.00
    #788, 1968 – 1969 (Maggie Mixup)..$300.00
    8", #505, reintroduced in 1990 – 1991 (Maggie) $75.00
Vintage Violet Silk Victorian — 8", #30405, 2001, pink dress $95.00
Violet — (see Sweet Violet)
Violet — (Nutcracker Ballerina) 10" Portrette, 1994 only..................................$80.00
Violetta — 10", #1116, 1987 – 1988, all deep blue (Cissette)..............................$70.00
Virgo — 8", #21380, pink pleated outfit, gold helmet...$90.00
W.A.A.C. (Army) — 14" compo., 1943 – 1944 (Wendy Ann) ....$750.00 up
W.A.A.F. (Air Force) — 14" compo., 1943 – 1944 (Wendy Ann).....................$750.00 up
W.A.V.E. (Navy) — 14" compo., 1943 – 1944 (Wendy Ann) ....$750.00 up
Waltz — 16", 1999, pink gown trimmed in marabou...$190.00
    8" h.p., #476, 1955 only (Wendy Ann) ....$750.00 up
Want — 8", #18406, 1996, Dickens (see Ghost of Christmas Present) (sold as set)
Washington, Martha — 1976 – 1978, 1st set Presidents' Ladies/First Ladies Series (Martha).....$250.00
Watchful Guardian Angel — 10", #10740, 1998 – 1999, blue, white outfit...........$190.00
Watchful Guardian Angel Set — 3 dolls, bridge, gift card $395.00
Wedding Wishes — 16", #28455, 2001, white gown with lace around hem,
    bouquet with red roses $250.00
Weeping Princess — 8", #11104, 1995 only, International Folk Tales (Maggie).....$65.00
Welcome Home — Desert Storm — 8", 1991 only, mid-year introduction, boy or girl
    soldier, black or white $55.00
Wendy — 8", 1989, first doll offered to club members only(see M.A.D.C. under
    Special Events/Exclusives)
Wendy Angel — 8" h.p., #404, 1954 (Wendy Ann)..$850.00 up
Wendy Ballerina — 8", (Wendy) 1999, pink trim on white lace tutu...................$80.00
Wendy (from Peter Pan) — 15" h.p., 1953 only (Margaret)...............................$550.00 up
    14" plastic/vinyl, #1415, 1969 only (Mary Ann)..$275.00
    8", #466 in 1991 – 1993; #140466 in 1994; Storyland Series, pom-poms on
        slippers (Peter Pan) $80.00
Wendy Cheerleader — 8", #16500, 1998, pleated skirt, red sweater....................$80.00
Wendy Elf — 8", #12818, 1995, Christmas Series $70.00
Wendy Shops FAO — (see FAO Schwarz under Special Events/Exclusives)
Wendy Loves Being Loved — 8", 1992 – 1993 only, doll and wardrobe................$150.00
(Wendy) Being Just Like Mommy — 8", #801, 1993, has baby carriage, #120801, 1994......$125.00
(Wendy) The Country Fair — 8", #802, 1993, has cow, #120802, 1994................$85.00
(Wendy) Summer Box Set — #805, 1993; #120805, 1994 ....$90.00
(Wendy) Winter Box Set — #120810, 1994, boxed doll and wardrobe $90.00
(Wendy) Learning to Sew — 8", #120809, 1994, in wicker case $125.00
(Wendy) Her First Day at School — 8", #120806, 1994 – 1995 ....$70.00
(Wendy) Being Prom Queen — #120808, 1994 ....$65.00
(Wendy) Her Sunday Best — 8", #120807, 1994 – 1995....................................$85.00
(Wendy) Her Sundress — #120804, 1994...$60.00
(Wendy) Goes to the Circus — 8", #12819, 1996 (Wendy Ann).........................$65.00
Wendy Learns Her ABC's — (see ABC Unlimited Productions under
    Special Events/Exclusives)
Wendy Makes It Special — 8", #31050, 1997 – 1998, pink satin dress.................$80.00
Wendy Salutes the Olympics — 8", #86005, 1996, Olympic Medal $150.00
Wendy Tap Dancer — 8", h.p., #13930, 1998, white jacket, gold tap pants.........$95.00

Wendy the Gardener — 8", #31400, 1998 – 1999, sunflower outfit, watering can, sunflowers ..$90.00
Wendy Visits World's Fair — (see Shirley's Doll House under Special Events/Exclusives)
Wendy Works Construction — 8", #31420, 1998 – 1999, includes tools and toolbox..............$90.00
Wendy's Special Cheer — 8", #16500, 1998 – 1999, cheerleading outfit...................................$80.00
Wendy Ann — 11 – 15" compo., 1935 – 1948...$325.00 – 575.00
    9" compo., 1936 – 1940, painted eyes..$350.00
    14", 1938 – 1939, in riding habit, molded hair or wig...$425.00
    14", any year, swivel waist, molded hair or wig..$425.00
    17 – 21" compo., 1938 – 1944 ....$550.00 – 950.00
    14½ – 17" h.p., 1948 – 1949..$600.00 – 850.00
    16 – 22" h.p., 1948 – 1950..$675.00 – 975.00
    23 – 25" h.p., 1949..$850.00
    8", #79516, 1995, 100th anniversary, wearing dress, coat, and bonnet, limited production $150.00
Wendy Bride — 14 – 22" compo., 1944 – 1945 (Wendy Ann) ....$325.00 – 500.00
    15 – 18" h.p., 1951 (Margaret) ....$600.00 – 875.00
    20" h.p., 1956 (Cissy) $800.00
    8" h.p., SLW, #475, 1955 (Wendy Ann) $600.00
Wendy Kin Baby — 8", one-piece vinyl body with hard plastic Little Genius head, 1954 ....$400.00
Wendy's Doll House Trunk Set — 8", #12820, 1996 ....$250.00
White Christmas — 10", #10105, 1995 only, Christmas Series...$85.00
White Christmas Pair — 10", #15380, Betty and Bob from the movie...................................$210.00
White Hat Doll — 8", #25315, 2000, Maud Humphrey design...$85.00
White Iris — 10", #22540, 1999 – 2000, (Cissette), white lace and roses.................................$160.00
White King — 8", h.p., #13020, 1997 – 1998, white suit, cape...$100.00
White Rabbit — 14 – 17", cloth/felt, 1940s...$500.00 – 750.00
    8", #14509, 1995, Alice in Wonderland Series $100.00
    8", #14616, 1996, White Rabbit in court...$75.00
Wicked Stepmother — 21", #50002, 1996, limited edition $310.00
Wicked Witch of the West — 10", #13270, 1997 – 2001, (Cissette), black witch costume $110.00
    21", #27760, 2000, black long costume with Dorothy globe $450.00
Wilson, Edith — 1988, 5th set Presidents' Ladies/First Ladies Series (Mary Ann) $125.00
Wilson, Ellen — 1988, 5th set Presidents' Ladies/First Ladies Series (Louisa) $125.00
Winged Monkey — 8" h.p. (Maggie) #140501, 1994 only..$250.00
    8", h.p. (Wendy), 2000, blue jacket, hat $70.00

Wendy Bride, 21", composition, 1944 – 1945. All original.

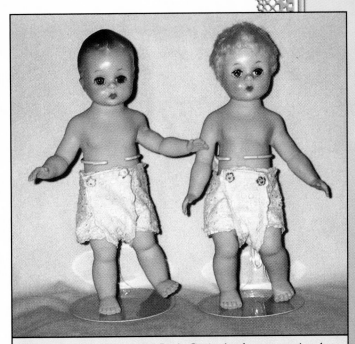

Wendy-Kin Babies, 8", 1954. Little Genius head on a one-piece latex body. The lace-covered plastic pants are tagged Wendy-Kin. The left doll has painted hair while the right has the caracul hair.

Winnie Walker — 15" h.p., 1953 only (Cissy) $275.00
    18 – 25", #1836 ....$350.00 – 650.00
    1953 – 1954, in trunk/trousseau ....$850.00 up
Winter — 14", 1993, Changing Seasons, doll and four outfits $150.00
    5", porcelain, #25865, 2000, fur trimmed white coat and hat................................$65.00
Winter Angel — 10", #28365, 2001, blue costume $110.00
Winter Fun Skater — 8", #10357, 1995, Christmas Series $65.00
Winter Sports — 1991 (see Shirley's Doll House under Special Events/Exclusives)
Winter Wonderland (Nashville Skater #1) — 1991 – 1992 (see Collectors United
    under Special Events/Exclusives)
Winter Wonderland — 10", #19990, 1999 – 2000, white satin, fur, jewels $120.00
Wintertime — (see M.A.D.C. under Special Events/Exclusives)
Wisteria Flower Girl — 8", 2001, (Maggie)..$90.00
Witch — 8", #322, 1992 – 1993, Americana Series $75.00
With Love — 8", #17003, 1996, pink gown, comes with a heart...................................$75.00
    8", #17001, 1996, same as above except African-American......................................$75.00
Witch/Halloween — (see Collectors United under Special
    Events/Exclusives)
Withers, Jane — 12 – 13½" compo., 1937, has closed mouth.............................$1,000.00 up
    15 – 17", 1937 – 1939 ....$850.00– 1,300.00
    17" cloth body, 1939 ....$1,500.00
    18 – 19", 1937 – 1939 ....$1,500.00
    19 – 20", closed mouth ....$1,400.00 up
    20 – 21", 1937 ....$1,600.00 up
Wizard of Oz — 8", mid-year special (see Madame Alexander Doll Co.
    under Special Events/Exclusives)
    8", #13281, plaid pants, green tailcoat, 1998 – 2000 ....$95.00
    8", with state fair balloon, #13280, Wizard, 1998 – 2000..$150.00
Workin' Out with Wendy 1980 — 8", #17810, 1999, BK, striped bodysuit.............$75.00
1860s Women — 10", h.p., 1990 (see Spiegel's under Special Events/Exclusives) (Beth)
Wynkin — (see Dutch Lullaby)
Yellow Butterfly Princess — 8", #25680, 2000 – 2001, (Maggie)..............................$75.00
Yellow Daffodil — 10", #25620, 2000, white and yellow long gown $120.00
Yellow Hat Doll — 8", #25320, 2000, Maud Humphrey design..................................$90.00
Yes, Virginia, There is a Santa Claus — 8", #20200, 1999 – 2001, green dress with
    lace collar and trim..$90.00
Yolanda — 12", 1965 only (Brenda Starr) $375.00
Yugoslavia — 8" h.p., BK, #789, 1968 – 1972 (Wendy) $90.00

Winnie Walker, 18", hard plastic, #1836, 1953, (Cissy). Navy blue cloth hat and coat over a red taffeta dress.

Yugoslavia, 8", #589, 1984, (Wendy).

8" straight leg, #0789, #589, 1973 – 1975, marked "Alex" $65.00

8" straight leg, #589, 1976 – 1986, marked "Alexander" $60.00

8", 1987 (see Collectors United under Special Events/Exclusives)

Yuletide Angel — (see Tree Toppers)

Zorina Ballerina — 17" compo., 1937 – 1938, extra make-up, must be mint
condition (Wendy Ann) ....$1,900.00 up

ABC Unlimited Productions

Wendy Learns Her ABC's — 8", 1993, wears blue jumper and beret, ABC blocks
on skirt, wooden block stand, limited to 3,200 ....$125.00

Belk & Leggett Department Stores

Miss Scarlett — 14", 1988 ....$150.00
Rachel/Rachael — 8", 1989, lavender gown $75.00
Nancy Jean — 8", 1990, yellow/brown outfit $75.00
Fannie Elizabeth — 8", 1991, limited to 3,000, floral dress with pinafore $95.00
Annabelle at Christmas — 8", 1992, limited to 3,000, plaid dress, holds Christmas cards $125.00
Caroline — 8", 1993, limited to 3,600 ....$100.00
Holly — 8", 1994, green eyes, freckles, wears red top with white skirt $100.00
Elizabeth Belk Angel — 8", #79648, 1996, red velvet $150.00

Bloomingdale's Department Store

10", 1997, coral and leopard Cissette with Bloomie's big brown bag $110.00
Golden Holiday Treetopper — 1999, limited to 1,000 pieces, gilded gold and silver
embroidery on satin $140.00
Millennium Angel Treetopper — 10", #27955, 2000, gold lamé dress with jewels $140.00

Celia's Dolls

David, The Little Rabbi — 8", 1991 – 1992, 3,600 made, 3 hair colors $85.00
Child at Heart Easter Bunny — 8", 1991, limited to 3,000 (1,500 blondes,
750 brunettes, 750 redheads) $325.00
My Little Sweetheart — 8", 1992, limited to 4,500 (1,000 blondes, 1,000 brunettes
w/blue eyes, 1,000 brunettes w/green eyes, 1,000 redheads w/green eyes, 500 blacks) $85.00
Trick and Treat — 8", 1993, sold in sets only (400 sets with red-haired/green-eyed
"Trick" and black "Treat"; 1,200 sets with red-haired/green-eyed "Trick"
and brunette/brown-eyed "Treat"; 1,400 blonde/blue-eyed "Trick" and
red-haired/brown-eyed "Treat.") ....$250.00 set

Christmas Shoppe

Boy & Girl, Alpine — 8" twins, 1992, in Alpine Christmas outfits, limited to 2,000 sets ....$200.00 pr.

Collectors United (C.U.)

C. U. Gathering (Georgia)

Yugoslavia — 8", F.A.D., limited to 625 ....$100.00
Tippi Ballerina — 8", 1988, limited to 800 ....$425.00
Miss Leigh — 8", 1989, limited to 800 ....$125.00

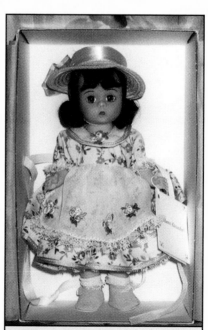

Lindsey, 8", #28920, 2001, Nashville
C.U. Special doll. Limited to 100.
Named for Gary and Dian Green's
granddaughter.

C.U. Gathering (Georgia), continued

Shea Elf — 8", 1990, limited to 1,000 ....$175.00
Ringmaster — 8", 1991, limited to 800 ....$100.00
Faith — 8", 1992, limited to 800 ....$250.00
Hope — 8", 1993, limited to 900, blue dress (1910 style) $175.00
Love — 8", 1994, limited to 2,400, has gold necklace and pearls on cap $100.00
Diane — 8", 1995, limited to 800, Back to the Fifties $125.00
C.U. Varsity Sweater — white sweater, 1995, special event souvenir $50.00
Olympia — 8", 1996, pants costume, with flag, limited to 800 ....$150.00
Olympic Bag — 1996, special Alexander event souvenir $60.00
C.U. Salutes Broadway — 8", 1997, burgundy theatre outfit $175.00
Black Fur Stole — 1997, special Alexander event souvenir $50.00
Polynesian Princess — 8", 1998, print skirt and top $175.00
Grass Skirt — 1998, special Alexander event souvenir $50.00
Fortune Teller — 1999, 8", red print costume trimmed in gold $175.00
Fortune Teller — 1999, 21", red print costume trimmed in gold $600.00
Fortune Teller Accessories — scarves and bangle bracelets, 1999, special event $50.00
Carnival Queen — limited to 24, 1999, 16", pink or blue gown $350.00
Majestic Midway — 21", 1999, gold costume ....one-of-a-kind

C.U. Nashville Winter Wonderland

Nashville Skater — 8", 1991, F.A.D., limited to 200 (Black Forest) $175.00
Nashville Skier — 8", 1992, F.A.D, limited to 200 (Tommy Tittlemouse) $100.00
First Comes Love — 8", 1993, limited to 200, F.A.D. $250.00
Captain's Cruise — 1994, limited to 250, with trunk & wardrobe $225.00
Nashville Goes Country — 8", 1995, western outfit with guitar $150.00
Nashville Sunny — 8", 1996, yellow raincoat, hat $200.00
Miss Tennessee Waltz — 8", 1977, long ball gown, coat $200.00
C.U. Goes to Camp — 8", 1998 ....$150.00
Irish Cissy — 21", #27460, 2000, limited to 200, green gown, silver cape $375.00
Shannon — 8", #27255, 2000, green costume $95.00
Lindsey — 8", #28920, 2001, print dress, straw hat, limited to 100 ....$85.00

C.U. Greenville Show

Bride — 8", 1990, F.A.D. of Tommy Snooks, limited to 250 (Betsy Brooks) $125.00
Witch/Halloween — 8", 1990, F.A.D., limited to 250 (Little Jumping Joan) $100.00
Oktoberfest — 8", 1992, F.A.D., limited to 200 ....$125.00
C.U. Columbia, S.C. Camelot — 8", 1991, F.A.D. (Maid Marian), limited to 400 ....$125.00
C.U. Columbia S.C. Homecoming Queen — 21", #28205, 2000, white gown,
limited to 200 ....$350.00
C.U. Columbia S.C. Homecoming Queen — 21", 2000, African-American,
limited to 24 ....$700.00
C.U. Jacksonville — 8" Greta, 1996, black doll, blue sundress $225.00

C.U. Doll Shop Exclusives

Cameo Lady — 10", 1991, limit: 1,000, white dress, black trim $125.00
Le Petit Boudoir — 10", 1993, F.A.D., limited to 700 ....$100.00
America's Junior Miss — 8", 1994, white gown, medal-lion, limited to 1,200 ....$75.00
Fitness — 8", 1995, tennis outfit $75.00
Judge's Interview — 8", 1996, limited to 500 ....$75.00
Talent — 8", 1996, gold tuxedo jacket, black shorts $75.00
Easter of Yesteryear — 8", 1995, comes with rabbit $75.00
Sailing with Sally — 8", 1998, white dress, wooden boat $100.00
Gary Green — 8", 1998...$75.00
Christmas Morn — 8", 1999, #80130, nightgown, teddy bear, limited to 411 pieces $75.00
Sterling Light, Sterling Bright — 8", #30721, 2000, Silver Angel lighted treetopper $150.00
Katy — 8", #28925, 2000, printed dress, straw hat, limited to 100 ....$85.00

Colonial Southwest

Tanya — 8", 1999, limited to 550, honors M.A.D.C. former president Tanya McWhorter ...$200.00

Colonial Williamsburg

Charlotte — 10", #26985, 2000, pink taffeta, 18th century dress.......................$150.00

Disney, Walt

Disney World Auction — 21" one-of-a-kind dolls, therefore no prices shown.
Sleeping Beauty — #1 in Series, 1989, 21", long blonde hair, in pink with rhinestones and pearls
Christine (Phantom of the Opera) — #2, 1990, blue/white outfit with white mask (Jacqueline)
Queen Isabella — #3, 1991, green/gold gown, long red hair (Jacqueline)
It's A Girl — #4, 1992, comes with 8" baby in carriage (Cissy, Baby Genuis)

Disney, Walt, continued

  Emperor and Nightingale — #4, 1992, 8" winged Wendy Ann (23" Emperor bear by Gund)

  Women in the Garden — #5, 1993, four dolls (Cissette) dressed like 1867 Monet painting

  Cissy Bride — 1923 and 8" Flower Girl and Ring Bearer, #5, 1993

  Romeo & Juliet — #6, 21" h.p., 1994, using 1950s bald nude "Maggie" dolls, rewigged,
      dressed in blue, burgundy, and gold

  Sir Lancelot duLac — #7, 1995, 1950s doll dressed in burgundy and gold

  Queen Guinevere — #7, 1995, 1950s doll dressed in burgundy and gold

  Chess Set — 35 dolls from 8" to 21" on a satin chess board

  Mary Poppins and Children — 1999, 21" Mary Poppins, 14" Jane and Michael

Disney Annual Showcase of Dolls

  Cinderella — 10", 1989, #1, blue satin gown, limited to 250 ....$750.00

  Snow White — 12", 1990, #2, limited to 750 (Nancy Drew) $175.00

  Alice in Wonderland/White Rabbit — 10", 1991, #3, limited to 750...............................$400.00

  Queen of Hearts — 10", 1992, #4, limited to 500 ....$400.00

  Alice in Wonderland/Jabberwocky — 11 – 12" (Lissy) 1993, #5, limited to 500 ....$375.00

  Tweedledee & Tweedledum — 8", 1994, #6, wear beany hats with propellers,
      names on collar, limited to 750...$350.00 pr.

  Morgan LeFay — 10", #797537, 1995, #7, limited to 500...$350.00

  Bobby (Bobbie) Soxer — 8", 1990 – 1991...$225.00

  Mouseketeer — 8", 1991...$225.00

  Roller Blades — 8", 1992, "Thoroughly Modern Wendy"...$150.00

  Round Up Cowgirl — 8", 1992, blue/white outfit $195.00

  Annette (Funicello) — 14" porcelain portrait sculpted by Robert Tonner, 1993,
      limited to 400..$475.00

  Monique — 8", 1993, made for Disney, limited to 250, lavender with lace trim $600.00

  Snow White — 10", 1993, Disney crest colors...$200.00

  Belle — 8" h.p., gold gown, 1994..$125.00

  Cinderella — 14", 1994, Disney catalog, has two outfits, limited to 900 ....$200.00

      14", 1995, different gown, no extra outfits...$200.00

  Wendy's Favorite Pastime — 8", 1994, comes with hula hoop $85.00

  Sleeping Beauty — 14", 1995, waist-length hair, blue gown from movie and
      two other outfits...$275.00

  Blue Fairy Tree Topper — 10", #79545, 1995 catalog exclusive (Cissette) $175.00

  Snow White — 14", 1995...$200.00

  Mary Poppins — 10", 1996, #79403 ....$125.00

  Alice — 14", 1996, limited to 1,500, catalog exclusive $175.00

  Knave — 8", 1996, #8, limited to 500, wears 2 of Spades card...$175.00

  Toto — 8", 1997, #9, limited to 750, comes with wooden basket $175.00

  Goldilocks and Baby Bear — 8", 1998, #10, purple print costume with Raikes Bear............$275.00

  Mouseketeers — 8", 1999, Alex and Wendy as Mouseketeers, #11 ....$250.00

  My Little Buttercup — 8", 2000, #12, yellow dress and hat trimmed in
      flowers and ribbons, #30320, limited to 200..$175.00

  Sleeping Beauty — 8", 1999, pink satin gown, limited to 1,000..$150.00

  Snow White — 8", 1999, Disney crest colors, limited to 1,000 ....$150.00

  Ariel — 8", 1999, #25085, long red hair, green mermaid costume.....................................$100.00

  Belle — 8", 1999, #25075, yellow ball gown with gold trim..$125.00

  Cinderella — 8", 1999, #25080, blue satin gown, limited to 1,000....................................$125.00

  Michael and Jane Banks — 8", 1999, #80450, 8" girl, boy limited to 200...........................$175.00

  Jasmine — 8", 1999, #25095, lavender chiffon harem outfit $150.00

Dolls and Ducks

  Ice Princess — 8", 1999, silver gown and tiara $125.00

Doll & Teddy Bear Expo

  Madame (Alexander) or Shadow of Madame — 8", 1994, in blue,
      limited to 500 first year...$250.00

  Madame With Love — 8", #79536, 1995, has hat with "100" on top, limited to 750 ....$100.00

  Maggie's First Doll — 8", 1996, pink cotton dress, carries cloth Alice doll $225.00

  Miss Eliza Doolittle — 21", 1996, white lace dress, auction piece ....one-of-a-kind

  Josephine Baker — 21", black Cissy, 1996, banana costume, auction piece....................one-of-a-kind

  Gingerbread outfit — outfit only for 8" doll..$75.00

  Love is in the Air — 8", Bride, 1999, limited to 100...$100.00

  Holiday Magic — 8", 1999, limited to 100, red and gold metallic gown $150.00

  American As Apple Pie — 8", #27490, 2000, 100 pieces, (Maggie) $150.00

  America the Beautiful Outfit — 2000, with boots $75.00

Doll & Teddy Bear Expo, continued

Wild, Wild West — 8", #27495, 2000, limited to 100...$185.00

Doll Finders

Fantasy — 8", 1990, limited to 350 ....$200.00

Dolls 'n Bearland

Pandora — 8", 1991, limited to 3,600 (950 brunette, 950 redheads, 1,700 blondes) $150.00

Dolly Dears

Bo Peep — 1987, holds staff, black sheep wears man's hat, white sheep wears
    woman's hat (sheep made exclusively by Dakin).......................................$225.00

Susannah Clogger — 8", 1992, has freckles, limited to 400 (Maggie)........................$325.00

Jack Be Nimble — 8", 1993, F.A.D., limited to 288 ....$125.00

Princess and the Pea — 8", 1993 limited to 1,000..$125.00

Elegant Doll Shop

Elegant Easter — 8", 1999, pink check with bunny $135.00

Heart of Dixie — 8", 1999, red and lace outfit $100.00

Enchanted Doll House

Rick-Rack on Pinafore — 8", 1980 limited to 3,000 ....$300.00

Eyelet Pinafore — 8", 1981 limited to 3,423 ....$325.00

Blue or Pink Ballerina — 8", 1983 – 1985, F.A.D., blonde or brunette doll in trunk
    with extra clothes $175.00

Cinderella & Trunk — 14", has glass slipper, 1985...$275.00

25th Anniversary (The Enchanted Doll) — 10", 1988, long gown, limited to 5,000...............$175.00

Ballerina — 8", 1989, blue tutu, limited to 360 ....$175.00

Vermont Maiden — 8", 1990 – 1992, official Vermont Bicentennial doll,
    limited to 3,600 (800 blondes, 2,800 brunettes) $100.00

Farmer's Daughter — 8", 1991, limited to 4,000 (1,000 blondes,
    1,500 redheads, 1,500 brunettes) $100.00

Farmer's Daughter — 8", 1992, "Goes To Town" (cape and basket added),
    limited to 1,600 ....$125.00

FAO Schwarz

Pussy Cat — 18", 1987, pale blue dress and bonnet $150.00

Brooke — 14", 1988, blonde or brunette (Mary Ann) with Steiff Bear.......................$125.00

David and Diana — 8", 1989, in red, white, and denim, with wooden wagon......................$225.00 set

Samantha — 14", 1989, white with black dots (Mary Ann)....................................$150.00

Me & My Scassi — 21", 1990, dressed in all red Arnold Scassi original (Cissy)................$375.00

Sailor — 8", 1991 ....$125.00

Carnavale Doll — 14", 1991 – 1992 (Samantha) $185.00

Beddy-Bye Brooke — 14", 1991 – 1992 (Mary Ann) $125.00

Beddy-Bye Brenda (Brooke's sister) — 8", 1992, sold only as set with 14" doll......................$225.00 set

Wendy Shops FAO — 8", 1993, red/white outfit, carries FAO
    Schwarz shopping bag...$125.00

My Secret Garden — 8", trunk with wardrobe, 1994...$350.00

Little Huggums — 12", red dress, bib & headband, has FAO logo horse 1994 ....$65.00

Little Women — 8", 1994, dressed in outfits from movie, limited to 500
    sets (5 dolls) and 700 of each girl..................$125.00 ea., $750.00 set

Princess trunk set — 8", #79526, 1995 ....$275.00

Fun with Dick & Jane — 8", #70509, 1995, limited to 1,200 pieces................................$275.00 set

Lucy Ricardo — 8", limited to 1,200...$250.00

I Love Lucy — 8" Fred, Ethel, Lucy, and Ricky, sold as set only, limited to 1,200 ....$700.00 set

The Little Rascals — 8" Alfalfa, Darla, Spanky, Buckwheat, and dog, Petey, 1996,
    limited to 2,000 sets ....$550.00 set

Singing in the Rain — 8" Gene Kelly, Debbie Reynolds with lamppost, 1996, 1952 film.......$300.00

I Dream of Jeannie — 8", harem outfit, 8", military uniform $275.00

Lucy and Ethel — 8", 1997, candy factory episode $200.00

The Honeymooners — 8", 1997, Ralph & Alice Norton, Trixie, limited to 2,000 sets $425.00

Grease — 1998, 10", Danny and Sandy in leather outfits $175.00

Fay Wray with Steiff King Kong — 1998, 10" doll...$500.00

Silver Sensation — 16", Alex fashion doll, limited to 100 ....$300.00

Gallery Opening Alex — 16", limited to 500 ....$150.00

Publisher's Metting Alex — 16", limited to 200..$150.00

Magnificent Mile Alex — 16", 2000, limited to 40 pieces $700.00

First Modern Doll Club (N.Y. Doll Club)

Autumn in N.Y. — 10", 1991, F.A.D., red skirt, fur trim cape/hat/muff/skates,
    limited to 260..$175.00

Home Shopping Network

Blue Angel — 8", 1997, #19972, dark blue and gold dress and halo, resin wings, limited to, 3000...$200.00

Horchow

Pamela Plays Dress Up — 12", 1993, in trunk with wardrobe, limited to 1,250 (Lissy) $350.00

Pamela Trousseau — 12", 1994, trunk and trousseau, limited to 265 ....$375.00

14" trunk set, 1995..$250.00

Mary Ann Dances for Grandma Trunk Set — 14", 1996 ....$300.00

I. Magnin

Cheerleader — 8", 1990, F.A.D., "5" on sweater $100.00

Miss Magnin — 10", 1991 – 1993, limited to 2,500, (Cissette)...$150.00

Little Huggums — 12" with cradle 1992..$125.00

Little Miss Magnin — 8", 1992, with tea set and teddy bear, limited to 3,600......................$225.00

Bon Voyage Miss Magnin — 10", 1993, navy/white gloves, has steamer trunk, limited to 2,500...$225.00

Bon Voyage Little Miss Magnin — 8", sailor dress, carries teddy bear/suitcase, limited to 3,500, 1993..$175.00

Little Miss Magnin Supports the Arts — 8", 1994, pink painter smock, wears red ribbon for AIDS Awareness $175.00

Imaginarium Shop (I. Magnin)

Little Huggums — 12", 1991, special outfits, bald or wigged, 2 wig colors $50.00

Jacobsons

Wendy Starts Her Collection — 1994, has bear, limited to 2,400 ....$150.00

Little Huggums — 1995 ....$65.00

Jean's Doll Shop

Suellen — 12", 1992, F.A.D...$135.00

Wendy Walks Her Dog — 8", #79549, 1995, limited to 500 pieces......................................$90.00

Lenox China Company

My Own Bell — 8", #27475, 2000, holiday dress with bell, limited to 1,000 ....$125.00

Lillian Vernon

Christmas Doll — 8", #79630, 1996, green and gold holly print dress $100.00

Miss Millennium — 8", 1999, #80580, blue ball gown, watch...$80.00

Christmas 2000 — 8", #27555, 2000, gown of white net with silver flecks, angel wings, silver crown, Christmas 2000 banner $80.00

St. Valentine's Day — 8", #26410, 2000, red and white outfit, limited to 2,000....................$100.00

Easter — 8", #26150, 2000, white dress, plush bunny..$80.00

Halloween Magic — 8", #27750, 2000, black velvet top $80.00

Nutcracker — 8", #27560, 2000, Nutcracker outfit..$100.00

Abigail Adams, 10", #31510, (Cissette), 2001, M.A.D.C. Convention Doll. Blue dress with lavender underskirt.

Evening at the Pops Cissy, 21", #31735, 2001, M.A.D.C. Cissy Luncheon Souvenir Doll. Lavender dress, jacket, and hat.

Lord & Taylor
  Victoria — 14", 1989 ....$85.00
Madame Alexander Doll Club (M.A.D.C.) Convention Dolls
  Fairy Godmother Outfit — 1983, for 8" non-Alexander designed by Judy LaManna............$350.00
  Ballerina — 8", 1984, F.A.D., limited to 360..$250.00
  Happy Birthday — 8", 1985, F.A.D., limited to 450 ....$325.00
  Scarlett — 8", 1986, F.A.D., red instead of green ribbon, limited to 625 ....$250.00
  Cowboy — 8", 1987, limited to 720 ....$450.00
  Flapper — 10", 1988, F.A.D., black outfit instead of red, limited to 720 ....$225.00
  Briar Rose — 8", 1989, uses Cissette head, limited to 804 ....$300.00
  Riverboat Queen (Lena) — 8", 1990, limited to 925......................................$300.00
  Queen Charlotte — 10", 1991, blue/gold outfit, limited ,to under 900...................$375.00
  Prom Queen (Memories) — 8", 1992, limited to 1,100 ....$200.00
  Drucilla — 14" 1992, limited to 268 ....$225.00
  Diamond Lil (Days Gone By) — 10", 1993, black gown, limited to 876.....................$325.00
  Anastasia — 14" 1993, F.A.D., available at convention, limited to 489..................$225.00
  Navajo Women — 8", 1994, comes with rug, sheep, and Hopi Kachina, limited to 835........$350.00
  Flower Girl — 8", companion to 1995 souvenir doll, could be purchased separately $125.00
  Folsom, Frances — 10", 1995 convention doll, #79517, (married Grover Cleveland) $275.00
  Showgirl — 10", 1996 convention doll, pink, blue, green, lavender, white feathers $350.00
  10", 1996 convention, black feather, limited to 20 pieces $500.00
  A Little Bit of Country — 8", 1997, #79080, with guitar $250.00
  Rose Festival Queen — 8", #79450, 1998, white gown, cape with roses $275.00
  Margaret O'Brien — 1998 Convention Companion doll,
  8", #79590..$200.00
  Orange Blossom — 10", 1999, long peach dress and gold straw hat $225.00
  Electra — 8", 1999, Convention Companion doll, silver costume $90.00
  Lilly Pulitzer — 21", 1999, Cissy Luncheon centerpiece doll, limited to 25 ....$850.00
  Cissy Accessories — 1999, no doll, accessories for 21" doll............................$40.00
  Little Miss Bea — 2000, #26410, 8", honors Madame Bea Alexander, limited to 500..........$100.00
  Going to M.A.D.C.C. — 8", #26415, 2000 convention doll, black bodice, ecru tulle,
      limited to 700...$250.00
  Seaside Serenade Gala 2000 — 16", (Alex), long blue gown with rhinestones.............$350.00
  Abigail Adams — 10", #31510, 2001 convention doll, blue and lavender dress, (Cissette)......$250.00
  Evening at the Pops Cissy — 21", #31735, 2001, luncheon doll, lavender dress, hat..............$400.00
  Seaside Serenade Gala 2000 Centerpiece — 16", #27510, pink dressing gown, (Alex)............$450.00
  Charles River Regatta Alex — 16", limited to 310, 2001 ....$300.00
  Cissy Gala — 21", 2000 luncheon doll, long blue and silver gown, limited to 300 ....$550.00

Seaside Serenade Gala 2000 Centerpiece, (Alex), 16", pink dressing gown. Made for San Diego Fashion Doll Luncheon.

Charles River Regatta Alex, 16", 2001, Boston Fashion Luncheon Souvenir doll. First Alex produced with bend knees.

Cissy Gala 2000 Centerpiece — 21", #27265, 2000, lavender dress, blonde $700.00
Skating Into Your Heart — 8", #26250, 2000, Travel Party $150.00
Cissy Diva — #31730, 2001 centerpiece doll, limited to 45 ....$700.00

M.A.D.C. Dolls, Exclusives (available to club members only)

Wendy — 8", 1989, in pink and blue, limited to 4,878 ....$175.00
Polly Pigtails — 8", 1990 (Maggie Mixup) limited to 4,896 ....$150.00
Miss Liberty — 10", 1991 – 1992, red/white/blue gown (Cissette) $125.00
Little Miss Godey — 8", 1992 – 1993..$125.00
Wendy's Best Friend Maggie — 8", 1994 ....$90.00
Wendy Loves Being Best Friends — 8", name embroidered on apron, 1994.........................$90.00
Wendy Loves the Dionnes — 8", one-of-a-kind set of 5 dolls, made for
    1994 convention ....not available
Ultimate Cissy — 21", one-of-a-kind for 1996 convention ....not available
Wendy Joins M.A.D.C. — 8", #79552, 1995 ....$250.00
Wendy Honors Margaret Winson — 8", 1996 postmistress outfit, honoring first
    M.A.D.C. president $85.00
From the Madame's Sketchbook — 8", 1997, replica of 1930s Tiny Betty.......................$85.00
Skate with Wendy — 8", 1998, plaid skating outfit, silver key...................................$80.00
Electro — 8", 1999, (Maggie) silver space costume, boy...$80.00
M.A.D.C. Angel — 8", 2000, pink gown, limited to 800...$100.00
M.A.D.C. Ballerina — 8", 2001, blue ballerina $75.00
Springtime Darling — 8", 1999, blue dress, pink trim $75.00
Summer Blossom — 8", 1999, bikini, skirt, sandals $75.00

M.A.D.C. Symposium/Premiere

Pre-Doll Specials (M.A.D.C. Symposium)
Disneyworld — 1984 – 1985 (1984 paper doll)..$60.00
Wendy Goes to Disneyworld — #1 Sunshine Symposium, 1986, navy dress with
    polka dots, Mickey Mouse hat, pennant (costume by Dorothy Starling), limited to 100 ...$125.00

Snowflake Symposium

1st Illinois, 1986, tagged orange taffeta/lace dress, metal pail, and orange, limited to 200........$85.00
2nd Illinois, 1987, tagged, little girl cotton print dress (costume by Mary Voigt) $85.00
3rd Illinois, 1988, tagged, gold/white print dress, gold bodice
    (created by Pamela Martenec)...$85.00
4th Illinois, 1989, tagged, red velvet ice skating costume (created by Joan Dixon) .$95.00
5th Illinois, 1990, bride by Linda's Bridal Shop (also Michelau Scarlett
    could be purchased)..$95.00
Scarlett — 8", 1990, #6, F.A.D. (white medallion* – Snowflake Symposium;
    red medallion – Premier Southern Symposium), limited to 800 ....$175.00
Springtime — 8", 1991, #7, floral dress, scalloped pinafore,
    straw hat, limited to 1,600...$200.00
Wintertime — 8", 1992, #8, all white, fur trim and hat (six locations),
    limited to 1,650...$250.00
Homecoming — 8", 1993, #9 car coat with color trim (8 different
    colors – one for each location), limited to 2,000 ....$225.00
Setting Sail for Summer — 8" 1994, #10 (eight locations), limited to 1,800 ....$175.00
Snowflake — 8", #79404, #11, 1995 (6 locations) gold skater, limited to 1,200 ...$175.00
Wendy Starts Her Travels — 8", 1996, #12, (3 locations), trunk set, different color
    checked coat each location $225.00
Bobby Takes a Picture — 8", 1996, limited to 215 pieces, California companion doll.$150.00
Cheshire Cat — 8", 1996, limited to 215 pieces, Texas companion doll $200.00
Wendy Tours the Factory — 8", 1996, New Jersey companion doll $150.00
Wendy's Tea Party — 8", #13, 1997 (4 locations), pink organdy dress, tea set.....$175.00
Boo — 8", 1996, 150 pieces, ghost costume over Mother's Day doll, Illinois event ...$125.00
Diamond Pixie — 8", 1998, #14, (3 locations), red Pixie costume........................$225.00
Starlett Glamour — 10", 1999, #15, black evening gown $225.00
Millennium Wendy — 8", 2000, #25155, blue dress, straw hat, watch...............$175.00
On the Town Alex — 16", 2001, gold dress and coat...................................$225.00
Evening on the Town Alex — 16", 2001, centerpiece doll, black long gown, stole ...$350.00

M.A.D.C. Friendship Luncheon (outfit only)

Friends Around the Country — print dress and pinafore outfit, 1997 ....$50.00
Wendy Plays Masquerade — 1998, pink butterfly costume..................................$50.00
Wendy, Out and About with Friends — 1999, brown felt coat,
    leopard tam and purse $50.00

* Medallions: Midwest, rose; Southwest, peach; Southeast, blue; Northeast, lavender; West Coast, yellow; Northwest, green.

Cissy Diva, 21", #31730, 2001, Cissy Centerpiece Doll. Limited to 45. Lavender gown with fur stole lined in the same fabric.

Special Events

M.A.D.C. Friendship Luncheon (outfit only), continued

Wendy Emcees Her School Play — pinafore, print dress, pink tam, standing microphone, limited to 700..$50.00

Madame Alexander Doll Company

Melody & Friends — 25", 1992, limited to 1,000, designed and made by Hilegard Gunzel, first anniversary dolls...$700.00 up set

Courtney & Friends — 25" & 8" boy and girl, 1993, second anniversary, limited to 1,200, by Gunzel ....$725.00 up set

Rumpelstiltskin & Miller's Daughter — 8" & 14", #1569, 1992 only, limited to 3,000 ....$325.00

Special Event Doll — 8", 1994, organza and lace in pink with special event banner, ribbon across body, front of hair pulled back in curls................................$85.00

Wendy Makes it Special — 8", 1998, #31050, pink and white dress, hat box........................$100.00

Wendy Salutes the Olympics — 8", #86005, 1996, Olympic medal $150.00

Maggie Mixup — 8", 1998, #31000, Post Office commemorative, blue gingham...................$65.00

75th Anniversary Wendy — 8", #22420, 1998, pink outfit $110.00

Wendy's Special Cheer — 8", #16510, cheerleader, 1999 ....$75.00

George and Martha Washington — 8", 1999, limited ....$200.00 set

Mary McFadden Cissy* — 21", 1999, black and gold gown ....one-of-a-kind

Isaac Mizrahi Cissy* — 21", 1999, gray skirt, red sweater ....one-of-a-kind

Carmen Marc Valvo Cissy* — 21", 1999, long evening gown ....one-of-a-kind

Nicole Miller — 21", 1999, dress and fur coat..one-of-a-kind

Diane Von Furstenberg Cissy* — 21", 1999, black dress, fur coat ....one-of-a-kind

Yeohlee Cissy* — 21", 1999, black skirt, long black coat ....one-of-a-kind

Betsy Johnson Cissy* — 21", 1999, black short dress trimmed in pink ....one-of-a-kind

Scaasi Cissy* — 21", 1999, white lace gown, red coat with feather ....one-of-a-kind

Jessica McClintock Cissy*† — 21", 1999, #22780, long gold ball gown $450.00

Fernando Sanchez Cissy*† — 21", 1999, #22720, white long gown $450.00

Josie Natori Cissy*† — 21", 1999, #22730 ....$450.00

Anna Sui Cissy*† — 21", 1999, #22590, has braids, brown dress, coat................................$450.00

Linda Allard for Ellen Tracy Cissy*† — 21", 1999, brown skirt, long black coat.....................$450.00

Dana Buchman Cissy*† — 21", 1999, green dress, coat $475.00

Donna Karan Cissy*† — 21", 1999, long black dress $475.00

James Purcell Cissy*† — 21", 1999, long white gown with black circles $450.00

Madame Alexander Celebrates American Design Cissy*† — 21", 1999, #22560 ....$400.00

Badgley Mischka Cissy*† — 21", 1999, #22740, long evening gown $450.00

Marc Bouwer Cissy*† — 21", 1999, #26125, African-American doll, long gown...................$500.00

Carolina Herrera Cissy*† — 21", 1999, #26121, red and white ball gown $450.00

"An American Legend" Book and Doll in display box $250.00

Mid-Year Specials for Madame Alexander Doll Company

Welcome Home — 8", 1991, black or white, boy or girl, Desert Storm Soldier.......................$50.00

Wendy Loves Being Loved — 8", 1992, doll and wardrobe...$150.00

Queen Elizabeth II — 8", 1992, 40th anniversary of coronation...$150.00

Christopher Columbus — 8", 1992, #328, burgundy and brown costume $125.00

Queen Isabella — 8", 1992, #329, green velvet and gold gown $125.00

Santa or Mrs. Claus — 8", 1993..$125.00 ea.

Scarlett O'Hara — 8", 1993, yellow dress, straw hat $175.00

Wendy Ann — 8", 1995, 100th anniversary, pink coat and hat $150.00

Sir Lancelot DuLac — 8", 1995, burgundy and gold knight's costume.................................$125.00

Queen Guinevere — 8", 1995, burgundy and gold gown $125.00

Wizard of Oz — 8", 1994, green metallic costume, black hat $150.00

Dorothy — 8", 1994, emerald green checked dress $175.00

Wicked Witch — 8", 1994, green face, black costume..$200.00

Marshall Fields

Avril, Jane — 10", 1989, red/black can-can outfit (tribute to T. Lautrec) (Cissette)................$150.00

Madame Butterfly — 10", 1990, blue brocade kimono, gold obi $150.00

Metroplex Doll Club

Spring Break — 8", 1992, 2-piece halter/wrapskirt outfit, limited to 400, beach bag $225.00

Meyers 80th Year

8", "Special Event" doll with banner, 1994 ....$75.00

Modern Doll Convention

Modern Romance Alex — 16", 2000, long strapless dress, limited to 200 ....$350.00

Modern Romance Alex centerpiece — 16", 2000, long strapless henna dress, limited to 20..$700.00

The 1999 designer Cissys and the original Cissys were auctioned for "Fashion Targets Breast Cancer."

†*Cissys made in limited editions for 1999.*

My Doll House

Southern Belle — 10", 1989, F.A.D., all pink gown with parasol and picture hat, limited to 2,300...$150.00

Queen Elizabeth I — 10", 1990, limited to 2,400 ....$150.00

Empress Elizabeth of Austria — 10", 1991, white/gold trim, limited to 3,600 (Cissette) $150.00

Neiman-Marcus

Doll with four outfits in trunk — 8", 1990, called "party trunk," limited to 1,044 ....$275.00

Caroline Loves Storyland — 8", 1993, trunk and wardrobe $275.00

Caroline's Adventures — 8", 1994, trunk and costumes for USA, China, Germany, Kenya (Maggie) $275.00

Anne Series — 8", 1994, trunk set, character from Lucy M. Montgomery books...................$275.00

ABC Huggums — limited to 650 pieces $70.00

Miss St. John — 21", 1998, limited to 750...$650.00

Crayola sets — 1999, dolls from regular line in ethnic sets $70.00

Holly Day — 8", #28195, #28196, #28197, 2000, red velvet dress...$100.00

New England Collector Society

Noel — 12", 1989 – 1991, porcelain Christmas doll, limited to 5,000.....................................$250.00

Joy — 12", 1991, porcelain Christmas doll, limited to 5,000...$225.00

New York Doll Club

Autumn in New York — 10" F.A.D., limited to 260...$175.00

Penney, J.C.

At the Hop — 8", #27860, 2000, skirt with hoops...$95.00

Paris Fashion Doll Convention

City Lights Alex — 16", 2001, white long gown, limited to 200 ....$700.00

City Lights centerpiece — 16", 2001, limited to 20 ....$1,500.00

QVC

Summer Cherry Picking — 8", #79760, 1998 (Wendy), cherry print dress, limited to 500 .....$250.00

Betsy Ross — 8", #79990, 1998 (Wendy), red striped dress, limited to 500 ....$100.00

Pilgrim Girl — 8", #79980, 1998 (Wendy), long blue dress, limited to 500 ....$100.00

Home for the Holidays — 10", #79800, 1998 (Cissette), limited to 400 ....$175.00

A Rose for You — 8", 1999, (Wendy), lace trimmed white dress with rose..............................$95.00

Lavender Rose — 10", 1999, lavender ball gown...$150.00

Pollyanna — 8", 1999, (Maggie), blue check dress, straw hat, limited to 500 ....$95.00

Blossom — 8", 1999, pink print dress (Wendy), limited to 500...$95.00

Little Bo Peep — 8", 1999, pink gown trimmed in lace, limited to 700 ....$100.00

Investigator Wendy — 8", 1999 (checked coat and hat), limited to 500 ....$100.00

Autumn Breeze — 8", 1999..$80.00

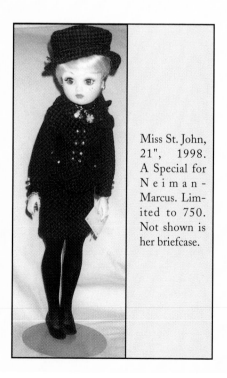

Miss St. John, 21", 1998. A Special for Neiman-Marcus. Limited to 750. Not shown is her briefcase.

Noel, 12", 1989. First Madame Alexander porcelain Christmas doll. Made for New England Collector Society. Limited to 5,000.

QVC, *continued*

Alice — 8", 1999 ....$80.00
Kiss Me, I'm Irish — 8", 1999..$95.00
Ladybug Garden — 8", 1999...$80.00
Fun at Halloween — 8", 1999, limited to 500 pieces $80.00
Golden Light Tree Topper — yellow and black costume.................$150.00
Spring Flowers — 8", 1999..$80.00
Fourth of July — 8", 1999 ....$80.00

Saks Fifth Avenue

Christmas Carol — 8", 1993, tartan plaid taffeta dress with velvet bodice $150.00
Joy of Christmas — 1994, 2nd in series, forest green taffeta dress $150.00

Sears-Roebuck

Little Women — 1989 – 1990, set of six 12" dolls (Nancy Drew) ....$600.00 set

Shirley's Doll House

Angel Face — 8", 1990 (Maggie Mixup), blue gown, white wings, limited to 3,500..............$125.00
Winter Sports — 8", 1991, F.A.D. (Tommy Snooks), skates, tagged hat, limited to 975 ....$75.00
Wendy Visits World's Fair — 1993, 100th anniversary Chicago World's Fair,
    limited to 3,600...$100.00
Winter Angel — 1993, has cape with hood, wings, and holds golden horn, exclusive: 1,000 ..$125.00
Maypole Dance — 8", 1994, shop's 20th anniversary doll, pink organdy dress and
    blue pinafore, limited to 3,000 (Wendy Ann)..$75.00
Grandma's Darling — 8", 1996, #79617, yellow dress, white blanket........................$90.00
Little Collector — 8", 1999, #79820, navy dress, straw hat, basket........................$90.00

Shriner's 1st Ladies Luncheon

8" boy, 1993, wears fez, jeans, shirt, vest/Texas star on back, limited to 1,800........................$450.00

Spiegel's

Beth — 10", 1990, 125th anniversary special, 1860s women, pink brocade gown....................$125.00
Christmas Tree Topper (also called Merry Angel) — 8", 1991, gold and red
    velvet angel costume...$150.00
Joy Noel — 8", 1992, tree topper angel, white satin/net with gold dots, gold lace,
    halo & skirt, limited to 3,000 ....$125.00
Mardi Gras — 10", 1992, elaborate costume of purple/gold/royal blue, limited to 3,000 ....$150.00

U.F.D.C. – United Federation of Doll Clubs

Sailor Boy — 8", 1990, gray gabardine outfit, limited to 260 ....$750.00
Miss Unity — 10", 1991, cotton eyelet dress, limited to 310...................................$400.00
Little Emperor — 8", 1992, elaborate silk and gold costume, limited to 400........................$500.00

U.F.D.C. "Me and My Shadow," Annette, 10", 2001, #31475, (Cissette). Plum silk dress with pink sash.

U.F.D.C. "Me and My Shadow," Annie, 8", 2001, #31480, (Wendy). Plum silk dress with smocked bodice.

Turn of the Century Bathing Beauty — 10", 1992, U.F.D.C. Region Nine Conference,
  F.A.D. (Gibson Girl), old-fashion bathing suit, beach bag, and umbrella,
  limited to 300...$275.00
Columbian 1893 Sailor — 12", 1993 (Lissy) $225.00
Gabrielle — 10", 1998 (Cissette), limited: 400, black suit, dressmaker's stand $325.00
One Enchanted Evening — 16", 1999, #80260, limited to 310 ....$450.00
Windy City Chic — 16", 2000, pink and black gown, limited to 350....................................$300.00
Susan — 8", #27465, 2000, doll, three outfits, case, limited to 400......................................$250.00
Me and My Shadow Annette — 10", 2001, plum silk dress, limited to 360 ....$175.00
Me and My Shadow Annie — 8", 2001, plum silk, limited to 250 ....$150.00
Eloise in Moscow centerpiece — 8", #27735, 2000, yellow coat, black hat............................$125.00

Informing Today's Collector

For over two decades we have been keeping collectors informed on trends and values in all fields of antiques and collectibles.

BOOKS ON DOLLS—

4631	**Barbie Doll** Boom, 1986–1995, Augustyniak	$18.95
2079	**Barbie Doll Fashion**, Vol. I, Eames	$24.95
4846	**Barbie Doll Fashion**, Vol. II, 1968–1974, Eames	$24.95
5672	The **Barbie Doll** Years, 4th. Ed., Olds	$19.95
3957	**Barbie Exclusives**, Rana	$18.95
4632	**Barbie Exclusives**, Book II, Rana	$18.95
5352	**Barbie Doll Exclusives** & More, 2nd Ed. Augustyniak	$24.95
5155	Collector's Ency. of **American Composition Dolls,** Mertz	$24.95
2211	Collector's Ency. of **Madame Alexander Dolls**, Smith	$24.95
4863	Collector's Encyclopedia of **Vogue Dolls**, Izen/Stover	$29.95
5148	Collector's Guide to **Barbie Doll Vinyl Cases**, Kaplan	$12.95
5160	Collector's Guide to **Ideal Dolls**, 2nd Edition, Izen	$24.95
4707	Decade of **Barbie Dolls** & Collectibles, 1981–1991, Summers	$19.95
5821	**Doll Values**, Antique to Modern, 5th Ed., Moyer	$12.95
5599	**Dolls of the 1960s and 1970s**, Sabulis	$24.95
1799	**Effanbee Doll** Encyclopedia, Smith	$19.95
5829	**Madame Alexander** Price Guide #26, Crowsey	$12.95
5611	**Madame Alexander** Store Exclusives & Ltd. Eds., Crowsey	$24.95
5050	**Modern Collectible Dolls**, Volume II, Moyer	$19.95
5269	**Modern Collectible Dolls**, Volume III, Moyer	$24.95
5612	**Modern Collectible Dolls**, Volume IV, Moyer	$24.95
5833	**Modern Collectible Dolls**, Volume V, Moyer	$24.95
5689	**Nippon Dolls** & Playthings, Van Patten/Lau	$29.95
5059	**Skipper**, Barbie Doll's Little Sister, Arend/Holzerland/Kent	$19.95
5253	Story of **Barbie**, 2nd Ed., Westenhouser	$24.95
1817	**Teddy Bears & Steiff Animals**, 2nd Series, Mandel	$19.95
2084	**Teddy Bears & Steiff Animals**, 3rd Series, Mandel	$19.95
5371	**Teddy Bear** Treasury, Yenke	$19.95
5049	Thirty Years of **Mattel Fashion Dolls**, Augustyniak	$19.95
1808	Wonder of **Barbie**, Manos	$9.95
4880	The World of **Raggedy Ann** Collectibles, Avery	$24.95
1430	World of **Barbie** Dolls, Manos	$9.95

BOOKS ON TOYS, MARBLES & CHRISTMAS COLLECTIBLES—

2333	Antique & Collectible **Marbles**, 3rd Ed., Grist	$9.95
5607	Antiquing and Collecting on the **Internet**, Parry	$12.95
5353	**Breyer Animal** Collector's Guide, 2nd Ed., Browell	$19.95
5608	Buying, Selling & Trading on the **Internet**, 2nd Ed., Hix	$12.95
5150	**Cartoon Toys** & Collectibles, Longest	$19.95
4976	**Christmas Ornaments**, Lights & Decorations, Johnson	$24.95
4737	**Christmas Ornaments**, Lights & Decorations, Vol. II	$24.95
4739	**Christmas Ornaments**, Lights & Decorations, Vol. III,	$24.95
4559	Collectible **Action Figures**, 2nd Ed., Manos	$17.95
2338	Collector's Encyclopedia of **Disneyana**, Longest/Stern	$24.95
5149	Collector's Guide to **Bubble Bath Containers**, Moore/Pizzo	$19.95
5038	Coll. Gde. to **Diecast Toys** & Scale Models, 2nd Ed., Johnson	$19.95
5681	Collector's Guide to **Lunchboxes**, White	19.95
5621	Collector's Guide to **Online Auctions**, Hix	$12.95
5169	Collector's Guide to **T.V. Toys** & Memorabilia, Davis/Morgan	$24.95
4651	Collector's Guide to **Tinker Toys**, Strange	$18.95
4566	Collector's Guide to **Tootsietoys**, 2nd Ed., Richter	$19.95
5360	**Fisher-Price Toys**, Cassity	$19.95
4945	**G-Men & FBI Toys** & Collectibles, Whitworth	$18.95
4720	Golden Age of **Automotive Toys**, Hutchison/Johnson	$24.95
5593	Grist's Big Book of **Marbles**, 2nd Ed.	$24.95
3970	Grist's Machine-Made & Contemporary **Marbles**, 2nd Ed.	$9.95
5684	Hake's Price Guide to **Character Toys**, 3rd Edition	$35.00
5267	**Matchbox Toys**, 3rd Ed., 1947 to 1998, Johnson	$19.95
5830	**McDonald's** Collectibles, 2nd Edition, Henriques/DuVall	$24.95
5673	Modern **Candy Containers** & Novelties, Brush/Miller	$19.95
1540	Modern **Toys**, 1930–1980, Baker	$19.95
3888	**Motorcycle Toys,** Antique & Contemporary, Gentry/Downs	$18.95
5365	**Peanuts Collectibles**, Podley/Bang	$24.95
5693	Schroeder's Collectible **Toys**, Antique to Modern, 7th Ed.	$17.95
5277	**Talking Toys** of the 20th Century, Lewis	$15.95